AUTHOR	CLASS
MORGAN, M.	940.5423 MOR

TITLE
Sting of the scorpion: the inside story
of the Long Range Desert Group

STING
OF THE
SCORPION

THE INSIDE STORY OF THE LONG RANGE DESERT GROUP

MIKE MORGAN

Foreword by Major General David Lloyd Owen DSO MC

SUTTON PUBLISHING

They caused us more damage than any other enemy unit of comparable strength.

Rommel, on the Long Range Desert Group

First published in 2000 by
Sutton Publishing Limited · Phoenix Mill
Thrupp · Stroud · Gloucestershire · GL5 2BU

British Library Cataloguing in Publication Data
A catalogue record for this book is available from the British Library

ISBN 0 7509 2481 0

Typeset in 11.5/14 pt Garamond.
Typesetting and origination by
Sutton Publishing Limited.
Printed and bound in England by
J.H. Haynes & Co. Ltd, Sparkford.

Contents

Dedication

This book is dedicated to my late father, Jack Morgan, a desert veteran of 2nd SAS, who later served with distinction in Italy working on the intelligence of Major Roy Farran's famous missions, the secret planning for the behind-the-lines drops in France after D-Day and the liberation of Norway, and to every soldier and officer who served in the Long Range Desert Group.

It is also a tribute to three brave men from Middlesbrough who fought alongside the legends of the wartime Special Forces:

Arthur Arger, Y Patrol LRDG – David Lloyd Owen DSO, MC;

Denis Bell, L Detachment, SRS and 1st SAS – David Stirling DSO and Paddy Mayne DSO and three bars;

Bill Hackney, SAS and SBS – Anders Lassen VC.

Foreword

MAJOR GENERAL DAVID LLOYD OWEN
CB, DSO, OBE, MC

The Long Range Desert Group is best known for its work in the vast area of the Libyan Desert, which is roughly the size of India – 1,200 miles by a thousand. Not many people know that, when that campaign ended in April 1943, the Group was reorganized to operate in Italy and the Balkans. They were trained and equipped to work in jeeps, on foot and on skis, reaching their targets by parachute or by sea.

In September 1943, the LRDG was sent to the Dodecanese, where it became involved in the seemingly pointless disaster which resulted in the fall of Leros and the loss of a complete brigade as well as one third of the Mediterranean

Outside the Farouk Hotel at Siwa's wartime LRDG base, David Lloyd Owen DSO, MC stands in front of one of the LRDG's 30-cwt trucks with the redoubtable Titch Cave at the back, November 1941. (IWM HU25299)

Fleet. The LRDG lost about a quarter of its strength of around 400 either wounded, killed or captured. But many of those taken prisoner eventually escaped and rejoined the unit.

The Leros debacle was a devastating blow, especially as the New Zealand Government decided to withdraw the squadron of those magnificent men who had played such a significant part since Colonel Bagnold formed the LRDG in June 1940. That story is well told in his own words at the beginning of this book.

However, we recovered and with renewed enthusiasm we moved across to Italy in early 1944 to harass enemy lines of communication, to support Partisans and to report on the movement of enemy shipping in the Adriatic. Our patrols operated continuously until the end of the war in Greece, Albania, Yugoslavia and Italy, carrying out over 100 successful sorties.

I remember so well the day in 1945 when we knew that the LRDG was to be disbanded after five years of war. We were stationed on the east coast of Italy and I called everyone together to discuss the formation of an Association before we were dispersed and scattered all over the world.

There was complete agreement because we were all determined to achieve two things. The first was to keep in touch. This would be done through reunions and an annual newsletter. The second was to look after any of our members who might fall on hard times. We have followed these objectives faithfully since. Similar arrangements were made in New Zealand and Southern Rhodesia.

We have always had wonderfully willing honorary secretaries to look after our affairs, and to compile the newsletter in which there has been a wealth of fascinating information, because our members have been encouraged to recall some of their wartime experiences. Mike Morgan has selected stories that have intrigued him as a professional journalist and has put this book together as a result. He has also managed to find some interesting photographs, some of which have never been published before.

I think that the reader will sense throughout this book the very strong *esprit de corps* that existed in this unique unit made up of officers and men from the Brigade of Guards and many other regiments and corps of the British Army, from the 2nd New Zealand Expeditionary Force, from Southern Rhodesia and from the yeomanry regiments of the 1st Cavalry Division sent to Palestine in 1939.

That those of us who survive still keep in touch with each other, and have met in London and in New Zealand every year, can only be a reflection of the friendships formed more than half a century ago.

I believe that Mike Morgan has captured something of that spirit and of the great qualities of the men who volunteered to serve with the LRDG.

David Lloyd Owen

Tributes

MAJOR ROY FARRAN
DSO, MC AND TWO BARS, LEGION OF HONOUR, CROIX DE GUERRE WITH PALM, US LEGION OF MERIT, ITALIAN GOLD MEDAL, GREEK WAR MEDAL

The LRDG will be remembered in history, like the Special Air Service to which it was so closely allied, as a manifestation of the adventurous spirit ever present in the British heart.

The challenge of navigation in a vast featureless desert was awesome. Crossing the soft Sand Sea in four-wheeled vehicles required courageous innovations, and the huge distances from sources of supply were bravely confronted.

The LRDG made David Stirling's early SAS raids on distant enemy airfields possible. No other way of reaching enemy targets had proved feasible by day or by night at that time.

Having struggled myself to navigate accurately by sun compass and the stars, I can appreciate the expertise of the LRDG. The boldness with which they posted their reconnaissance patrols to overlook the long coastal road was in itself remarkable, as one remembers the vulnerability to air attack of isolated and often conspicuous vehicles in the open desert.

As an old friend, I salute the LRDG and send my best wishes for the success of this history of their gallantry.

Roy Farran
Calgary, Alberta
Canada

GENERAL SIR PETER DE LA BILLIERE
GULF WAR COMMANDER

General Sir Peter de la Billiere, Gulf War commander and former president of the SAS Association, wrote the following to Major General David Lloyd Owen, former commanding officer of the LRDG, as a special tribute to mark the 50th anniversary of the LRDG Association in 1995. He specifically recalled the formation of the SAS in the Western Desert in 1941 and the crucial part the

LRDG played in the unit's early missions, transporting David Stirling's SAS raiders to their targets by truck when the initial plan to parachute in and attack on foot proved disastrously impracticable when gale force winds caused many men to be lost on the inaugural mission:

> I know David Stirling would wish me to re-emphasise the tremendously close relationship that existed between our two Regiments. I would like to say how very much the modern generation [of SAS] appreciate that we owe our existence in many ways to the help and support that we received from the LRDG in those early tumultuous days of our history.

In the savage desert war against Saddam Hussein's Iraq, modern observers were amazed at the uncanny similarity of the highly successful deep-ranging SAS motorized columns to that of their LRDG forebears of the Second World War.

Who dares forget, the Scorpion bears a lethal sting . . .

Beware the Scorpion's Bite

THE ORIGIN OF THE UNIT'S BADGE

The Scorpion was chosen for the unit's badge from the early days of the LRDG's existence and has become a proud and lasting symbol of a force which has never been surpassed in its expert field of operation and which has often been envied, imitated and admired. The lethal desert creature which strikes with lightning and paralysing force was a wise and appropriate choice for the unit's cap badges and insignia, and the means by which the badge originated is typical of the colourful characters which made up the teak-tough ranks of the desert raiders.

Bluey Grimsey of T Patrol was stung by a scorpion — and, contrary to what can often happen in the circumstances, when serious illness ensues or even life is threatened, it was the unfortunate beast that died! Bluey pickled its body in spirit — reputedly whisky — and it became his good luck talisman. The powers-that-be got wind of the tale and the rest is history.

The scorpion is a potent symbol of power in many units, but especially for small, close-knit groups such as the LRDG. Its menacing appearance and ability to strike suddenly and with great effect has led to it being selected as an emblem by many other forces. But no scorpion badge has won greater fame than that worn by the veterans of the LRDG.

Scorpions have lived on Earth for 500 million years, idolized yet feared by man. They are truly remarkable creatures. Among their peculiarities are the ability to survive with little water and no food and to live immersed in alcohol for periods of several hours. In this respect, the ferocious little arachnids show amazingly similar propensities to their human LRDG counterparts . . .

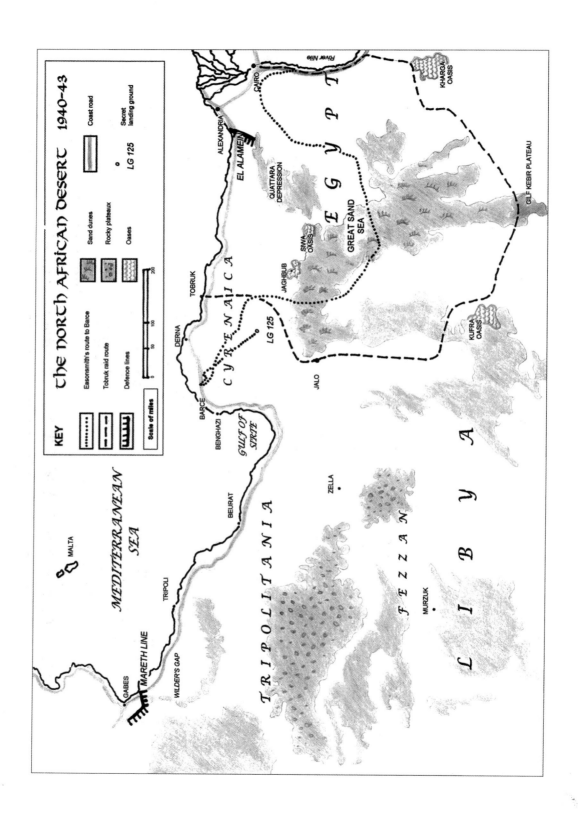

The North African Desert 1940–43

KEY

Easonsmith's route to Barce

Tobruk raid route

Defence lines

Sand dunes

Rocky plateaux

Oases

Coast road

LG 125 Secret landing ground

Scale of miles
0   50   100   200

MEDITERRANEAN SEA

MALTA

TRIPOLITANIA

GULF OF SIRTE

CYRENAICA

EGYPT

LIBYA

FEZZAN

GABES
MARETH LINE
WILDER'S GAP
TRIPOLI
BEURAT
ZELLA
MURZUK
BENGHAZI
BARCE
DERNA
TOBRUK
LG 125
JALO
JAGHBUB
SIWA OASIS
GREAT SAND SEA
QUATTARA DEPRESSION
EL ALAMEIN
ALEXANDRIA
CAIRO
River Nile
KHARGA OASIS
GILF KEBIR PLATEAU
KUFRA OASIS

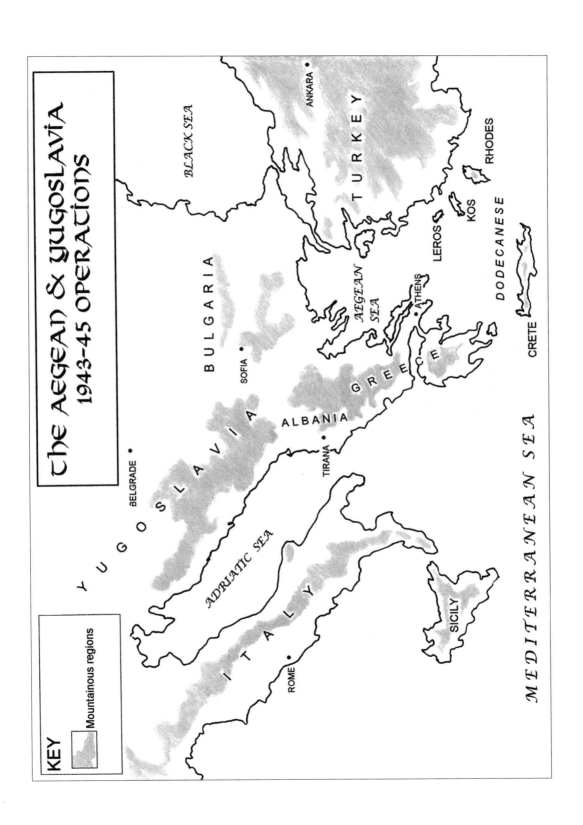

The Aegean & Yugoslavia 1943–45 operations

KEY

Mountainous regions

BLACK SEA

ANKARA

TURKEY

RHODES

KOS

LEROS

DODECANESE

BULGARIA

AEGEAN SEA

ATHENS

SOFIA

GREECE

CRETE

ALBANIA

YUGOSLAVIA

BELGRADE

TIRANA

ADRIATIC SEA

ITALY

ROME

SICILY

MEDITERRANEAN SEA

Acknowledgements

The year 2000 is the Diamond Jubilee of the LRDG's formation in 1940. It is already certain that the unit has forever won a unique place in the history of warfare and especially so in connection with its most famous area of operation, the Western Desert. This book has therefore been compiled with the full authorization of the LRDG Association as a historical tribute to all those who served in the LRDG in the Second World War, of every rank, creed and country.

It would have been impossible to assemble all these colourful stories and facts without the diligence of the veterans themselves in recording their experiences on the various raids, in such diverse and dangerous theatres of war. Likewise, without the LRDG Association's newsletters, spanning over fifty years, many of these tales would have been lost forever instead of now being available to all.

It has been decided that from the end of the year 2000, the LRDG Association will merge with the SAS Association and that the 2000 LRDG Annual Reunion will be the last, although members will meet at future SAS reunions.

Special thanks must therefore go to all the Association secretaries over the years and especially to the current – and last – secretary Jim Patch, whose name justifiably graces several of the exciting adventures which, together with those of many comrades, are now an indelible part of military folklore.

Sincere thanks must also go to Major General David Lloyd Owen, one of the finest and most respected former commanding officers of the LRDG and Chairman of the LRDG Association. Without his backing, knowledge and wholehearted support, this project could not have come to fruition.

Lastly, special acknowledgement must be made for the heartfelt tribute expressed by a stalwart and loyal friend of the LRDG, wartime SAS Major Roy Farran, DSO, MC and two bars, one of the truly legendary heroes of behind-the-lines action in the Second World War. As he has said, without the LRDG, the SAS – arguably the most famous military unit of all time – could not have got off the ground.

Mike Morgan

Raiders of the Desert

The Long Range Desert Group (LRDG) was the original desert Special Force, carrying out many daring behind-the-lines operations in the white-hot cauldron of the Second World War.

In the most destructive conflict of modern times, many Special Force units sprang from the ranks of the British Army as it fought for its life against overwhelming odds. These also included the Special Air Service, Popski's Private Army and the Special Boat Service.

Perhaps the reason why the LRDG is best remembered is the undeniably romantic image with which they became associated – the Arab head-dresses, the beards, the wild-looking brigands carrying out their audacious acts of piracy in the awe-inspiring wastes of the desert.

But its members came from the elite regiments of the British Army and from far-flung reaches of the Empire, on which the sun had still to set.

There were ramrod-straight soldiers from the Coldstream and Scots Guards who had been stationed in Egypt before the outbreak of war. They were joined by crack troops from the Cavalry Brigade which went out to Palestine in January 1940, soldiers of famous units such as the Yorkshire Hussars, the Yorkshire Dragoons and the North Somerset, Staffordshire, Cheshire and Warwickshire Yeomanry Regiments.

There were some of the toughest troops in the ranks of the LRDG – such as the superbly courageous, hardy and versatile New Zealanders, who would carve an indelible reputation in the history of the desert war, along with equally tough

Graham Warrington in Arab head-dress at Zella, January 1943. (IWM HU25078)

counterparts from Rhodesia and volunteers from far and wide, even from America.

When the 11th Scottish Commando was disbanded after heavy losses in 1941, at the costly battle of the Litani River in the Lebanon, against Vichy French forces, its members were given the choice of joining the LRDG, SAS, other Commando units, or returning to their original regiments. Many put their special skills in explosives, close combat and raiding to good use in the LRDG.

Ford and Chevrolet trucks – and later jeeps – were heavily armed with Vickers machine-guns, Lewis guns and Browning heavy calibre weaponry, plus a formidable array of small arms, Tommy guns, rifles, grenades, mines and explosives. The machine-guns, where appropriate, were oil cooled for ease of traverse and to prevent overheating in the fierce desert temperatures. Patrols consisted of four or five trucks as the optimum workable unit, although on occasion patrols joined forces for big raids. Experiments were even carried out with field guns and anti-aircraft weapons carried on the back of trucks to stiffen firepower even further.

The foundations of this unique, hard-hitting fighting unit had been laid down by a previous generation of British forces more than thirty years before when the Duke of Westminster Yeomanry roamed the desert in converted Model T Fords.

The illustrious history of the LRDG thus has its roots in the First World War, when these pioneering British Army units, known as Light Car Patrols, first traversed the arid wastes, never before crossed by military motor vehicles.

In their rickety, but surprisingly robust, Model T Fords, they ran far south into the Western Desert of Egypt, beyond the range of the camel explorers, to guard Gen Allenby's flank from hostile Arab tribes.

This was the era when Lawrence of Arabia became a living legend by blowing up railway lines, hitting the enemy with stunning force, then melting away into the desert to fight another day – just like the LRDG.

Besides romantic desert-lore, the car patrols left their successors two primitive, but essential, inventions – the sun compass for navigation and the first water condenser for trapping and recycling coolant into vehicle radiators. Without this simple, yet effective contraption, vehicles would soon overheat in the ferocious desert heat, wasting valuable water resources and limiting the range and reliability of their engines.

Later, in the 1920s, a group of enthusiasts in the Middle East, led by Major, later Brigadier, R.A. Bagnold, the founder of the LRDG and the man who knew more about sand and its effects on vehicular travel than anyone else, took to desert exploration. They too mastered the intricacies of desert travel and added to the maps of the unforgiving terrain.

Meanwhile, Bagnold perfected the sun compass and invented the prototype of the sand mat for extricating bogged down vehicles from soft sand. These were later used during the Second World War with great effect by the LRDG and Special Air Service patrols. The LRDG particularly were loath ever to abandon their precious vehicles in the desert, often towing broken down trucks back to base.

In 1939, Bagnold was posted from England to East Africa, but his ship collided with another in the Mediterranean and put into Alexandria for repairs. Bagnold took a trip to Cairo, where General, later Field Marshal, Wavell, heard of his arrival, was highly impressed by the desert pioneer and promptly had him transferred to Middle East Command.

Wavell, one of Britain's finest and most under-rated generals, knew a good man when he saw one, and his confidence was repaid by Bagnold a thousand-fold. Countless lives were saved by the vital intelligence gleaned by the all-seeing eyes of the LRDG, which roamed at will among the enemy rear ranks.

It was not until after the Italians had declared war in 1940, however, that Bagnold was able to sell his idea of an LRDG to the more sceptical high command. By then, the growing threat to Britain's empire from Italian and later powerful German forces, created a desperate need for new and untried measures. The LRDG scheme to raid deep behind the enemy lines, causing panic, confusion and wasteful enemy reinforcement over vast and scattered areas, suddenly became extremely attractive to the high command, whose troops were outnumbered and over-stretched.

Bagnold, given the go-ahead at last, was only able to recruit two of the peacetime desert veterans he already knew to create a backbone of officers for the unit – Pat Clayton, who had been in the Egyptian Government Survey, and the highly respected W.B. Kennedy Shaw, whose classic book, *Long Range Desert Group*, later told of some of the exciting exploits of the LRDG in the Western Desert, North Africa.

Most of the original unit members were New Zealanders, outstanding soldiers whose natural-born qualities of toughness and love of the outdoor life made them easily adaptable to the hardships and privations of desert war.

From numerous unorthodox sources, the new unit collected its equipment – including trucks from the American Chevrolet company, logarithm tables for vital navigational calculations from demure schoolmistresses in Cairo and binoculars from wealthy horse racing fans. In just five weeks, the men were ready for duty and raring to go into action. The unit proved its worth almost from the start in highly effective intelligence gathering and in hard-hitting raids.

They were able to operate in the desert hundreds of miles further from bases than any other unit. The LRDG's primary task initially was reconnaissance behind the enemy lines, which it reached by travelling across almost unknown country far south of the coastal belt. Patrols would bring back invaluable information about the enemy, his lines of communication, the trustworthiness

LRDG veteran Jack Davis, in another version of the Arab head-dress. (IWM HU16522)

of the local Arab population and maps of vast areas of desert never before surveyed.

One of its most valuable contributions as a reconnaissance unit was the road watch at 'Marble Arch' in Tripolitania, especially later in the campaign, when it operated deep behind Rommel's rear in the desert. Many miles behind the enemy lines, small teams of LRDG kept constant vigil on all truck and troop movements, radioing the results of their handiwork back to British Army headquarters in Cairo. For two periods in 1941 and 1942 totalling nearly six months, the LRDG kept constant check on enemy vehicles moving along the coast road a full 400 miles behind the front line.

A patrol, usually two-man, would hide up in a wadi and before dawn they would settle down under whatever cover they could find within a few hundred yards of the road and stay motionless, patiently watching and recording until nightfall. With powerful binoculars and up-to-date photographs of enemy vehicles, they noted down everything that passed along the road and reported it back to HQ, where the high command was notified and appropriate action taken, sometimes with devastating effect by the desert air force of the RAF.

The LRDG soon played an important part in other forces' operations. Its specially converted trucks transported men and supplies to points all over Libya for espionage, link-ups with the Arabs, or for helping prisoners to escape.

This 'taxi service' was also used by the Special Air Service in its early days before it had its own transport, literally propelling the now world-famous force into action and its own date with history. LRDG veterans were involved in many of the SAS's wild adventures which caused massive panic and destruction in the rear of the enemy ranks.

After one of these trips, a combined group set off to beat up Marsa Brega, a shallow anchorage used by the enemy to land supplies from coastal vehicles in a supposedly safe area. Driving along in their own convoy, they mingled with enemy convoys on the coast road, the only approach, shouting greetings in the dark to trucks driving in the opposite direction. Arriving at Marsa Brega, they opened up with all their machine-guns on vehicles parked by the road, dropping 'sticky bombs' into trucks further away, killing everyone who stood in their way, before speeding off along the road before the stunned enemy could gather reinforcements to chase them.

To discourage pursuit, the commander in the last truck laid mines in the road and heard several explosions before they got out of earshot. By dawn, the party was camouflaged in the desert, watching enemy planes searching in vain for them.

But the LRDG had plenty of wild adventures of its own. As part of its task of constantly keeping the enemy guessing, the LRDG linked up with Free Frenchmen from the Chad and attacked the Murzuk oasis in the Fezzan, where the Italians had a small fort, a landing field and a garrison of about 150 heavily armed troops.

The attack was launched while the garrison was enjoying an after-lunch stroll and several of the Italian troops, including the commander, were killed before they knew what had hit them. Then, while one party kept the main strength of the garrison busy in the fort, another went off to the airfield and destroyed the waiting planes, hangars and equipment.

Raiders from the LRDG withdrew almost unmolested. This lightning attack took place many hundreds of miles behind the fighting front and caused widespread fear among the Italians, causing large numbers of troops to be diverted to guard airfields, ammunition dumps and other military installations well behind the lines, helping take vital pressure off the British Army's front-line fighting units.

Later on, when the Eighth Army was preparing its great comeback battle at El Alamein, the LRDG was busy disrupting Rommel's communications and panicking districts all over the rear areas.

Among its operations at this time was one of its most destructive attacks. A squadron of LRDG approaching Barce from the south, cleaned up a traffic control post shooting the Italian officer in command, cut the telephone wires, knocked out a couple of light tanks defending the road and drove to a crossroads just outside the town, where it split up.

A New Zealand patrol went to the airfield, shot down Italians at the gates, threw grenades into the mess windows and then, with a jeep and

Tough-looking LRDG Tpr Franks in Arab head-dress, smoking a well-earned pipe of tobacco. (IWM HU16513)

A seasoned desert veteran engrossed in a letter from home. (IWM CBM 2217)

four 30-cwt trucks, drove in single file around the airfield firing incendiary bullets at each aircraft while a man in the last truck used short delay action bombs to deal with any which did not catch fire. They destroyed at least twenty aircraft and damaged a dozen more. The patrol got clean away with the exception of one truck. A second patrol, of Guards, went to the barracks, killed the sentries and stormed through the buildings throwing grenades into windows, doors and slit trenches, from which Italians were wildly returning fire. Meanwhile, the commander of the squadron and his driver, drove into the town causing further chaos with their twin Vickers, wrecking a dozen vehicles.

Before dawn, the group was reunited outside the town and ran into an ambush in which three men were wounded. Finally, enemy aircraft found them and attacked until dusk, by which time the LRDG had six wounded men and only one 30-cwt truck and two jeeps left. During the night both jeeps were put out of action. The medical officer with a driver, fitter and navigator set off in the truck with the wounded to a secret landing ground from where they were picked up. The rest had to walk. It was not the first nor the last time that LRDG men found themselves stranded behind the lines with no vehicles and precious little food or water and yet still managed to get home. This operation cost the Axis about thirty aircraft and numerous casualties. The LRDG had six wounded, all of whom recovered, and lost ten prisoners and fourteen vehicles. The unit was awarded two Distinguished Service Orders (DSOs), one Military Cross (MC) and three Military Medals (MM) for this one raid alone.

The headaches of operating in the desert behind enemy lines became routine for the LRDG. It found its own routes, many never navigated before, made its own maps, evolved a technique of driving in the desert, established its own food, water and fuel dumps, had its own repair shops for vehicles and, partly as a counter to the constant danger of being caught badly wounded far from friendly territory, had its own aeroplanes to fly wounded out and bring personnel in.

In Eighth Army's final triumphant advance, the LRDG played a truly decisive part. Mapping the country as they went, patrol members pioneered new 'impassable' southern routes into Tripolitania and Tunisia, providing guides for each of the New Zealand Division's famous left-hooks around the near-impregnable Mareth Line. This brilliantly successful operation effectively finished off the Axis as a major force in North Africa, saving thousands of lives in a costly frontal attack on formidable prepared positions, and enabled the eventual total victory of the British and Commonwealth Army and American forces advancing from Algeria and Morocco.

Withdrawn from Tunisia in April 1943, the LRDG went into training for reconnaissance in mountainous country, moving either in jeeps or on foot. The 30-cwt trucks which had served them faithfully in the desert were replaced by sturdy jeeps armed to the teeth principally with Vickers K machine-guns, as used by the SAS and Popski's Private Army in Italy and elsewhere. One patrol in each squadron became a mule patrol and the men who had been used to the burning desert heat learned to use skis on snow. They also started to take a parachutists' course, but just after it had begun most of the LRDG was ordered off to action again, in the Aegean.

Their headquarters were established on Leros, where Allied LRDG patrols stiffened the garrison, went out on reconnaissance trips to other islands and kept a shipping watch, similar to the 'Marble Arch' road watch. The group had many more adventures – one patrol on Stampalia was let down by the Italian garrison when the Germans attacked and had to hide for a month before it could get away in a caique boat. Another patrol that stayed on the German-occupied island of Seriphos for nearly a month lived for the last week on a diet of beans and marrows. On the first anniversary of Alamein, a party of fifty set off to liquidate the German garrison on the island of Levitha, at the request of the Royal Navy. However, it ran into a strong German garrison in prepared positions and was forced out of the island with the loss of two officers and thirty-nine other ranks.

On Leros itself, 125 LRDG scattered all over the island saw a lot of fighting, much of it in an infantry role. One party, at the top of Mount Clidi, retook the position from which it had been forced out by crack parachutists and held it until well after British forces surrendered. A party of seventy got away from Leros and most of those left behind in the islands managed to filter back to freedom later. In addition, the LRDG helped other troops to get away and LRDG officers returned to organize other troops to escape.

The impulse to escape was a common feature among the LRDG when captured. These free spirits, so used to operating boldly and using their own initiative, did not take well to being locked up and usually made a break for freedom at the earliest opportunity, no matter what risks were involved. Many of these daring escapes and risky periods on the run are recorded in this book.

Once out of the Dodecanese, the LRDG prepared for further operations in other theatres of war, completing its training as parachutists. The elite New Zealanders left the unit and tough Rhodesians took their place, but some of the Kiwis came back to the LRDG in Italy, unable to resist their burning desire to fight the Germans.

The LRDG had only one operation on the Italian mainland and that, because something went wrong with the drops, was only partly successful. For the rest of the war, its territory was on the other side of the Adriatic, from the Austrian frontier to the southern Greek island of Kythera. Based on Adriatic islands, the LRDG took to the ocean waves. A headquarters schooner, the *Kufra*, named after one of the desert bases, appeared on the scene to transport men and supplies to the various hot spots.

The heavy truck section, which had supplied them in the desert, became the crew of the MV Palma, which was skippered by a Yeomanry officer who had learned to navigate in North Africa. He had as boatswain an NCO who was a farmer in civil life. The light repair squadron turned its attention from vehicles to boat building and was outstanding at shoe horning unwieldy jeep engines into speed boats!

Greece, Albania and Yugoslavia became what the desert had been to the LRDG. Its role here was much the same, except that now it was co-operating with fighting partisans. The group even ran a Balkan 'taxi service' on the same lines as the old Libyan version. Duties included lying patiently watching enemy shipping. Owing to Allied air superiority, vessels could move only at night and the men lay up, camouflaged, in inlets during daylight. LRDG patrols on islands and the mainland reported the whereabouts of enemy vessels by radio to the RAF and Royal Naval stations in the area. Lightning fast and heavily armed MTBs would turn up at night and bottle the ships up in inlets. Rocket-firing planes would then attack soon afterwards during daylight and wipe them out. Between them, the RAF and Royal Navy accounted for well over 100 vessels as a result of LRDG vigilance. One officer stationed along the Adriatic coast had a huge bounty of £1,000 put on his head by the Germans, but none of the partisans with whom he worked gave him away, even though he was there for four and a half months.

But coast watching was not the LRDG's only function in the area. There were plenty of reconnaissance trips and raids in the old style to keep the enemy on his toes. One officer, with a wireless operator, went from an island in the northern Adriatic to the mainland and through the Denaric Alps and nearly to Trieste and back – more than 500 miles on foot through enemy country.

As the Germans pulled out of the Balkans, it became the LRDG's job, in co-operation with other units, to hinder the retreat. A small party of LRDG, with partisans, cut and held the El Basan toTirana road in Albania for three weeks.

Jeep-borne LRDG followed the Germans out of Greece, some of them getting as far as the Adriatic, to Athens and even Salonika. Others went due north from Greece to link up with more LRDG who had been dropped by parachute in southern Yugoslavia. Meanwhile, on the European mainland, one squadron of LRDG had undergone intensive training in mountain warfare, ready to help take Hitler's mountain fortress in Bavaria if needed. In the event, Hitler committed suicide in his Berlin bunker and so the end of the Axis in the Balkans meant the end of operations for the LRDG.

For a while there was talk of the unit going to the Far East to fight the Japanese, who were still fanatically resisting the inexorable British and American advance. Around 80 per cent of the LRDG loyally volunteered for service there, but the war on Japan was brought to an abrupt end with the dropping of the atomic bombs on Hiroshima and Nagasaki and final victory was assured at last.

The glorious story of the LRDG, who won admirers from all sides during the war, came to a close after five action-packed years and the famous unit was disbanded with great sadness, praise and regret in July 1945.

CHAPTER 1

Piracy on the High Desert

HOW IT ALL STARTED: RALPH BAGNOLD, FOUNDING GENIUS OF THE LEGENDARY DESERT FORCE

The late Ralph Bagnold was the brilliant originator and first commanding officer of the Long Range Desert Group. He was a man of uncanny vision, expert in the movements of the remorselessly shifting sands, with vast practical experience in negotiating the treacherous, arid wastes in motor vehicles, surmounting daunting difficulties with clever innovation, skill and guile.

Pirates of the desert! Jubilant members of Y Patrol celebrate a successful sortie behind enemy lines on the way back to Kufra. Left to right, back: Trp Tankie Babb, RTR; Cpl Jack Harris, Somerset Yeomanry; Gnr James Patch, RA; Sgt Derek Hutchins, Somerset Yeomanry; L/Cpl Arthur Titch Cave, MM, Somerset Yeomanry; L/Cpl Brian Springford, Somerset Yeomanry; Tpr Ken Tinckler, Cheshire Yeomanry; Craftsman Alf Tighe, MM, REME; Tpr 'Jesus' Armstrong. Front. Pte 'Darkie' Divine; Pte John 'Daisy' McKay, Seaforths; Tpr F. Gordon; Harry Harrison, Yorkshire Hussars; Pte William Fraser, Seaforths; Tpr Micky Coombs, Somerset Yeomanry; Tpr Robert Davies; Tpr 'Bomski' Cashin, Cheshire Yeomanry. (IWM HU25277)

LRDG raiders use sand mats to extricate one of their trucks from the clutches of a soft sand quagmire. (IWM E12394)

Simple, yet effective sun compasses, and portable mats to help vehicles drive themselves out of the clutches of soft, sinking sand were just two of Bagnold's refinements and inventions, without which the LRDG could not have functioned with such telling effect. Meticulous maps of the desert areas of operation, made before the war, came into their own, together with key survival techniques and knowledge of hidden sources of water. The experience of First World War Light Car Patrols in the Western Desert also provided much key information.

Bagnold's own account of the origin of the LRDG was reproduced as part of the LRDG's 50th anniversary celebrations in 1995, privately circulated in the veterans' own newsletter. His words, as the first commander and founder of the LRDG, remain as the definitive statement of the proud and pioneering LRDG tradition, the original and most charismatic of the British Army's Special Forces.

His study into the relentless shifting sands of the North African desert was made in the turbulent years in the run-up to the Second World War, when war seemed inevitable to many. However, the wide-open spaces of the desert were the last places on earth it was expected that such a terrifying conflict would envelop . . .

I had no idea at the time that our travels could have any serious scientific outcome. It was only later that it dawned on me that the natural mechanism we had become so familiar with, whereby the wind blowing on loose dry sand grains creates and activates the huge dune forms, was as yet entirely unknown. I became so interested that on my retirement from the Army in 1935 I built at home a suitable wind tunnel of plywood and glass panes and equipped with simple wind-measuring instruments. With this, some sieves and a supply of builder's sand, I embarked on the first scientific study of the mechanism. I felt it was really just exploring in another form.

Lt Col Ralph Bagnold, legendary founder of the LRP and LRDG, is pictured in 1944 by Walter Stoneman in this superb study. (Courtesy of the National Portrait Gallery, London)

The Physics of Blown Sand and Desert Dunes was finished in 1939 and published shortly afterwards. To my astonishment it soon became the standard textbook on the subject and still remains so. Indeed, when NASA's spacecraft were able to examine the Martian landscape at close range, the book was found to allow the sand-driving mechanism to be adapted to the very different and far more tenuous atmosphere of Mars.

Although most of us were young army officers, not one of us in the 1920s dreamed for a moment that war could ever come to the vast, waterless and lifeless Libyan Desert. We simply enjoyed the excitement of pioneering into the unknown. But the Second World War was declared almost as soon as the physics book was finished. I had served in the First War in the trenches in France as an engineer officer and, as a recompense, spent two happy years at Cambridge. Now, as a reservist, I was recalled to the Army in the autumn of 1939 and posted to East Africa. It was by the pure accident of a convoy collision in the Mediterranean that I was landed at Port Said to await another troop ship.

Seizing the opportunity, I took a train to Cairo to look up old friends. That visit, again accidentally, resulted in my posting being changed to Egypt, a country I was at home in.

HQ British Troops in Egypt [BTE] was just the same as I had known it. Its role having long been confined to internal security it seemed as yet to have given no thought to the defence of the country against attack from outside. Training had always been for a war in some temperate climate rather than in the desert on its doorstep. The staff seemed to be obsessed with the danger of any soldier getting lost, to the frustration of the more enterprising troops under it. The 700-mile western frontier with Libya, running south nominally along longitude 25E, was unguarded and unpatrolled, the Light Car Patrols of 1916 having been disbanded long before, and most types of army vehicle were unsuitable for desert going.

I wrote a three-page memo on what my experience suggested should be done in a small way, such as re-forming an up-to-date version of the Light Car Patrol. My General thoroughly agreed and sent the memo to HQ BTE. The idea was turned down angrily as though it was impertinent! Even the idea of driving out into the desert seemed to appal them as impossible, insane or at least reckless.

In the spring of 1940 things began to change. General Sir Archibald Wavell became an overlord, as C-in-C Middle East Land Forces with responsibilities from India to West Africa. A fresh staff was arriving from England to form his new GHQ, so HQ BTE sank to a subordinate position. All this time we knew that a great Italian army was massing on the Libyan coast ready to invade Egypt and another equally large army lay in Ethiopia ready to invade the Sudan. But on our side, no overt preparations were allowed, in the vain hope that Mussolini would remain neutral.

Then came June 1940. France collapsed. Italy declared war on us. The Mediterranean was closed, so we were cut off from England except by the long slow shipping route round the Cape. I felt impelled to do my bit. Pulling out the last copy of my former memo I added a few paragraphs and persuaded a friend in Ops to lay it on the C-in-C's own desk. I was sent for within an hour.

Wavell was alone. He put me at ease in an armchair and invited me to talk. Here, I felt almost at once that I had at last found a man of vision and vast knowledge who understood. I told him of the possibility of an enemy raid on Aswan from their southern-most outpost of Uweinat only 500 miles away across ideal desert going. I had myself done the journey in a day and a half. Such a raid would cut our vital link with the Sudan. If attacked, the raiders would simply threaten to open all the sluices of the Aswan Dam and cause disastrous floods in Egypt. Moreover, if Lorenzini was still in Libya, he would be just the man to do it. He and I had discussed that very thing during our strange desert meeting years ago. (Major Lorenzini was an adventurous Italian officer whom Bagnold had met before the war. He boasted he could take vehicles across the desert from the Libyan/Sudanese border from Uweinat to destroy the Aswan Dam.) We had now no means of knowing what the Italians might be preparing away in the far south.

I proposed that a small group of modernised Light Patrols should be created, specially equipped, manned by specially trained volunteers in really desert-worthy vehicles. By applying all the techniques our former little private parties had learned, we would have the extreme mobility of 1,500 miles of travel entirely self-contained, with water and food for several weeks. We could get into

An awesome panorama of undulating dunes in the Great Eastern desert. (IWM HU16487)

the emptiness of inner Libya by a back door I alone knew of, through the heart of the sand barrier. We would then track-read both the routes leading south. 'What', asked Wavell, 'would you do if you were to find no signs of unusual activity?' Without thought I said, 'How about some piracy on the high desert?'

At the word piracy the rugged face that had seemed a bit stern suddenly broke into a broad grin. 'Can you be ready in six weeks?'

I said, 'Yes.'

'Of course,' he said, 'there'll be opposition and delay.' He pressed a bell. His Chief-of-Staff, General Sir Arthur Smith, came in. 'Arthur,' said Wavell, 'Bagnold seeks a talisman. Get this typed for my signature right away: "To all heads of departments and branches. I wish any request made by Major Bagnold in person to be met at once without question."' Then to me, 'Not a word of this must go out. There are 60,000 enemy subjects here. Get a good cover story from my DMI [Director of Military Intelligence]. When you are ready, write your own operation orders and show them to me personally.' That was all.

I had been given complete carte blanche, presumably to make trouble anywhere in Libya. Clearly, any threat to the 900 mile unguarded desert flank of the enemy's supply route along the North African coast would be taken very seriously. The C-in-C had conceived a big bluff.

There was much to do, but little time. Three of the old gang were available. Rupert Harding-Newman was on the spot in Cairo, Pat Clayton was surveying somewhere in Tanganyika and Bill Shaw was in Jerusalem, curator of the

Palestine Museum. The latter two were extricated, flown to Cairo and commissioned captains within 48 hours. Meanwhile, Rupert collected thirty 1½-ton commercial Chevrolet chassis from local dealers and elsewhere, and he and I set to work making all the detailed designs needed for ordnance workshops to make the many conversions we wanted. Bill Shaw became our intelligence officer and chief navigator and set to work acquiring and improvising all the instruments.

There were to be three patrols, each self-contained and capable of independent action. A special ration scale was drawn up and authorised, as also were special footwear (sandals) and special Arab headdress for face protection against sandstorms. I raided the GHQ reserve of stores for machine-guns and suitable long-range radio transmitters. A very bright wireless officer volunteered to join, as also did a doctor.

General Freyberg agreed to ask his New Zealand Division for volunteers for an 'undisclosed mission of some danger'. There was a great response. Two officers and some 150 other ranks we had asked for arrived just as the first trucks were coming out of the workshops — tough, self-reliant and responsible people with many useful skills. They were just what we had hoped for. Training was largely combined with cross-country journeys to Ain Dalla to make a forward dump of petrol there, as we had done in the old days. The New Zealanders were astonishingly quick to learn a new, and to them a very strange, way of life.

I laid great stress on conservation. We were going a very long way without the possibility of obtaining anything anywhere. So there must be no losses and no breakdown involving the abandonment of a single vehicle.

We were ready on time. The C-in-C came himself to see us off and wish us good luck. The 150-mile sand dune barrier was crossed twice over in order to start fully loaded from the Libyan side. Then, on the very day, 15 September, the Italians crossed the Egyptian frontier going east along the coast, two little patrols crossed the same frontier going west into Libya, 300 miles further south.

Mitford's patrol penetrated so far west as to cross and examine both the enemy's southward routes to Kufra and Uweinat. Finding no signs of activity on either, he turned pirate, drove southward and burned unguarded aircraft and aviation petrol dumps. A small convoy was intercepted carrying supplies and mail to Kufra. The crew and mail were captured and the trucks were made to disappear without trace.

Meanwhile, Clayton took a more southerly route across southern Libya to make contact with a French outpost of Chad Province. He too found no trace of enemy activity. Both patrols returned triumphantly to Cairo having covered 60,000 truck miles in enemy territory without losing a single truck.

As a result, three more patrols were ordered to be raised, with volunteers from the Guards and from the Rhodesian and Yeomanry regiments. More raids took

An LRDG patrol member keeps guard with heavy machine-gun on a truck in desert wastes to avoid surprise attack while his comrades relax. (IWM E12408)

place during the next few months. Isolated garrisons were shot up. On one occasion two posts, up to 300 miles apart, were attacked on the same day by mysterious troops who appeared from nowhere and disappeared. The Italian invasion was halted for a vital period.

Wavell's bluff paid off.

As a final stroke in the Italian phase of the Libyan campaign Clayton, Shaw and I decided to raid the Murzuk oasis in the far south-west 1,400 miles away, provided we could induce the French to help us with supplies. They were an unknown quantity to us. Douglas Newbold was then head of the Sudan Government. I flew to Khartoum to see him. With his secret backing, I flew on to Chad.

A contract was signed, with the provincial governor's blessing, between Lieutenant Colonel Bagnold and the French Army whereby they would supply all we wanted on condition we let them join us with a token contingent consisting of the army commander himself and a captain. By implication, Chad Province would rebel and openly join the Allies and De Gaulle. The raid was

Free French hero Gen Leclerc, later created a Marshal of France. (via LRDG)

very successful, though sadly the gallant French commander Colonel d'Ornano was killed. De Gaulle immediately sent as his replacement Colonel, soon afterwards the famous General, Leclerc. The latter and I became friends and cooperated closely till he left to join our Eighth Army on the coast.

In the summer of 1941, Guy Prendergast arrived from England. I had wanted him badly from the start. Now, I felt, I could hand over to a younger man.

The LRDG continued to play its unique role until the end of the North African campaign. It was the first of several 'private armies'. Its speciality remained, as it had begun in the old pre-war days, extreme mobility and accurate navigation. Occasionally, two private armies would cooperate, as when the LRDG carried David Stirling's SAS, who then had no transport, to do their sabotaging of enemy aircraft on the ground.'

LONG RANGE PATROL – FORERUNNER OF THE LRDG

Little has been written about how the LRDG began. Brigadier Teddy Mitford MC, late officer commanding W Patrol, who was one of the last remaining original members of the unit in the UK, wrote a fascinating account about the Long Range Patrol, forerunner of the LRDG, showing how founder Ralph Bagnold produced the unique unit from virtually nothing in a remarkably short time.

The germ of the idea for the unit started during Bagnold's tour of duty in Egypt in the years up to 1932 when, having read extensively about the Light Car Patrols of the First World War which operated successfully in the desert, he organized parties of civilian and army friends and travelled many hundreds of miles into unknown country.

Bagnold gained an immense amount of valuable experience of desert travel which he later described in his book *Libyan Sands*. Brigadier Mitford takes up the story . . .

The Italians entered the war in June 1940. At that time Ralph found himself back in Egypt and managed to obtain an interview with the then GOC-in-C, General Wavell, on the subject of producing some form of counter to possible Italian threats in the desert to the south. The General was very sympathetic to his ideas and agreed that patrols should be specially formed as soon as possible. Some of the necessary equipment was very unorthodox.

The British Army in Egypt considered it to be difficult and quite possibly dangerous to travel out of sight of the pyramids, but we did have annual manoeuvres a few miles into the desert. We always knew where they would take place because the sappers put up water points for the cavalry and petrol points for the armour. Neither of these could meet during the exercise in case the tanks frightened the horses!

I was posted to 3rd Armoured Company in 1932. There were three mechanised units in Egypt and some wheeled transport in supply units, but everyone else, including artillery, Royal Engineers, signals etc, were horsed or on foot.

Almost every year from 1935, parts of the army went to Mersa Matruh, by train, owing to some international crisis. When the crisis subsided we returned to Cairo, also by train. I soon caught the desert motoring disease and bought a Ford car, which I fitted with fat desert tyres. I was able to carry out a few journeys across Sinai in 1935 to Aqaba, Petra, Jerusalem and back to Cairo and in 1938 to Kufra via Gialo (Jalo) and back. This, with some fairly short-range military recces, gave me a little more experience than some. None of this in any way compared with Ralph Bagnold and those who accompanied him on his desert travels.

Ralph, having received the go-ahead from General Wavell and, armed with his signed talisman, got to work forming what were then known as the Long Range Patrols. It was decided to form a small HQ and three patrols each of two officers and thirty men carried in eleven vehicles, also a small supply section of three large trucks for building forward dumps. He was very fortunate in obtaining the transfer from the New Zealand Divisional Cavalry of five officers and about 110 other ranks, all volunteers, who were in every way suitable for carrying out the tasks required.

Ralph had transferred to LRP as officers Pat Clayton from the Egyptian Desert Survey and Bill Kennedy Shaw from Palestine. Tim Heywood came from the Middlesex Yeomanry as Signals Officer and Captain Edmundson from NZ Medical Corps. The three patrols were commanded by Pat Clayton, Captain Don Steele from NZ infantry and myself. I had been transferred very willingly from 7th Armoured Division. Rupert Harding-Newman, Royal Tank

Regiment, could not be extracted from the Egyptian Military Mission but was of great value to Ralph in organising the lists of stores required.

The immense task began of equipping this unit. Vehicles were produced mainly from civilian sources, navigation equipment from friends in Egyptian government departments and more normal stores from the army using the talisman signed by the General. The three patrols were formed and as soon as they received their equipment they started training. There was no time to waste. The vehicles arrived complete with box bodies, which had been designed during the early Bagnold trips. The armament was one Vickers machine-gun per patrol and some Lewis guns, First World War type, as seen in television's *Dad's Army*. I think I was the only one to know anything about the Lewis gun, having been taught its use at Sandhurst twelve years before. My patrol was also given a Polish anti-tank 37-mm gun with little ammunition and dubious sights. We managed to discard this after our first training run.

Navigators were trained by Pat Clayton and Bill Kennedy Shaw, signals operators by Tim Heywood and medical orderlies by Dr Edmundson. Shorty Barrett, our quartermaster from NZ Divisional Cavalry, was winning the battle against military bureaucracy and collecting all the stores, waving the talisman in the faces of an astonished Q Branch and saying that they were required *now*, if not sooner.

Our vehicles had painted on them the 7th Armoured Division red rat to disguise our real purpose. Ralph produced a camouflage pattern of very broad dark and light stripes, different for each truck, which would help in areas of rock and scrub. It was difficult to fire a Vickers MG into the air against aircraft without the ammunition causing stoppages by slipping out of the belt. Ralph produced a metal plate welded to the belt box carrier, which kept the belt in line. A fitting was also put on each vehicle on which the Lewis gun was fixed.

Finally, the work was completed. We made training runs in all conditions of desert and tried out all our equipment. There is the much-quoted story of how Ralph had noticed that the tyres of a vehicle had not been pumped up to the correct pressure. He demanded this should be done against the pleas of the New Zealand driver that he had already done so. Ralph walked on and the driver was heard to say – and I give the expurgated version – 'The trouble with that joker is that he's always right.' And of course he was.

Ralph Bagnold got the green light from General Wavell in mid-June 1940 and the patrols left Cairo on their first operational journey on 3 September. This was a really incredible achievement.

LRDG FORMED

In November 1940, LRP became LRDG. Three more patrols, Guards, Yeomanry and Rhodesian, were formed. The LRDG was initially due to one

An LRDG patrol disappears into the desert wastes on a vital clandestine mission. (IWM HU16490)

man, Major Ralph Bagnold, who made it work and inspired those under his command to carry out his ideas. The New Zealand troops who formed the LRP were first class and, with the experts at HQ, they were responsible for the early successes, which continued when the Group was expanded and new patrols equipped and trained.

The spirit of this extraordinary unit is a tribute to the man who thought it out and produced it.

KEY DISCOVERER OF THE QATTARA DEPRESSION – BY MODEL T FORD

The late Captain Claud H. Williams MC was a remarkable man and it is generally accepted that he was the first to 'discover' the Qattara (Quattara) Depression in modern times, one of the key geographical features of the campaign in the Western Desert in the Second World War and a vital part of the extensive knowledge of the LRDG patrols. This gave them a huge advantage over Rommel's opposing enemy forces.

The Depression is a vast area of sand dunes and impassable salt marsh hundreds of square miles in extent and at its lowest point 400 feet below sea level. At Alamein, the southern flanks of the opposing British and Commonwealth and German and Italian Axis armies rested on the Depression, which made it impossible for either army to turn the flank of the other – thus the turning point Battle of El Alamein in 1943 became a frontal grinding struggle, so brilliantly won by General, later Field Marshal, Montgomery.

During the First World War, Williams, of the Pembroke Yeomanry, commanded No. 5 Light Car Patrol, one of the forerunners of the LRDG, operating in the desert in Model T Fords, to provide a mobile scouting force with which to help counter the possibility of an Arab advance through Siwa and other oases.

With Turkish help, Arab forces had invaded Egypt in 1915, but near the coast within reach of water, they were repelled by British horsed yeomanry and camel corps.

Williams started out on a recce to see if the Senussi [tribe] in Siwa could be attacked from the east. He failed to get through the salt marsh, but realized the totally impenetrable nature of the Depression to wheeled vehicles and reported this vital fact to the Egyptian Government Desert Surveys. However, it was a full ten years before they made a proper survey and could verify Williams's key discovery, about which he wrote a War Office handbook – *Report on the Military Geography of the North Western Desert of Egypt*.

Williams died in about his ninetieth year in Gisborne, New Zealand in the late 1960s, but his pioneering contribution to the war effort will long be remembered in LRDG circles.

PHONEY WAR, MI5 AND AN UNNERVING MEETING WITH 'BAGGERS' BAGNOLD

Tim Heywood reflects on the birth of LRDG signals. It all began for Tim when he went to see his father in Wormwood Scrubs, of all places, in August 1939. As a Wireless Officer, of the 1st Middlesex Yeomanry, Tim had a plan to keep first-class wireless operators, mostly ex-GPO men, amused and in training by using their receivers for interception work. The problem was what to listen for and what to do with the results . . .

The Regiment's job at this time was to provide emergency communications for London Area Defence in the event of the cataclysmic bombing of the city that was expected on the outbreak of war. My immediate responsibility was a chain of radio stations strung out across central London from a police station in Kensington to a dugout in the Royal Docks. Interspersed were stations in strange places such as Leaf Yard in Hyde Park and Duck Island in St James's Park. Control was in the basement of the War Office with an aerial on the roof that always gave trouble.

It is interesting to note that the politicians of the day so underestimated the quality and fortitude of the inhabitants of the East End that they expected them to riot and loot the West End when the bombing started. To stop this a few First World War Rolls Royce armoured cars were strategically placed in police stations near my wireless sets. Later on, when I saw their tracks in the desert, I wondered if they were the same vehicles. They certainly looked like it.

Such was my lack of security in those days that I wrote to my father at home in Northumberland telling him all about where I was, what I was doing and mentioning my ideas of how to keep the chaps happy. Little did I know that he too had been mobilised and was also in London. I was somewhat mystified and intrigued to receive a telephone message that Major Heywood was in Wormwood Scrubs and would I visit him there as soon as possible! On arrival at the gate, I was greeted with the information that he was with MI5 – the first I had heard of it – and that I would find him in the chief warder's office in A Block, the general direction of which was pointed out to me.

Eventually, I found the place, knocked on the door, marched in, saluted and said good afternoon. Whereupon the balloon went up. Apparently, a *Daily Mirror* reporter had got in the day before with a photographer. The story had been suppressed with difficulty, security had been tightened and no one was allowed in without a pass and an escort.

After the furore had died down, I was taken round and introduced to some interesting people who, saying that I could be of great use to them, asked if I was prepared to leave the Regiment and be seconded to them. Although of course I agreed, alas, it was not to be. The War Office was not prepared to lose good cannon fodder such as a healthy young Territorial Officer. So things took their course. The Regiment, relieved of its job in London, was sent to Retford to prepare for overseas service. On Boxing Day 1939 we set off and after a most uncomfortable journey by land and sea reached Palestine in early January as 1st Cavalry Divisional Signals stationed at Nathanya and later Haifa.

Six months followed with little to do except ride, shoot, bathe and lie on the beach at Nathanya or sail dinghies at Haifa, while we lived off the fat of the land washed down with champagne at 10 shillings a bottle. My wireless sets were only used once on manoeuvres in the Hebron hills. It was enough for me. Lady Astor at the time rudely referred to us in a speech to the House [of Commons] as 'the drunken and licentious soldiery basking on the beaches of the Holy Land'. There was a war on and I wrote to my father in despair. The Army Post Office was swift in those days and I got a reply very quickly. It would be useful, it said, if I visited Cairo soon and went to a certain address, where I would meet someone I had met in prison.

Coincidentally, in a day or so I was due to attend a short course with the 11th Hussars in Cairo on the use of wireless in tanks and armoured cars – the division was expecting to be mechanized. So a few days after the letter arrived, I was able to go to a house in a quiet street behind GHQ Middle East. There I found M04, later to be SOE, and one of the people I had met in the Scrubs. After a short chat, I was taken round and introduced to Colonel Bagnold and Captain Kennedy Shaw. The former I found somewhat unnerving at first, a small wizened figure with piercing eyes and an abrupt manner. My interview with him went something like this . . .

'Do you know the Number 11 set?'

'Yes, sir.'

'Well?'

'Yes, pretty well. We are equipped with them.'

'What is their range?' Then I noticed his Royal Corps of Signals lapel badges and became cautious.

'Officially about 20 miles,' then proudly, 'However, recently, using two of them, I have managed to communicate with our HQ in Haifa from Beersheba, which is about 120 miles.'

'That's nothing. I expect you to manage over 1,000 miles,' he said. Then with a winning smile, 'Don't worry, I'll show you how.'

And that was the end of my first interview with the great man. Bill Shaw was utterly charming, explaining a little of the history of the Long Range Patrols, he swore me to secrecy and sent me back to M04. There I was asked whether I was prepared to volunteer as Signals Officer for the emerging organisation. I replied that of course I would but that I was very much afraid that my Colonel back at Haifa might have other ideas. I was told not to worry, to return to my Regiment and say little of what had happened. Everything would be arranged.

On reaching our Officers' Mess in General Allenby's old house on Mount Carmel, there was a message for me to report to the CO at once. My Colonel and his second in command were absolutely furious. I was asked what the devil I had been doing in Cairo as they had just received orders for me to report at once to the Signals Officer-in-Chief Middle East. It was breaking up the Regiment, they fumed, and they would not have it. I was then told that the Divisional Commander wanted to see me.

This made me anxious for, although I knew General Clarke quite well, having served as a deck hand on his yacht, I wondered what he would say. I need not have worried. He rose from his desk with hand outstretched and greeted me with 'How much he wished he was a young man like me, how lucky I was' etc.

Back at Regimental HQ, some thought me mad, others were envious. All said goodbye as if I was going to my death. But it was done and in early October I reported to the Citadel in Cairo. There I met Sergeant Potts and a Signalman. LRDG Signals Squadron was born!

THE FIRST LONG RANGE PATROL

Major Pat Clayton arrived in Cairo from Tanganyika on Saturday 27 July 1940, a 45-year-old civil servant of low medical category, in response to a vague message apparently offering a safe chair-borne job in Cairo. On arrival, however, he found he was to report to his old friend Ralph Bagnold, who asked him that same morning to make a bold patrolling programme while a new unit of 'enormous and terrifyingly fit' New Zealanders began to draw equipment. Pat Clayton explained just what the mysterious and exciting experience felt like . . .

An obvious start was for a small patrol to drive across the Italian routes leading from the coast to Kufra and the south and see from the traffic and tracks what the Italians were up to. A couple of cars would do and no wireless, anyway the latter was not yet ready. On the Sunday evening, Bagnold came back with the Chief-of-Staff's initials approving it. 'Fine,' said I, chair-borne and still a civilian. 'Send me the poor mutt who is to go and I'll put him wise.'

'Oh you're going,' said Bagnold, laconically and he being Bagnold, on 7 August 1940, I went!

The party was six New Zealanders in two Chevrolet pick-ups, Lance Corporal Hamilton, Croucher, Tinker, Spottiswood, Elmslie, Curtis and myself and Ali Said Fudail, an old driver friend of mine from Desert Survey days, borrowed from Murray. We had a Lewis gun mounted on each car.

Care had to be taken to leave behind nothing to disclose to the Italians that invasion had begun, so army toilet paper was refused and old Italian newspapers garnered from our lady friends in the censorship, to whom was said, 'If I told you what it was for, you wouldn't believe me!'

I reported to General O'Connor at Bagush and then went on to Siwa, where Tom Bather of the Egyptian Frontiers Administration provided a party of three cars and Sudanese crews under a keen young Egyptian officer, not too heavily loaded with petrol. We set off south from Siwa through the Sand Sea on August 10 and by midday on the 11th were through and close to the two 'Mushroom Hills', where we dumped petrol and the Frontiers people turned regretfully back on their tracks to Siwa. My orders had been most strict that they were not to pass out of Egyptian territory, so I only took them about 25 kilometres across the frontier.

The little patrol of two cars then struck due west, exploring and made the unwelcome discovery of a large strip of sand sea between the frontier and the Jalo-Kufra road. The Chevrolet clutches began to smell a bit hot by the time we got across, but the evening saw us near the Kufra track.

The next two days were spent in the neighbourhood — it was very hot — gathering proof that no Italian build-up had commenced towards the vulnerable Aswan dam, or Wadi Halfa, and by the 16th, we were back in Siwa and our news was in Cairo. We left Siwa on the 18th to Cairo for lunch on the 19th, by the fast route across the Qattara Depression which Ali Fudail and I knew so well from our detailed survey work there twelve years before.

We had, as hoped and intended, not fired a shot or seen the enemy, bar one or two peacefully occupied planes. But we had proved that LRDG could go and come back to a strict timetable and General Wavell, who sent for Bagnold and me on 20 August, made up his mind then and there to give us his strongest backing.

That was the LRDG's first trip, 1,600 miles in 13 days, three of which we rested.

As related in detail in a following section, later that year Clayton was to command the famous Murzuk raid in the Fezzan, in Italian Libya, after linking up with the Free French 1,600 miles away in Chad. During this truly remarkable patrol, a small group of mainly 15-cwt LRDG trucks mounting heavy machine-guns covered an amazing *4,500 miles*, from Boxing Day 1940 to early February 1941, successfully assaulting a fort, capturing an airfield and destroying enemy aircraft, hangars and other posts. Clayton was, unluckily, captured in a subsequent attack on Kufra on the homeward leg when his truck was hit by enemy aircraft, but the remainder of the patrol made it back to Cairo, proving once and for all the LRDG's unstoppable worth.

Y Patrol, Desert Spies and Danger

Patrick McCraith, formerly of the Sherwood Rangers Yeomanry, raised, trained and commanded the LRDG's Y Patrol from the autumn of 1940, later taking agents deep behind enemy lines into the heart of territory held by the elite Afrika Korps, as just one of the daring missions carried out in the earliest days of the unit. His story accurately illustrates the gritty determination of the men of the LRDG.

I was wounded on our first mission south of Barce on 1 April 1941 which was the day that Rommel and his German troops first appeared in the Western Desert. The subsequent British retreat was immediate and chaotic but after near-capture I eventually arrived in hospital in Cairo. In early June, I returned to my patrol, which was then based with the Guards Patrol at Siwa oasis.

On my second patrol after returning, I was ordered to take a British agent, Captain Taranto, up to the Gebel south-east of Slonta some 200 miles within enemy held territory, the main line being then on the Egyptian/Libyan frontier, to a rendezvous with a pro-British Arab sheikh who was one of Taranto's sub agents. I took five trucks and, much against my better judgement, permitted Taranto to take with him his un-desertworthy and spareless light van which he wanted to use when he arrived up there to save himself a long walk in the great heat.

A truck negotiating steep dunes in the desert. (IWM HU16499)

The period during which I served in the LRDG was one of espionage and reconnaissance. Unlike during other more offensive periods of sabotage and destruction, it was then comparatively easy to penetrate far into enemy territory even in daylight without arousing suspicion.

The outward journey of over 350 miles took two and a half days of hard driving, uneventful except that on the first night Taranto produced a bottle of Weasel brand gin which appeared to be pure alcohol and, in crossing an unavoidable and notoriously difficult area of rock and stone, we broke five or six main springs and thus used up all the spares we carried. We arrived in the hills of the Gebel without incident and leaguered at a point in the hills (Bir en Ngar?) beyond which we could go no further because of the fearful going. I agreed to Taranto's request for a volunteer fitter to accompany him on his mission. But I would not agree to his suggestion that they both dressed up in German helmets and jackets, which we had found among the debris of earlier battles on our way up. To have done so would have risked death had they been captured, as it would be assumed that they were spies.

Taranto set off saying he would return in three days. Our leaguer, although fairly well hidden, was one from which it would not have been easy to fight our way out had we been spotted either from the ground or from the air. But there was no other suitable hideout. My anxiety was increased when Taranto did not return by the end of the third day. I began to suspect that he had been captured and I imagined the subsequent suspicion and search that such capture might arouse. I decided to wait a further 24 hours.

On the fourth day, Taranto and the fitter returned exhausted and on foot, the van having been irreparably damaged. It had taken Taranto much time to find the sheikh due to the fact that he had lost his way soon after leaving me. To prevent further delay, he had been compelled to ask directions from an Italian soldier and thereafter to drive a considerable distance along the main road, mingling with enemy convoys.

I was most anxious to leave for we had stayed long enough and the longer we remained the more likely it was that we might be given away by hostile Arabs or otherwise discovered. Furthermore, my medical orderly had a temperature of 105° and another soldier a temperature not much lower and both were delirious. But before leaving we were compelled to move across very difficult country to the abandoned van to camouflage it and pinpoint its position for collection by the next patrol to visit the area.

An hour later, on re-entering the rock and stone area, my truck broke a mainspring. With no further spares its abandonment seemed inevitable but my Patrol Sergeant, who was a skilled and ingenious fitter, bound and wedged the spring with leather bootlaces, wire, metal and wood. He told me to stop every quarter of an hour so that he could tighten up his Heath Robinson contraption and he bet me a bottle of whisky he could get the truck safely back to Siwa if I did so.

The constant halts to attend to the spring and the delirious patients were most tedious. The return journey was otherwise uneventful except that I was lucky enough to get within 30 yards of a black panther and her three cubs sitting beneath a small bush in the middle of a large salt pan before they sped away. This was the second time within a few weeks that black panthers had been seen by an LRDG patrol and it was confirmation that these rare, swift and graceful creatures were not, as was hitherto believed, extinct in the Western Desert.

We duly arrived safely in Siwa and my Patrol Sergeant received his bottle of whisky!

The beards we wore were not an affectation. Not only was there no water for washing or shaving, but a beard protected one's face from the intense heat, wind and dust. To those at base we stank most fearfully on returning from any but the briefest patrol and I sometimes had to burn my clothing. I returned to my Regiment in late September 1941, handing over my patrol to David Lloyd Owen, who eventually commanded the LRDG.

A Little Bird Told Me It Was Time to Go to War

Derek 'Hutch' Hutchins was on Y Patrol's first mission out into the desert, when the LRDG was ordered to face Rommel's mighty conquering Panzers armed with machine-guns and Bofors two-pounders in what would have been a suicide encounter. Luckily for Derek and his LRDG comrades, the fates had other ideas in store . . .

The first operation that Y Patrol took part in was south of Barce on 1 April 1941 and how near it came to be a complete write-off before we'd hardly started! I think I could fairly say that nobody in Y Patrol at that time had had any experience of the desert and we had been severely warned in a lecture beforehand of the traps and pitfalls caused by the excessive heat and lack of water during the summer in the desert.

Most of us had spent the previous year in Palestine with the 1st Cavalry Division under almost peacetime conditions, exercising our horses and trekking round the Arab and Jewish settlements to show the flag.

Out of the blue came the order to prepare for action as we were moving up into the desert at short notice to take on we knew not what. Y Patrol then operated as a single unit before it was split into Y1 and Y2 and formed part of the squadron under Major Mitford. We arrived just south of Msus, where all appeared to be chaos, and awaited orders. It appeared that the Afrika Korps under Rommel had recently arrived in the desert and was pushing the 8th Army back towards Egypt in no uncertain manner. Our orders were to act as a decoy to divert the German Panzer columns away from Msus, where there were large dumps of stores and supplies of every kind, in order to give the engineers more time to blow them up or get them away. This appeared, even to my un-military mind, to be rather a tall order, especially considering our heaviest armament was one two-pounder Bofors per patrol plus several Vickers .303 machine-guns and Lewis guns and rifles. However, such is the way of the British Army that nobody appeared to be daunted.

The Squadron moved forward across the open desert in line abreast to meet the German Panzers and, as I thought, probably our maker as well. Eventually, the order was given to stop, turn the trucks with the rear or fighting end facing the enemy, and await results. While I was sitting on the back of our Ford 30-cwt open truck, crouching over my Vickers gun, musing to myself as to whether the next world was likely to prove any kinder to me than the present one, a small sparrow-like bird suddenly appeared from nowhere and settled on the barrel of my gun. Such was the absurdity of the situation that I can remember thinking that this poor little wretched bird was going to get in the way of my first shot at the Germans since the war started. Consequently, I lunged at it and the poor, startled creature flew quickly out of harm's way.

The sequel to this unlikely, but quite truthful story, is that we accomplished our mission in as much as we succeeded in diverting some of the German attention upon ourselves. This was unpleasant and although we all made it back to Siwa, we were somewhat chastened.

Keeping a tense watch on enemy movements in the Western Desert from the mobile platform of a 30-cwt LRDG truck. (IWM E12383)

I like to think that this incident might have been the origin of Bomski Cashin's party piece 'Tit Willow', a really heart-rending ditty when sung by Bomski after several rum punches round the camp fire after return from patrol . . .

STIRLING TELLS THE LRDG OF HIS HISTORIC PLAN
TO FORM THE SAS

Alastair Timpson spent sixteen months leading G Patrol of the LRDG during the desert days. Here, he describes his first meeting with his new Commanding Officer, Colonel Guy Prendergast and the latter's first fateful meeting with David Stirling, the legendary commander of the wartime SAS. (Lieutenant Stirling was formerly of the Scots Guards and 8 Commando, part of Layforce.)

I was posted to the LRDG on 10 September 1941, so the casualty list reports, and indeed I was a casualty, in the 15th General (Scottish) Hospital at Cairo. Not a good start, nor calculated to make a good impression on entering this hardy unit. However, I luckily got out in time not to get sacked on the start line.

To go back a little, I had been sent by my battalion, then in the Sollum area, to take over from Captain Crichton-Stuart as Scots Guards officer in G Patrol, now under the command of Captain Tony Hay, Coldstream Guards. Therefore,

I had with me my excellent soldier servant Thomas Wann and a poisoned foot, my own. We made the welcome journey to Cairo to receive instructions from Michael Crichton-Stuart and my new Commanding Officer, Colonel Guy Prendergast.

The latter received me in his room at Shepheards. Though it was indeed siesta time and the Colonel was in fact resting, one could hardly call it by the name that denotes the period of time dividing lunch, say at the St James, and cocktails at Gezira. My CO had actually lunched at Bagush (Western Desert Force HQ near Matruh) after breakfasting at Siwa and lunching the day before at Kufra. He had piloted his own aircraft 1,200 miles.

The astounding distances over which the LRDG operated with very

The dashing David Stirling near an LRDG truck on one of his early raids. (IWM HU24994)

little fuss fascinated a newcomer and this impression of measureless mobility was further heightened for me at dinner that evening. Straight from the desert it was always entrancing to sit in Shepheards garden with good food and wine, blue and red lights, evening dresses and tangos. These delights were memorable above all others of their kind for the colour they gave to Colonel Guy's story and for the contrast they provided against the background of war in distant places. It was the extreme contrast of oasis and desert that makes both, in their way, agreeable to some people at least.

Here, in Cairo, was the supreme oasis of peace and plenty, where one stayed for a while between the long spells in the west with its dust and rock and camel thorn, its battles of advance and of retreat. When away, one longed for oasis life; but if one stayed too long, one felt one did not deserve more and must be on the road again. This alternation of life gave a spur and sustenance to one's activity, of which one was conscious even at the time, and makes understandable the nostalgia of those who served in that part of Africa. It kept one going in a war which, in 1941, showed no reason to end.

So, at Shepheards that evening, as I listened to the description by my new CO of what the LRDG was trying to do, I was not a little thrilled by the vista and expectations aroused. Nor should I fail to record that it was on this evening that David Stirling first met Colonel Guy, sat at our table and told him of his plans to form a new parachute unit which he intended to use in the forthcoming offensive and would require LRDG co-operation.

We hardly dreamed at the time that we would have contributed, in the course of the next year, towards the destruction by L Detachment, SAS, of nearly 300 enemy aircraft as well as scores of vehicles, ammunition dumps, hangars and enemy personnel.

STIRLING'S FIRST DESERT RAID REMEMBERED

Arthur Arger, of Ormesby near Middlesbrough, is one of the founder members of the LRDG's Y Patrol, which picked up David Stirling's SAS raiders from their ill-fated, but daring, inaugural parachute raid on an enemy airfield near Tobruk. Like the rest of the LRDG, Arthur is part of an extremely rare breed, as at any one time only about 200 soldiers made up the Group's strength.

Corporal Arger joined the Yorkshire Hussar's Cavalry Regiment as a Territorial in 1938 and was called up in September 1939 and sent to France to fight the

Germans on horseback! This idea was, sensibly, rapidly abandoned and Arthur was sent with the 5th Cavalry Brigade to Palestine, from where he joined the newly formed LRDG.

He told me: 'It was said that at any one time, up to 10,000 German and Italian troops were looking for us, such havoc did we create behind the enemy lines! We shared the Siwa and Kufra oasis bases with the SAS and often took out SAS patrols into the desert and picked them up again afterwards.'

Arthur said of the devastating first-ever parachute mission for the SAS: 'There were very high winds and Stirling and his men were blown all over the place. Many were lost and never seen again. The raid was a disaster and we were ordered to pick up the survivors as we came back from a patrol Derna way.

A brilliant study of Popski, Lt Col Vladimir Peniakoff DSO, MC, commander of the famous Popski's Private Army desert force, who often crossed paths with the LRDG on his own behind-the-lines missions in the Western Desert. (via LRDG)

A famous photograph of officers and wild-looking desert LRDG brigands regrouping for another mission. The soldier on the right with arms folded is wearing goggles on his head – an essential item for driving in windblown sand and sandstorms. Arthur Arger is standing third from right at the back. (IWM CBM1218)

'Stirling was cursing his luck and never dropped by parachute again. Later the jeeps came into use. Stirling was a real gentleman, quietly spoken, but very determined.'

The LRDG veteran also knew the fiercely courageous Popski before he even formed his famous Private Army. Popski was a Russian, born in Belgium, who was commissioned into the British Army because he was so skilled with languages and knew how to deal with the Senussi tribesmen in the desert and persuade them to help the British. 'Popski's Private Army ranged far behind enemy lines like we did, but they weren't so good at navigating,' Arthur quipped.

Arthur was photographed by Cecil Beaton with other patrol members, unshaven and filthy after returning from one lengthy mission behind enemy lines, one of many historic photographs now in the Imperial War Museum.

LRDG members manned their trucks with a crew of three — a driver, gunner and another crewman, all of whom could alternate roles, he recalled. Each column had a specialist navigator. Machine-guns were oil cooled, as water-cooled weapons would have become useless after a while in the extreme conditions of heat and dust, and were also difficult to traverse cleanly on a moving truck with all the necessary accessories for water cooling.

Initially, the main purpose of the LRDG was reconnaissance for the main army, Arthur said, but it soon became clear that the Group could create mayhem in the rear areas way out of proportion to its size and strength. This soon became one of its prime roles.

Arthur said: 'I've no regrets. We were never in big battles and there was no room for any army bull, but I wouldn't have missed it for the world!'

CHAPTER 2

The Western Wilderness

MONKEYING AROUND WITH LECLERC ON THE WAY TO ZOUAR

By December 1941, the LRDG was flexing its muscles and trying more ambitious schemes. The commanders had the idea to follow the tracks of a French expedition that a year earlier had commenced at Kayugi and skirted the main massif to Bardai in northern Chad. Plans were all very vague, but nevertheless a patrol entered the wadi at Kayugi to meet up with the French under Philippe Leclerc, later to win fame as General Leclerc of the Free French 2nd Armoured Division, which captured Strasbourg and reached the Rhine under Patch's US 7th Army towards the end of the war, as Germany reeled towards total defeat.

As it set out on its desert mission, the LRDG patrol noted some muddled tracks, possibly left earlier by the French Colonel d'Ornano, but these soon disappeared in the rocky terrain of the wadi and the LRDG men were on their own, as usual, relying on instincts honed in active service. They were maintaining radio contact with Cairo, more than 1,000 miles away; a tribute to the skill of the LRDG wireless operators.

Dick Croucher tells how the New Zealand R2 Patrol sampled French cuisine, showed their Free French allies the secrets of desert navigation and inspected the delights of a French desert post at close hand. But, as the LRDG men soon found, Beau Geste was never like this! More testing adventures were soon to follow . . .

As the wadi itself looked most promising and led in the direction required, we followed it despite the fact that the going was atrocious and involved low gear work all the way. By late afternoon we had travelled about 50 kilometres and seemed to have come to a dead end. The wadi had a reasonably well-defined camel trail showing up in the odd soft patches but, when we arrived at the head of the wadi, the camel tracks went up the side of the slope over a saddle into a fine sandy plain. The trouble was that the track was only camel width!

Shooting a dune, LRDG style. (IWM HU25293)

We were really in a predicament. Checking up on our fuel supply, we had used far more than expected through all the low gear work and the situation was not good. We had another look at the track over the saddle and decided we could widen it sufficiently to take a Chev (lorry) with a bit of luck, in three days, all pitching in. Meantime, Clarkie Waetford and his brother Tommy had other ideas. It was getting dark by then but, working their way along the crest of the hills, they found a branching-off wadi a couple of kilometres back which we had passed without noticing. Next morning we went to see and found we could get out that way with only minor moving of a couple of boulders. There were terrific sighs of relief all round.

Out we went on to that glorious sandy plain dotted with small conical hillocks rather like a moonscape. We headed across the plain in the direction of Bardai (we hoped). Half way across we came on a wandering old Tibou man and his wife. I don't know who was the most surprised. We gave him some cigarettes and were pleased to learn from him that we were on the right track. Shortly after, we climbed a fairly steep dune and came upon the French Poste of Bardai. From there to Zouar the track for vehicles was quite well defined and initially somewhat of a climb. The road skirted the rim of an extinct volcano, Mount Toussidee. The crater was about 5 miles across and half a mile deep. Having come off the mountain, we were met by the French with great enthusiasm and were escorted into the wadi where they had their HQ.

When we were there, there were at least a dozen French officers beside the then Colonel Leclerc. Also, there were George Mercer Nairne and Bill Barlow, liaison officers. R2 Patrol was allocated a spot amongst the acacia bushes where we set up camp. The next amusing thing was the allocation of rations . . . French rations. We were issued with dried beans, flour, tinned meat, singe (*monkey*), which resembled a ball of twine soaked in vinegar, and potent palm toddy, which they called Mehrissee. The first thing to go wrong was that the beans, which were put in the stew, were as hard as rocks and bitter. The grog, which had the kick of a mule, was vile to the taste. The only way to cope with it was to shut one's eyes and hold one's nose. Of course, such matters never deterred a Kiwi. After some discussion with the French Commissariat, we found that the beans were not haricot but coffee beans which we were supposed to roast on a tin plate over the fire and then crush with a bottle! The grog was supposed to be used as rising when making bread with the flour. Needless to say, our chaps made dampers and disposed of the liquor in more direct fashion.

The rations included the occasional 'fresh' meat brought up by camel from Fort Lamy. The Kiwis in R2 were over-resourceful and did the odd supplementing by barter with the local Tibous for goat kids. Unfortunately, the locals became rather too greedy for their own good, which led to the adoption of other methods. It was a daily occurrence for a little boy to drive a herd of goats and kids down the wadi to feed. On one particular day, two of our chaps hid themselves in the thicket and, on the arrival of the herd, quick as a flash, a nice young specimen was extracted and whisked away into the depths of the bush while the goatherd was being distracted by others on the other side. Before the boy was out of sight, the beast was slaughtered, skinned, gutted and into the biscuit tin oven in a hole under the fire. All traces of blood and skin were cleaned up and buried without trace. A most expert performance. I'm sure some of our forebears were sheep rustlers! Some of us, though, regretted the incident later when a man, presumably the lad's father, dragged him down by the ear searching for the missing beast. No evidence was left, but no doubt the lad got beans.

When it appeared we would not be moving up to the coast immediately, Leclerc asked me to give his officers instruction in astro navigation, so I ran daily classes. None of the officers taking part could speak any English so the whole thing had to be conducted in French; I was completely lost when it came to translating technical terms in spherical trigonometry.

When we received orders to return to base, we were all lined up for Leclerc to inspect us and bid us farewell. He was most gracious, made a nice little speech and then a couple of Askaris came forward with a box of lettuces and tomatoes, which he presented to us for our journey. It was a magnificent gesture because the little vegetable garden of the poste was only designed to feed four or five persons and was under considerable strain with all the additional inhabitants of the mess. Throughout the whole ceremony, Leclerc kept a very straight face but I noticed that a couple of our chaps seemed to be a little uncomfortable. It was not until much later that I found that two of the men had been apprehended by the guards while robbing the said garden in the early hours of the morning.

I had some correspondence with Leclerc in subsequent months and apologised, but he took it all as a joke.

I seemed to get on quite well with the French. Some of them I managed to keep in touch with, de Guillebon (later killed in action), Dio, a giant of a man, and Fabre, officer commanding the garrison at Faya. On our way through there on our return journey we stayed the night and had quite a convivial party. In the course of a poker game I won a magnificent white, red-lined, Spahi cloak from Fabre. It was obviously his pride and joy because next morning when we were lined up to depart he pleaded with me to let him have it back and I did not have the heart to refuse.

We looked in briefly at Tekro, which was not occupied, then travelled on and camped down for the night at Bishara. Clarkie and Tommy went for a wander around the dunes and came upon a 15-cwt Chevrolet civilian pick-up painted dark blue with narrow road tyres. There seemed to be nothing wrong with it except for a flat battery. In no time it was made mobile and Clarkie and Tommy transferred their bits and pieces to it. They painted on the sides 'Waetford Bros, Country Storekeepers' and it was officially incorporated into R2. I am not sure if it did much to assist the Entente Cordiale! The French at Kufra were in a cleft stick. It was obviously one of their vehicles left behind or lost on one of their sorties towards Kufra. On the other hand, they were not prepared to make an issue of it as it meant admitting they had abandoned or lost a perfectly fit vehicle. We kept it anyway.

It was on the run from Kufra to Siwa that we ran into rain in the Sand Sea. I had struck a course to come out on the track between Jalo and Jarabub. We had only just entered the strip of dune country between the gravel plain and the track when we had light rain. I cannot recall for how long but in the morning there was a definite low, green fuzz over the dunes and a crust had formed that made it possible to do the craziest of things in our trucks without getting stuck. Even the Waetford Chevy could climb the steepest of slopes with ease. I do not know what happened to the vehicle after all that. I wouldn't have put it beyond some of them to have flogged it to the natives!

BACK FROM THE DEAD – THE HOUDINI VC WINNER

There can be very few soldiers who have 'posthumously' won Britain's highest award for bravery – and lived to tell the tale. But Lieutenant Colonel Eric Wilson achieved this extraordinary feat, later joining the LRDG where he found individual character of his inimitable brand was much appreciated.

While serving with the East Surrey Regiment in the early period of the war, Wilson displayed extraordinary bravery in covering the British evacuation from

The pugnacious Eric Wilson VC poring over a campaign map in the North African desert. (IWM HU16452)

Somaliland, hammering away at the advancing Italians with machine-guns, his stubborn courage enabling many men to get away unscathed, before he was lost from sight and posted missing believed killed. A posthumous award for valour was deservedly presented in his memory and the tenacious Wilson much admired and lamented. Meanwhile, Wilson was very much alive and kicking and a prisoner, though he was later extricated from this unhappy predicament to join the ranks of the LRDG as a squadron commander, taking over from Teddy Mitford.

Incidentally, the redoubtable Wilson nearly scuppered the LRDG career of David Lloyd Owen in its fledgling stages. The then CO, Guy Prendergast, had ordered Wilson to keep a lookout on the newly joined Lloyd Owen on his first desert patrol. On the patrol's return, Prendergast made it clear to Lloyd Owen that Wilson had given a very unfavourable report on his performance, but that he was going to give him a fair crack of the whip in the hope that he would make the grade.

As David Lloyd Owen says in his book, *Providence Their Guide*: 'I know that Eric Wilson had been quite right, not only in the impression he had gained of my performance, but in reporting what he had seen to my commanding officer. What he did not know was that I simply had not got a clue as to what I ought to be doing and I was biding my time, watching everything diligently.'

The LRDG was a highly unusual and complex unit and many found it difficult to get used to it initially, after the rigid format of regular Army life. Later on, the converse would be the norm.

Fortunately for the later history of the illustrious unit, its outstanding future commander Lloyd Owen was not 'Returned To Unit' and his career continued on an ever-upward spiral. However, a couple of years later, Prendergast told Lloyd Owen, who was commanding the LRDG in his place, that his position in the unit soon after joining had been 'touch and go'. Lloyd Owen modestly says: 'Any credit for any success that I might have had later on was due as much as anything else to Guy giving me some well-timed encouragement when I most needed it.' The two became lifelong friends.

Sometimes even legends need a second chance . . .

STIRLING'S BUERAT RAID AND THE FATE OF THE MISSING G1 MEN

G Patrol played a glorious part in the history of the LRDG, especially in the early years in the desert, where the guardsmen were usually to be found in the thick of the action. Few have been able to fill in gaps in patrol history like Bill Anderson, who contacted the LRDG Association out of the blue after the best part of fifty years, having been seen last in December 1941 in the Wadi Tamet; after some prolonged bombing and strafing, Anderson and two others failed to turn up and everyone feared the worst.

The incident, as far as it was previously known, was described in Michael Crichton-Stuart's splendid book *G Patrol*. But the fate of the missing LRDG men involved was a mystery until Bill's eyewitness account completed the story of one of the key occasions when the unit effectively combined as 'taxi drivers' to the SAS.

Tony Hunter was, temporarily, commanding G1 when they were bombed all day in the Wadi Tamet. The task, which the patrol had been allotted, was to take David Stirling and a party of SAS to Buerat, at the western end of the Gulf of Sirte. During the bombing, Tony Hunter had his trucks dispersed and concealed and the crews were ordered to keep clear of them. However, at the end of the day when they reassembled, Guardsmen Anderson and Smith and Signalman Till failed to turn up. The patrol waited until the moon rose early in the morning before they moved off. Already they were late and it was necessary to get closer to their target.

Thanks to Bill Anderson, the veterans of the LRDG Association learned what had happened to the three missing men decades after the end of the war. When the patrol first arrived at the Wadi Tamet, the descent into the wadi was found to be so difficult that each truck had to make a controlled descent with only the driver on board and the rest of the patrol hanging on to it with a rope. When it came to Bill's truck, the rope gave way and the laden vehicle hurtled down the rocky, precipitous slope at enormous speed. Bill stayed at the wheel, terrified but bravely struggling to keep the truck under control. He managed to prevent it from somersaulting or being pitched on to its side but, although he arrived at the bottom more or less uninjured, a great tribute to his own strength and skill, the truck was very much the worse for wear.

The other trucks survived and were driven off up the wadi. Soon after, the bombing started. Bill grabbed his greatcoat and water bottle but left a new pair of boots on the truck. The boots he was wearing were old ones for driving. The bombing and strafing went on for a long time and, obeying orders, Bill, Smith and Till kept well away from the truck. When the bombing stopped, they couldn't find their way back and, when finally they did, they found their truck had been destroyed and the patrol had gone. In the wreckage they found a tin of jam and another of bully beef. The only water they had was in Bill's water bottle.

They started walking, but headed north-east instead of due north thus adding many miles to their journey and, after walking for seven days, finished up on the coast road near Sirte. They were very weak and had to give up an idea they had about stealing a vehicle. They found some water, which had collected on the tops of 40-gallon drums after recent rain, and tried to lap it up. It was while doing this that they were spotted and captured.

In a POW camp south of Naples, they met Tony Hay who was despondent, blaming himself for the disaster that had befallen G1 in December 1941. He cheered up a little when he learnt that at least some of the patrol had got away and had later been reformed.

One of the many mysteries of war surrounding the LRDG was solved at long last. But many still remain . . .

THE MURZUK RAID – THE SOLDIER'S STORY

Len Poole has supplied extracts from a diary kept by Frank Jopling, a New Zealander of T Patrol, who wrote his diary on the spot immediately after the following dramatic events. This story has been told in various books written by LRDG members, but never in such a detailed and graphic account, written by a man who was in the thick of it all.

Jopling's extract relates to the raid on Murzuk in the Fezzan by G and T Patrols in January 1941, led by Major Pat Clayton in which the French Colonel d'Ornano and Sergeant Cyril Hewson were killed.

Further extracts cover the battle of Gebel Sherif, twenty days after the attack on Murzuk. In this action, Clayton was wounded and captured, Rex Beech was killed, three trucks were destroyed, one was captured, and 'Skin' Moore started his epic march south with Easton, Winchester and Tighe. Again, Jopling was bang in the middle of the action and wrote up his diary the very next day.

Jopling's diary relates that, as the patrols approached the fort at Murzuk, the Italians started turning out the guard for them, presumably in the belief that

A colourful group study of LRDG veterans mixing with exotically dressed Free French soldiers during one of their longest patrols during the Murzuk raid into the desert in the Fezzan, near French Equatorial Africa. (IWM E12447)

they were a visiting friendly force. This belief was shattered when, at a range of 150 yards, the patrols opened up.

Frank Jopling was in the party detailed to raiding the airfield, and six trucks drove past the fort on to the landing grounds . . .

Taking advantage of rises in the ground, they engaged troops trying to man a number of pill-boxes scattered about, including an anti-aircraft pit. Then Pat Clayton drove his vehicle to circle the hangar and, as he rounded a corner, a machine-gun fired at the truck from only 20 yards. Colonel d'Ornano was shot through the throat and died instantly. An Italian signals sergeant who had been picked up and was in the back of the truck was an 'awful mess' and his body was thrown overboard. Rounds hit the theodolite on the running board, another went through the truck just behind the driver and another through the seat underneath him.

Orders were shouted to keep firing, but in the 'dickens of a noise' one thing that could be picked out was the 'ping' of a sniper's bullet when he got one close. The fort was on fire and, after two hours, a white flag was shown from the hangar and a prisoner was sent to order the occupants to come out with their hands up.

There were three Gibley bombers in the hangar, many bombs and much equipment such as parachutes and radios. Petrol was scattered everywhere and set fire to.

In the attack on the fort, Cyril Hewson, newly promoted sergeant, was killed when he stood up to clear a blockage in his Vickers but mercifully he never knew what hit him. Sadly, the wife and two children of the Italian commanding officer were killed with him as they tried to drive into the fort.

Two prisoners were selected from the many taken and the rest released. Then the patrols withdrew. Tony Browne had a round through the back of his boot but it only just broke the skin. A G Patrolman had a bullet just miss the back of his hand where it left a red mark. One or two had rounds pass through their trousers without touching their legs, another had a slight graze and another suffered a cut vein. On the French side, a captain received an in-and-out wound in his ear which he cauterised with his cigarette and took no further notice of it!

The diary then moves on to Gebel Sherif on 31 January. G Patrol were held in reserve near Sarra and Pat Clayton with T Patrol made his way towards Kufra, but at Gebel Sherif, in a valley, they were spotted by an aircraft and soon some vehicles appeared. These vehicles went behind a hill and Jopling was ordered to back his truck up to one of the entrances to the valley to see what was there. As he approached the entrance, the Italians came into view and fired at the truck from short range and Frank expresses wonder and thankfulness that they missed.

T Patrol managed to get out of the valley but three trucks were missing. Columns of smoke were seen, obviously from burning vehicles. Survivors were picked up running from the hills. One of them, Tommy McNeill, told how Rex Beech, corporal on his truck, kept on firing his Vickers at the enemy until he was hit dead centre by an explosive shell.

Skirting the hills looking for a target for the Bofors gun, they found none, then they were ordered to make for a pre-arranged rendezvous. Two more planes then appeared and the trucks made their hazardous way towards the rendezvous, successfully dodging bombs all the way.

When they arrived, Pat Clayton's truck and the wireless truck were missing. The latter crew arrived later with the story of being attacked from the air and being forced to abandon the truck. The attack was switched to Pat Clayton's truck and nothing was known about its fate except that a burst of machine-gun fire was seen to go right across the front seat.

THE MAN WHO TAUGHT THE LRDG'S ACE NAVIGATOR

The LRDG was as tough in a tight corner as any unit in the British Army. But fighting spirit was not much use behind the lines in the desert if units hadn't a clue where they were. Corporal Stuart 'Lofty' Carr was one of the best in the unit

LRDG and truck. (IWM HU69744)

at finding his way around the featureless wastes of the desert. Mike Sadler, one of his pupils, later became one of the LRDG's best-known navigators and went on to similar fame when he left the unit to serve with distinction in the SAS. However, few know that Mike's first lesson in taking star shots came courtesy of Lofty on the roof of the Abbassia Barracks in Cairo. Later, Mike could take his truck patrols to their destinations, by day or night, with uncanny accuracy, and he rightly became a legend. Mind you, he had a very good teacher . . .

August 1942, first day of a leave in Cairo. Told to forget it. I had been a navigator in LRDG from the formation of Y Patrol in 1940 by Captain Pat McCraith of the Nottinghamshire Yeomanry. So in August 1940 we set off from Faiyoum to cross the Qattara Depression south of Alamein.

It transpired that Popski was in trouble in the Jebel Akhdar between Benghazi and Tobruk 700 miles away from Cairo behind enemy lines. Jerries were searching for him day by day but fortunately the Arab guide they were using was one of ours, so each day he made sure that Popski moved from the area to be searched. This could not go on forever, so we had to snatch Popski from under their noses.

The Qattara Depression was tricky. Its salt marshes could turn to slush at night with the danger of our five trucks being lost in the quicksands. So we had to risk being seen by the Luftwaffe and cross by day. Up the pass at Qara to the top of the scarp, we headed west, north of Siwa oasis, where we shorted an enemy telegraph line and placed pencil mines around the telegraph poles to 'get' the enemy searching for and mending the faults.

Through the barbed wire marking the Egyptian/Libyan border and north-west across the gravel and rock to the Jebel Akhdar, driving into the rendezvous arranged through Popski's radio operator (one of us, from LRDG) we became aware of a number of figures moving among the rocks in the wadi. We thought it was an ambush, but luckily held our fire because some of the men were wearing LRDG Arab headdresses. It was Popski and company.

There was a camp full of British POWs nearby so we managed to contact and persuade three or four of

Seasoned members of Y Patrol at Kufra oasis with truck. (IWM HU25202)

them to escape and join us. We then set off for home looking forward to finishing a lovely leave in Cairo. We were told by radio that we could not use the short route by which we had come because Jerry was waiting to ambush us.

Knowing that they were lying in wait for us, we suggested that we should catch them on the hop and turn the tables on them and so get on with our leave. The suggestion was vetoed. We were told to make our way back by a long detour across the Sand Sea, south to our base at Kufra oasis. The problem was that we did not have enough petrol, tyres or spares to do this. It was decided that we should help ourselves from dumps of British supplies left behind in the retreat to Alamein now held by the enemy.

We chose a massive mixed dump. From it we got half shafts and track rods, which we were always breaking, plus tyres and petrol. We spent the day placing dozens of drums of petrol on the remaining supplies. We drove north through the mounds of materials, machine-gunning the petrol drums with incendiaries. These began to ignite and explode, setting fire to the remaining supplies.

We did an about-turn, to drive south through the fires again. Shells etc., in them started to explode. It was alarming, so we rapidly set off south into the scrub towards the desert, Sand Sea and Kufra oasis hundreds of miles away. After a while, I paused to take photos of the enormous fires we had started. I have never seen so many different coloured columns of smoke.

LRDG patrol members take a well-earned break at Kufra Oasis, Libya, 1941. The back row includes: Arger, Devonshire, Wise, Carr. Front, left to right: Denniff, Hutchings, Hurst, Scotty, Miller-Kerr, Sandle, Bartlett, Carningham, Chard, Davies, Barker, Grayham. (LRDG)

When we reached the Sand Sea we were lucky. These massive dunes are always on the move and are difficult to traverse. Recent winds had sorted them into long continuous dunes of soft sand, magnificent to look at. These had a hard sheet of sand in a corridor between, like a motorway. These corridors ran roughly in the direction in which we needed to travel. We were able to cruise very fast down them. It must have been the fastest crossing of the Sand Sea ever!

We had no charts of the Kufra area so I took star shots to fix our position when we emerged on the south of the Sand Sea. We radioed our position to HQ and they radioed back the bearing we needed. We reached Kufra in one piece apart from one of our rescued POWs. He saw a concrete pool at the oasis and dived in not knowing it was only a foot deep. He came up a changed man covered in blood. Oh! And that lovely leave of mine – well, 'they' said, 'While you're here at Kufra there's a job you might as well go on.' . . .

Moore's March – An Epic Tale of Grit and Survival

The barren wastes of the Gebel Sherif, south-west of Kufra, were the scene of a devastating Italian ambush of the LRDG in February 1941. T Patrol lost four trucks within minutes when attacked by their Italian LRDG counterparts, the

Auto-Saharan Company, plus three aircraft, while they were camped and effectively trapped in a small valley. Three trucks were blown up and three Italian prisoners held by the patrol were killed. Several of the LRDG men were wounded as they desperately fought back.

Some members of the patrol managed to get away in the confusion, but four men – Trooper Ronald Moore, Guardsmen John Easton and Alex Winchester, and Private Alf Tighe – were left behind, the others being convinced that they must have been either killed or made prisoner. In fact, all four were alive, although injured. The story of their epic march across the desert was broadcast from Cairo two months later and published in the *Scots Guards Regimental Orders* in London on 17 April 1941:

These four had in reality escaped to the nearby hills, where they hid to avoid capture by the enemy. Moore, a trooper of the New Zealand Cavalry, was wounded in the foot. Of the two guardsmen, Easton and Winchester, Easton had a bullet wound in the throat which caused him great pain. The fourth member of the party, an ordnance fitter named Tighe, was suffering from a former internal injury.

The following morning, the enemy had gone. Having discovered among the burnt-out wreckage one 2-gallon tin of water, but unfortunately no food whatsoever, the four men were faced with two alternatives. They could walk what was to them the comparatively short distance of 80 miles north-eastwards to Kufra and give themselves up to the Italians, as they could have done on the spot the day before, or they could retain their freedom at the expense of almost certain death by attempting to walk 290 miles, following the vehicle tracks along the way they had come, with the slender chance that they might be picked up by some Free French party. Rather than give in, they chose the latter course.

The rugged courage and determination of Tpr R.J. Moore DCM, of 'Moore's March' fame, is brilliantly captured in this superb drawing by Penny Morgan, inspired by a wartime study. Though wounded, separated from others of his unit, and with little water or food, he walked an incredible 210 miles through the burning desert towards his home base before being picked up – a superhuman feat.

Under the implicit leadership of Moore, they set out on their incredible march, carrying in turn the precious tin of water. That day, an Italian aircraft flew over them but apparently did not see them.

On the third day, they found a 2-pound pot of plum jam, dropped off one of the trucks on the journey northward. They ate the whole of it that day. On the fourth day, Tighe became very tired and on the fifth eventually persuaded his comrades to leave him and to go on, as he felt he was hindering their progress. Before going, they poured his share of the tiny water supply into a bottle, which they had picked up. Not until after they had left him did this unfortunate man discover that the bottle had contained some salty substance, which made the water undrinkable.

On the sixth day, a violent sand storm arose, but Moore, Easton and Winchester just managed to follow the fast-disappearing car tracks to Sarra. Here they spent some time in a ruined hut. They found no food, but with some motor oil, which had been abandoned, they managed to bathe their feet and to make a fire to warm themselves at night. They had walked 130 miles. The next morning, they continued on towards Tekro, still 160 miles distant. By now, the motor tracks had entirely disappeared over long stretches of the route, and it became extremely difficult to follow them up.

Meanwhile, Tighe, who had struggled on through all that seventh day, managed to reach the hut by nightfall, but was too exhausted to go further. He found one match in the sand and, with this and the oil, made a fire without which he would probably have died that night. On the evening of the ninth day, a French patrol, fresh from a reconnaissance of the enemy position at Kufra, found Tighe at Sarra. He was still conscious and, although he had been alone and without water for four days and consequently was in a dreadful state of exhaustion, his first thought was to explain that his three companions were ahead of him.

A search party was at once organised by the French, but was unsuccessful in following the track in the dark. The same day, two French aircraft spotted Moore and Winchester. By now, all water had given out and Easton was lagging behind. The aircraft dropped food and a bottle of lemonade, all they had with them, but neither Moore nor Winchester noticed the food, and the cork came out of the lemonade bottle on impact with the ground, so that only half an inch of liquid remained. After this, the two men went on independently, Moore ahead, and poor Winchester, semi-delirious, struggling after him. Finally, on the tenth day, another search party found first Easton about 55 miles south of Sarra and then Winchester 12 miles further on. Both could walk no more and were lying exhausted on the sand.

The party then caught up with Moore, 70 miles south of Sarra and 210 miles from his starting point. He was still plodding on with swinging arms. Perfectly clear headed and normal, he waved to them without stopping as if to an acquaintance during a walking race. He was determined to reach Tekro in the two days that he estimated he could last out – and he would probably have done so if he had not been found. With nothing to eat for ten days, except a little jam, and with only 4 pints of water to drink, wounded in one foot in which a shell splinter still lodged, Moore had not only walked this astonishing distance, but had for several days virtually carried with him two men who were physically weaker than himself, as well as poor Winchester.

That such a journey was humanly possible was due only to the fact that it was relatively cold. In hot weather, it is most unlikely that any man could remain alive in the desert without water for more than three days.

When found, Easton could scarcely swallow because of the wound in his throat, from which he had suffered continuously. Finally, with a great effort, he managed to get down a few drops of sweet tea. With a little smile he was heard to say, 'I don't usually take sugar with my tea.' He died shortly afterwards, despite all the doctor's efforts to revive him, having to the end displayed extraordinary courage and fortitude.

Moore, Tighe and Winchester recovered from their ordeal and Moore, for his outstanding determination and inspired leadership, was presented with a well-earned Distinguished Conduct Medal.

All four had shown a special brand of courage in adversity, over and beyond that which can reasonably be expected from the human spirit.

Spine-Tingling Sequel in the Desert

The well-known explorer John Blashford-Snell has recounted in his autobiography, *Something Lost Behind the Ranges*, a strange, inexplicable experience he had at a place that was almost certainly the site of the battle of Gebel Sherif, an experience which occurred more than twenty years after the LRDG action . . .

In the summer of 1963 I went along to help fellow sapper David Hall, who was leading an expedition of cadets in the far south of the Libyan Desert. Historically, this is a fascinating area, for it is here that a famous British Army unit, the Long Range Desert Group, fought a magnificent hit and run campaign against the Italians during the Second World War. Our task involved important mapping and scientific work directed by David, who was already a legendary figure in desert exploration. He was happy to leave me to handle the administration.

On one re-supply run from our remote base to the oasis of Kufra, I had a strange experience. I'd wanted to make Kufra by dark but now we hadn't a hope. At dusk we reached some low rocky hills, really just big piles of jumbled broken stones with numerous narrow passes running through them. The map wasn't very precise so I chose one at random, which turned out to be a little west of the usual route. The sand was soft and in the failing light we bogged down several times. Heaving the sand channels back aboard for the third time, I said, 'We should be able to get some shelter amongst these rocks', and my weary crew readily agreed that it was none too soon to call it a day. None of us felt like cooking, so we munched a few hard tack biscuits smothered in raspberry jam and washed them down with a mug of coffee. The night was clear and before turning in I went to commune with nature.

Squatting beneath the stars I swore I heard the sound of a voice. The first time, I looked back towards the dull outline of the Land Rover. The second time, thinking one of the crew had called, I said loudly, 'Just a minute.' Back at the car, I asked, 'What's the matter?'

John, cadet crew member, was already asleep, although his colleague looked up and said, 'Nothing, why?'

'Didn't you call?'

'No,' he replied.

'Funny,' I yawned, 'must have been the wind.'

I woke just after dawn with a shiver and bursting bladder. Standing up, I shook off the sand, rubbed my eyes and stretched stiff limbs in the half-light. I was only partly awake when I saw something odd. About 60 yards away was a truck, or rather the remains of one, and all around it were scattered bits of equipment dark against the white surface. I walked over to the Chevrolet, for even at this distance I recognised the familiar shape of the LRDG raiding vehicle. The debris consisted of cartridges, grenades, mortar bombs, broken rifles and parts of a machine-gun. Thirty feet to one side by a low mound lay a small wooden cross and pieces of splintered wood that had probably been another. Similar vehicles were 'parked' along the rock walls of the pass. Some had engines missing, all appeared to have been blasted apart by a single explosion in the back.

Combing the area, we made an interesting discovery high among the rocks; a faded canvas British Army haversack containing a rusty Kodak camera and a toothbrush. Nearby were scattered a pile of empty .303 cartridge cases. I now believe it was here that the LRDG's T Patrol was destroyed by its Italian opposite number, the Auto-Saharan Company, based at Kufra. According to W.B. Kennedy Shaw, in his book *Long Range Desert Group*, a running fight developed on 31 January 1941, when Italians, with a heavily armed motorized patrol and three aircraft, caught T Patrol advancing on Kufra, in the Valley of the Gebel Sherif.

Following the battle, a New Zealand Trooper, R.J. Moore, and three colleagues remained undetected among the rocks of the waterless hills. Almost everything they needed for survival had been destroyed. They were wounded and all the wells within 200 miles were either in enemy hands or filled with stones. The situation seemed hopeless. However, they managed to salvage a 2-gallon tin of water and, scorning any idea of walking a mere 80 miles north-east to surrender at Kufra, they buried the dead, then turned and marched south towards their allies.

The Free French Army's positions were known to be several hundred miles away across almost waterless desert. Their remarkable and heroic escape over an astonishing distance was typical of the soldiers of one of the finest special forces ever raised. Three survived and their leader, Trooper Moore, was found by the French, walking steadily after ten days, having covered 210 miles.

We tidied up the grave, re-erected the crosses, saluted, stood silent for a moment and drove off towards Kufra. I reported the matter in Benghazi and later heard that the Imperial War Graves Commission had visited the site.

But I never discovered the origin of the strange voice . . .

BAGNOLD'S BIG GUNS – THE LRDG'S ROYAL ARTILLERY UNIT

When attacking Italian forts in the Western Desert in 1941, the LRDG reasoned that it could do with some heavier armaments with which to 'persuade' the enemy to surrender from their defensive eyries, as its Bofors anti-aircraft guns were not quite up to the job. This was how the effective, but short-lived, Group Artillery Section came into being, commanded by Paul 'Blitz' Eitzen. The late Brigadier Prendergast had a high regard for the unit, which was disbanded because the LRDG ran out of Italian forts to attack! Here are his thoughts on the field guns that were undoubtedly one of the most unusual cargoes the LRDG ever managed to squeeze aboard its trusty workhorse trucks:

In August 1941 it was decided at GHQ in Cairo that it would be desirable to form more units of an LRDG type for use in the African and Syrian deserts. Ralph Bagnold was therefore told to hand over command of the LRDG to me and to set himself up as a full Colonel in an office in Cairo, with Rupert Harding-Newman as his assistant. Ralph kept a watchful eye on our activities and dealt with any admin problems we had. He also used to think of ways in which we might be helped. One of these ideas was the formation of the Royal Artillery [RA] Section. His idea was that it would be attractive to be able to knock holes in any Italian fort, which a patrol was detailed to attack, as our light weapons were not heavy enough for this purpose.

Second Lieutenant H.P. Eitzen RA was detailed to command this section, which was originally armed with a 4.5 howitzer carried in a 10-ton lorry and had also a light tank to be used as an armoured OP (Observation Post). The

4.5 howitzer, however, was handed over to Colonel Leclerc of the French Army and I think the tank was also handed over to the French for the defence of Kufra. The RA Section was then issued with a 25-pounder also porte (carried and fired on the back of an LRDG truck).

On 13 December 1941, John Olivey's S2 Patrol and the RA Section left Kufra on various tasks, one of which was to attack the fort at El Gtafia, at the track junction 25 miles south-south-west of Jedabia.

On the 15th, further reconnaissance took place of the Wadi el Faregh and also of the fort at Gtafia, which was sited in a hollow and in bad repair. The attack on the fort was made next day. The RA Section with the W/T (wireless) truck approached it from the south-west; two trucks (S.5 and S.10) took up a position south-east of it, and 2nd Lieutenant Olivey with the two remaining trucks moved round the west side to positions north and north-east.

The artillery opened at 1630 hrs and fired fourteen rounds with the result that four soldiers left the fort and went along a wadi to the north-west, where they were captured, and, the rest of the garrison having fled, the fort was entered and searched. No wireless or telephone was found, but two Fiat guns were taken and the ammunition was put into the well. Papers were removed and everything of value broken up. The party then camped 10 miles south-east of the fort, lay up during the 17th and signalled the results to Group HQ.

The unit's historians state that this was the only action in which the RA Section took part, but that the heavy gun certainly put the wind up the enemy on this occasion. Needless to say, Paul Eitzen and his men achieved much elsewhere, without their gun, later on.

A 25-POUNDER FIELD GUN – ON THE BACK OF AN LRDG TRUCK!

As has been seen, the desert veterans tried out all manner of weapons on the backs of their trusty Chevrolet and Ford trucks, including many types of light and heavy machine-guns as well as weapons of a much heavier calibre, including 37-mm Bofors and full-blown artillery. Although the extra weight and awkwardness of manoeuvring caused problems, these drawbacks did not deter the LRDG in the slightest, and the unorthodox experiments were more than justified by the devastating effect the extra firepower had on the unsuspecting enemy. Here, Bill Morrison explains another difficulty that was encountered . . .

Jim Patch and I landed at Royal Artillery Base Depot, Almaza, Cairo, in mid-1941. A notice on orders asked for volunteer signalmen for the LRDG and as usual we volunteered, not knowing what it stood for. After an interview with

Lieutenant 'Blitz' Eitzen, we arrived at the oasis of Siwa and met the gun crew — a Scots bombardier with two stripes, a South African lance-jack (he and Blitz sometimes conversed in Afrikaans) and three or four gunners. The equipment was a 25-pounder artillery gun mounted pointing over the tail of a 10-ton Mack truck, which also carried the men, their gear and a load of ammunition.

Blitz had an 8-cwt pick-up with Jim as his signalman and I was with the gun to keep communication by field telephone and a reel of cable. I recall the test firing into the Sand Sea south of Siwa and then setting out on our first job. We were with S2, led by John Olivey, and went through the wire, past Jarabub and followed a well-used track. The Mack was heavy. One track over a gap had been laid with heavy wire mesh but it rolled up under the lorry, pulling the leads from the air brakes and stopping everything.

We were not popular with the Rhodesians, but the firepower when we attacked the Italian fort at El Gtafia certainly was.

The Mack was kept out of sight behind a ridge while Blitz and Jim, unreeling the cable, went over the brow to have a view of the fort. The patrol trucks took up positions; Blitz worked out the range and gave the order to fire. A correction or two and the fun was over. All the others advanced on the fort and some time later returned to us with four prisoners.

We moved away from the area and the patrol went off on other jobs while we waited. The next day aircraft were about, probably looking for the enemy who had shelled their fort. We were inspected by a very low flying Messerschmidt, but the gun was hidden beneath the canvas canopy of the truck. We mostly looked like Arabs and we made the smartly uniformed Italian prisoners wave to the pilot. I could see his face quite clearly he was so low. But we were left alone.

Blitz had gone off with the patrol and our bombardier was in charge. That night we set a guard but next morning we only had three prisoners. One of the two Arab soldiers had vanished in the night.

A quick circle of the camp showed his footprints and a party set off in the pick-up after him, returning an hour or two later. He had shed items of his heavy uniform on the way and, when overtaken, was dressed in the completely white outfit of the typical Bedouin. And he had made a beeline for his home village! He was disciplined by the Italian corporal and made to put all his uniform on again.

When the patrol and Blitz returned, nothing was said of this incident and we set off back, travelling by night. The going was rough, mud flats surrounded by small hummocks, and the Mack rode them badly. The engine stalled and the battery was too flat to turn the heavy diesel motor over. We tried cranking her, but even with a rope and two teams of pullers it was too heavy. It didn't work and John Olivey wanted to move on, so eventually it was decided to abandon the truck. Blitz would not abandon his gun, though, and it was towed behind a patrol truck while the rest of us stowed ourselves among the other vehicles and we all returned to Jalo.

Desert dawns could be cold as ice. David Lloyd Owen in sheepskin, near Jalo, February 1942. (IWM HU25287)

The RA Section was camped on the edge of the oasis and we amused ourselves with captured equipment – Breda machine-guns, a Lancia truck with a wind-up starter (namely, a heavy fly wheel which could be engaged to turn the engine), and an anti-tank gun which was stripped and test fired into the desert. New Year's eve was a noisy affair with a lot of wasted ammo!

It was very cold. Jim and I made a bivvy for shelter which nearly caught fire one night from our reading lamp – a tin can filled with petrol with a hole in the lid for the wick. The mosquito net over the open front flared up but Jim swept it out on to the sand. When T2 Patrol arrived at Jalo with no kit, having walked for ten days after being shot up, we gave up some of our blankets for them. I went down with pleurisy but, fortunately for me, Doc Lawson (our medic) had reached Jalo and, with his care and attention and sulpha drugs, I survived, although I remember very little of the trip over the desert to Siwa and the Waco flight to hospital in Cairo.

At the convalescent camp at El Ballah on the Suez, I was summoned to the orderly room where my kit was examined and I was asked to explain the two red Italian hand grenades I had saved, thinking that one day I would make a pepper and salt set from them. To demonstrate they were harmless, I picked them up and unscrewed them but nobody stayed to see – the orderly room cleared like magic!

After a leave in Cairo, it was back to Siwa again, where I found the RA Section disbanded. Jim had joined Y Patrol, so I joined the Signal Section, eventually becoming a patrol operator, but on the strength as a driver. I was with T Patrol when Nick Wilder gave his name to Wilder's Gap, which enabled 8th Army to turn the Mareth Line – a famous operation I have seen quoted in many histories as typical of Monty's flair.

I eventually transferred to the Royal Corps of Signals, leaving Jim the only true representative of the RA Section.

A NEAR WIPE-OUT AT BENGHAZI'S GREEN MOUNTAIN

LRDG secretary Jim Patch relates a mission, unrecorded in official LRDG history, involving Geoffrey Arnold, best known for his exploits in navigating

LRDG Waco aircraft after landing supplies somewhere between Kufra and Siwa. These pilots regularly brought in special supplies, such as vehicle spares and personnel, and took out the sick and wounded, keeping open a vital link with the main British Army. (IWM HU25081)

the desert unit's Waco aircraft. Geoffrey was lent as navigator to a group of Commandos whose bold plan it was, in May 1942, to raid a place called Maraua in the Jebel Akhdar, the Green Mountain, east of Benghazi. The raiders were commanded by a Major Knowles with a Captain Powers as second-in-command. The mission was not planned with anything like the skill or thoroughness habitually employed by the LRDG, with near disastrous results. It is not recorded who devised this ill-conceived operation in the first place. But the raid is highly unusual in that David Lloyd Owen never heard of it and, if Alastair Timpson and G1 Patrol had not become involved by accident, the fate of the mission – and its brave men – could have been one of the mysteries of the desert to this very day. Jim summarizes Geoffrey's own report:

There were about sixty men in the raiding party. They sallied forth from Siwa travelling in four 3-tonners and twenty 15-cwt pick-ups. They made a forward base camp about 50 miles from their target, camouflaged the 3-tonners and left them there with a small party while the main party went on in the pick-ups, to a point 4 miles short of their destination. The Major and his intelligence officer went forward for a recce on foot but while they were away, the party was spotted by an Arab. This man refused to stop in spite of being shot at.

The incident persuaded the Major, on his return from his recce, to postpone the raid for a couple of days and retire to the forward base. For the journey back they split up into two parties with ten pick-ups in each. The first party made

Trp Ken Tinckler of Y Patrol demonstrates the difficulties of crossing rocky desert terrain in an LRDG truck. (IWM HU24988)

the distance successfully, but the second party was attacked by enemy aircraft and all the trucks were destroyed. The men were all rescued, and sent back to Siwa in one of the 3-tonners, then the Major, undaunted, took his ten remaining pick-ups to carry out the raid. They made it as far as the scene of the aircraft attack, but were then set upon from the air and all their trucks but one were finished off. They made a brave attempt to get back to the forward base with this one pick-up, but it hit a boulder and that was the end of that.

Geoffrey Arnold and the intelligence officer went on foot because they were close to an enemy held track and didn't want to put the whole party at risk. On the way they very fortunately met an LRDG truck of G1 Patrol under Alastair Timpson, who had heard the strafing and had sent the truck to investigate.

The patrol was doing a road watch but had been ordered to another job on the coast road and could not spare the time to be of much help, but the Commandos managed to get themselves together and drove back to Siwa in their remaining 3-tonners feeling somewhat deflated, if not a little relieved.

The only job done with efficiency in this whole dreadful business was the navigation but Geoffrey Arnold was far too polite to express an opinion about the conception and command of the raid.

To give a yardstick in comparison with LRDG raids, the desert veterans considered it a matter of necessity and honour to get all their trucks back to base employing their vast experience, camouflage and stealth, even if that meant they had to be towed.

The loss of even a single vehicle was something to be avoided at all costs — and often was. Transport in the waterless desert was often the difference between life and death and their precious trucks were the LRDG's best and most treasured friends.

Tobruk – Barce Raid

THE ASTOUNDING SUCCESS OF THE FAMOUS BARCE RAID

New Zealand and Guards LRDG patrols under Nick Wilder and Sergeant Jack Dennis had SAS-equalling success when they hit the enemy airfield at Barce, in a lightning raid under the overall command of the legendary Jake Easonsmith, widely accepted as one of the finest and most fearless of the LRDG desert commanders. The elated LRDG men left twenty-four enemy aircraft burning to destruction and a further twelve badly damaged by bombs and machine-gun fire.

The Barce raid was a crucial linking part of the ill-fated Tobruk raid, which cost many lives in a daring seaborne assault on the heavily defended port. Four

Tobruk raid hero Col John Haselden with an LRDG truck. (IWM HU24992)

Col John Haselden dressed as an Arab coming out of the desert to meet the LRDG after one of his daring reconnaissances of enemy positions. (IWM HU24997)

MTBs, two destroyers and an anti-aircraft cruiser were also lost. Stirling's SAS raiders met similarly stiff resistance at Benghazi, backed by John Olivey and his Rhodesian LRDG Patrol – the third linchpin in a complex and ambitious operation. Stirling suffered uncharacteristically high losses with eighteen jeeps and twenty-five other vehicles destroyed.

A further LRDG patrol under the command of David Lloyd Owen skilfully extricated itself from the Tobruk debacle after holding the eastern perimeter for twelve vital hours, preventing reinforcements from entering the town. One of the greatest tragedies of the Tobruk raid, designed to cripple key port facilities and guns before an organized withdrawal, was the loss of the ground force's commander John Haselden, who perished leading a brave counter-attack on the overwhelmingly superior and encircling enemy forces. Haselden was an audaciously unorthodox officer of the Special Forces, who at times even donned Arab clothing to reconnoitre enemy airfields and was well known to the LRDG from previous spying missions behind the lines.

D-Day for the overall operation, 13 September 1942, turned out to be a tragically unlucky one. A co-ordinated attack to seize Jalo four days later by the Sudan Defence Force (SDF) and one of the LRDG's Y Patrols under Tony Hunter also failed.

As David Lloyd Owen records in *Providence Their Guide*, the Barce plan incorporated a combined LRDG role involving the patrols of Easonsmith, Wilder and Alastair Timpson, with a minor supporting role for Popski of

David Lloyd Owen gleans vital information from friendly Arabs in the desert wastes. (IWM HU25258)

Popski's Private Army fame. However, Timpson's jeep was involved in a horrendous accident negotiating a razorback dune. His driver broke his back and was paralysed from the waist down and Timpson fractured his skull. The two had to be flown back to Cairo.

There was a widespread belief beforehand among the attacking forces that security surrounding the big Tobruk raid had been blown. It was known to be the talk of the spy-ridden bars in Cairo. Many felt they would be walking into a trap. Nevertheless, despite warnings to the powers that be, including from Stirling who felt his force was being drawn into an operation dangerously different from its usual role, the raid went on as planned.

After Stirling's forced withdrawal from Benghazi, the SDF failed to take Jalo, so the oasis was not available for the surviving SAS force on their homeward route, as planned.

Haselden and his Commando party tricked their way safely into Tobruk, under the guise of being prisoners held by a special 'suicide' squad of Allied

Guttridge's and Easonsmith's jeeps bristle with guns on the edge of the Sand Sea during the famous Barce mission, September 1942. (IWM HU16666)

volunteers in German uniform. They captured several gun positions before confused and heavy fighting broke out and the force was virtually annihilated. As a result, a seaborne force of Northumberland Fusiliers and Argyll and Sutherland Highlanders coming in to complete the job of wrecking Tobruk harbour was unable to land and the mission was doomed to failure.

It was a heartbreaking decision for Lloyd Owen and his men to have to leave the stricken Commando force, having travelled nearly 1,500 miles together since leaving the Fayoum on 24 August. But there was no choice. The LRDG men slipped back unmolested to a place of cover about 90 miles south of Tobruk to await further orders. Lloyd Owen is convinced the Tobruk defences were pre-alerted. A steamroller had been placed as a roadblock across the main route leading to the eastern perimeter of the town and an enemy patrol was encountered almost as soon as Haselden's force had departed at the start of the raid.

Meanwhile, at Barce, the brave Easonsmith led his men into the attack, calmly directing the patrols to their allotted tasks. Wilder led his patrol of four 30-cwt Chevrolets spectacularly in a jeep, skirting the town to the landing ground where soon all hell broke loose. In single file, the LRDG men poured tracer and bullets at each aircraft as they passed in a deadly and pre-arranged plan. The last of the trucks carried a pile of delayed action bombs which were liberally distributed to ensure an unstoppable blaze. The Italian garrison was caught totally by surprise and panicked, returning fire wildly and ineffectually. By this time, Wilder's men were running low on ammunition and it was decided to make a break-out in the direction the raiders had come.

However, several light tanks blocked the escape route. Wilder, by now in a Chevrolet, rammed the first tank and bounced at speed into a second. But a way through had been courageously forced. The gallant Wilder and crew were picked up by the following jeep and the Kiwi officer manned a machine-gun and furiously fired at the remaining two tanks. The jeep then overturned after hitting a kerb and Wilder was pinned unconscious underneath. He was dragged out and thrown aboard another truck, and the jeep and two trucks escaped the carnage, though the last New Zealand truck was cut off and lost with its crew.

Amazingly, not one of the survivors had been hit by enemy action.

After continued harrying from enemy aircraft, desperately short of transport, rations and water, the LRDG men eventually escaped to safety on re-grouping, mainly due to the prudent Easonsmith, who had left one Chevy, hidden and loaded with petrol and rations for such an emergency, around 60 miles south of Barce. The wounded were given priority and ferried by vehicle and the rest had to walk.

The party fortunately met up with Olivey's Rhodesians returning from Benghazi. He searched the area for several days for any stragglers and eight were found. Some others later turned up after being sheltered by friendly Arabs, and ten were taken prisoner. The group then made for the LG 125 forward landing ground, which was on bare, hard ground in the midst of the desert – a secret place for the RAF to pick up men and deposit supplies behind the lines without disturbance. Group HQ was contacted and the wounded flown out first.

Doc Lawson pictured by the legendary Popski himself in this rare and jubilant shot taken just after the highly successful Barce raid, September 1942. (IWM HU16647)

David Lloyd Owen and Doc Lawson at the secret landing ground LG 125 after the Barce raid, September 1942. The Germans never did discover its whereabouts, despite numerous searches. (IWM HU16466)

Almost three weeks after the LRDG men had left the Kufra oasis confidently expecting an overall success at Tobruk, they arrived back depleted and deflated on 23 September. Nick Wilder and Jake Easonsmith received well-deserved DSOs, Dick Lawson a Military Cross and Sergeant Dennis the Military Medal – all extremely hard won.

This is *the* classic tale in the annals of the LRDG, but its aftermath led to yet another stirring account of guts and survival . . .

A BATTLE TO THE DEATH WITH THE DEADLY DESERT

Roy Duncalfe MM, an eyewitness to the devastating Barce raid on 13 and 14 September 1942, tells his story of the danger-packed aftermath when survivors were not only strafed by enemy aircraft, but also had to walk to safety through the treacherous desert.

The day following the Barce raid we were shot up by enemy aircraft; having no vehicle, it was a case of 'these boots were made for walking'. Darkness came, with Paddy McNabola and me together and the prospect of a long walk to where a getaway truck had been left at Bir Gerrari.

Having no compass, we decided to walk mainly by night when it would be cooler and we would also have the aid of the stars to guide us. Our only water was a partly filled bottle and on the third day this had almost gone, so we decided to turn back towards the foothills of Cyrenaica. We were fortunate in reaching a Bedouin encampment but, because of the state we were in, we vowed not to attempt the walk again without an adequate water supply. The sheikh of the tribe informed us that a British officer had been there the previous day and had stated he would be back again in five days. The sheikh's son took us to a cavern about 3 miles away in the desert, leaving us with a supply of water, flour and salt. The reason for our exile was increased activity by Axis forces in the area.

After six days and no sign of the British officer returning, we decided to make our long trek again. The Bedouins supplied a 1-gallon tin of water and we had our full water bottle, which we used first, but, when we came to use the tin, to our dismay we discovered that the inside was coated with a yellow substance and the water was putrid. Rather than be tempted, we slung the tin and because we had covered a fair distance, we carried on, eventually reaching the Msus–Mechili track about half a mile east of the rendezvous point. As expected, there was no truck, but we did find three tins of runner beans and an 800 lire note which had been left. The liquid in the tins didn't have much kick and I have tasted better, but at least it was wet.

The water situation was now desperate. We discovered that the nearest well marked on our escape map appeared to be over towards Msus and this is where we headed for. Two days later we came upon a camel herdsman who, although not particularly friendly, gave us some camel's milk, half a bottle of water and made us a meal of dough boiled in camel's milk, which is called *oice* (or something like that). I only know that afterwards, without Rennies, had we lit a match, we would have become airborne!

From here we struck off north-east, since the herdsman did not appear to know of a well in the area and the best place we could think of was our Bedouin encampment. Again, we ran out of water. On the fourth day without food or liquid, the sun was very hot and when we both dropped down unable to go any further, each of us knew this was probably the end.

In retrospect, the body is a wonderful thing because, after the craving for water, the brain and the senses become numb and I believe that death from thirst is therefore made a little easier as one sinks into oblivion.

We must have lain there an hour or so when I thought I heard singing. Not angels, but native singing. The thought of hallucinations occurred to me but I got to my feet and, shielding my eyes from the sun, I could see two camels moving in the far distance. I roused Paddy. We could not shout because our throats were parched and our swollen tongues like lumps of lead but, taking off our shirts, we waved them with new-found energy.

Sure enough, after a few minutes, we could see the camels were heading towards us. When they arrived, the two natives with them gave us water, put us on board the camels and took us to the foothills where they removed two slabs of stone, revealing lovely clear water beneath. These two Bedouin had undoubtedly saved our lives but, because they retired a short distance away conversing in whispers, casting furtive glances towards us and appearing very shifty, I became suspicious. They then told us to stay where we were and they would come back.

Immediately they had gone, Paddy and I also moved and that evening came to our previous Bedouin encampment. We gave the sheikh the 800 lire note and he agreed to us taking up residence in our previous apartment. We remained there several weeks, being supplied with sufficient flour etc. to make one chappati per day between us for five days at a time.

On one occasion our supply was two days overdue, so I decided to find out what the trouble was. I arrived at the encampment after dark and sat down outside deciding on my next move, when I saw a *bint* (native woman) coming in towards the camp. Thinking that if I startled her she might scream and I might find myself on the wrong end of a Bedouin blunderbuss, I hesitated before quietly calling her. She came over and we held a whispered *tête-à-tête* as I tried to convey to her that I wished to speak to Hirihem, the sheikh's son. When she appeared to understand, and in view of her calmness, I thought I must reward her. The only thing I possessed was a 50 piastre note in my wallet which was Egyptian money and probably useless in Libya anyway. I gave her this note and away she went. Hirihem arrived soon after with flour and water. Because the camp had been visited recently by Italian troops, he was rather agitated.

I returned to Paddy. The Bedouin desert dwellers' menu is extremely frugal at the best of times but even more so at Ramadan when they fast between sunrise and sunset. Trust us to pick this particular time for our holidays! When Ramadan had ended we often received bowls of *oice* and occasionally had a meat dish, which was probably goat. Hirihem could write in Arabic and tried to teach me the alphabet. He was very interested in the Senussi/Arab Force, which operated in Libya on behalf of the Allied Forces.

Towards the end of October we were told of much 'boom boom'! We realized our troops were fighting their way back from Alamein. At the first sight of one of our fighter planes we started to walk north towards the coastal road. Arriving at a village one evening we were told the Germans had moved out about an hour previously and the day following, in the morning, we were picked up by a 25-pounder crew who opened their emergency rations to feed us.

Some days later, we arrived at Mersa Matruh transit camp where the CO told us to attach ourselves to the master cook while he attempted to discover the location of our unit. Several days later we were summoned to the CO's office where, to our surprise, we found Hirihem. We told the CO of his desire to join

Friendly Arabs often gave the LRDG useful information about the enemy's positions and strength. Here Arab informers meet Y Patrol in the desert. (IWM HU24983)

the Senussi Force and the next morning he was taken to Alexandria with a letter explaining what a staunch role he had played.

Before he went, Hirihem handed me half of the 50 piastre note with the message, 'My sister say one day you come back and join.' I do not think she was concerned about the note! This was something more romantic. But I still have the note and my sweat-stained wallet.

AN EYEWITNESS ACCOUNT OF THE TOBRUK DEBACLE

Medical Officer Doc Lawson and Derek Parker were part of the LRDG patrols involved in the various missions linking with the infamous Tobruk raid in 1942.

This costly failure, ironically, ensured the continuance and expansion of the SAS raiding force, which impressed the previous doubters among the top brass, who now perceived that the unit could operate successfully as part of a large-scale, combined services raid, much to the relief of founder David

Stirling. Stirling had from the outset fought a running battle to prevent his fledgling Special Force being disbanded, or swallowed up in some ill-judged amalgamation. Now General, later Field Marshal, Alexander decided the SAS should be given regimental status. No more would the SAS live from hand to mouth. This decision was repeatedly vindicated in the later invasion of Sicily and Italy, when SAS raiders enjoyed stunning success as seaborne shock troops, knocking out key gun emplacements and securing beachheads and objectives ahead of the main invasion forces, and later still in audacious behind-the-lines parachute and jeep raids in France, Belgium, Holland and Germany.

Meanwhile, as has already been seen, the over-ambitious Tobruk and Benghazi raids resulted in a disastrous waste of SAS, Commando and Royal Navy lives, including that of the raid's land forces commander, the courageous John Haselden, due it is thought mainly to appallingly bad security beforehand. The only positive things to come out of the Tobruk fiasco, like Dieppe, were hard but highly pertinent lessons for future operations.

A camouflaged wireless truck at Hatiet Etla, before Tobruk, September 1942. Left to right: Matthews, Harrison, Davies, Searle, and Fraser. (IWM HU24986)

But for his timely rescue, Derek Parker might not have recovered. It was a great privilege and pleasure to take part in a tribute to such a fine all-rounder as Air Marshal Sir William Coles.

THE STRANGE TALE OF THE PHOTOS OF THE INFAMOUS TOBRUK RAID

The disastrous raid on Tobruk on, ironically, 13 September 1942 was the bloodiest desert mission the LRDG or Commandos were involved in during the Second World War. The raid, which had modest beginnings, was originally conceived as a small affair, but was taken over by planners who let their imaginations run riot. The SAS was involved in an associated wrecking attack on Benghazi. As stated, security among some of the participating troops in Cairo hot spots, which were riddled with enemy informers, left a lot to be desired and the ambitious enterprise achieved nothing, with the loss of a cruiser, two destroyers and 750 casualties. Major General Sir Francis de Guingand (General Montgomery's Chief-of-Staff) is said afterwards to have called the operation 'woolly', adding that Monty had nothing to do with it and viewed the whole business with disfavour.

LRDG's part in the episode was to guide a group of Commandos under Colonel John Haselden – a very brave officer – to Tobruk from the Nile via Kufra. The Commandos were to enter the town and perform certain desperate tasks, then the LRDG (Y Patrol) was to enter after dark, on receiving a success signal, and perform equally demanding tasks. In the event, no success signal was received and the patrol spent the whole night on the perimeter, stopping traffic from entering or leaving the town.

The Commandos ran into terrible trouble. A large number were killed and most of the rest were captured. One of the officers killed was Lieutenant Michael Duffy, whose young brother Desmond produced a biography entitled *One of the Many*. This includes the story of the above journey across the desert, ending at Tobruk. Some vivid photographs illustrate the story and the way in which these came to light is quite uncanny.

A Captain Benciolini, of the Italian Army, took a camera from one of the wounded and captured Commando officers (Lieutenant Graham Taylor), removed the film from it and put it in his pocket. Incredibly, the film remained there until 1961, when it was found by the Captain's son, Giorgio. How it escaped notice during the near-twenty intervening years is a mystery. Giorgio recognized the film as British and, instead of having it processed locally, decided to send it to a British newspaper. The only one he knew was the *Daily Mail* and so that was where he sent it.

The film was duly developed, twelve pictures in all. The kilt figured in a few of them so the prints were sent on to the Scottish *Daily Mail* and on 21 and

22 April 1961 some were published. Two days later, most of the officers pictured had been identified, among them Michael Duffy. There was also a brilliant photo of David Lloyd Owen scanning the distance through his binoculars, standing on one of the LRDG trucks in the shadow of the Gilf Kebir, while the rest of the column waited for instructions.

Copies of the pictures came into the possession of the Duffy family via a nephew, Robin Findlay, who was a sub-editor of the London *Daily Mail*, and were reproduced in the biography by Desmond Duffy.

Thus culminated a truly remarkable, but true tale!

Hon Raid

Tighe watching Tinckler and truck negotiate rough ground approaching Hon for a raid on the landing ground, November 1942. (IWM HU24971)

A patrol resting after the Hon raid. (IWM HU25080)

A jokey sign draws attention to an 'invisible' newly camouflaged jeep! LRDG vehicles had their own unique and highly effective camouflage patterns, which made detection at a distance, or from the air, difficult. This one was Jimmy Patch's vehicle, snapped at Hon, 1 February 1943. (IWM HU16531)

A LAWRENCE OF ARABIA CONNECTION

Micky Coombs was one of the many cavalrymen who joined Y Patrol at the start of the desert war, when it became obvious that horses could no longer play a leading part in what was, essentially, a mechanized war of rapid movement. Micky's father Stephen had seen action with the RFC as a pilot in Palestine in the First World War, flying Bristols and Sopwith Camels, when a certain mechanic, named Lawrence, was working on machines in the squadron. No one paid much attention to the lowly ranked serviceman who was obsessed with fast Brough Superior motorcycles, speed, danger and excitement. A year or so later and the same Lawrence had become a living legend as he led the Arab revolt against the Turks in Hejaz and Palestine from 1916 to 1918 . . .

Micky joined the North Somerset Yeomanry and at the outbreak of war, like his father, he was sent out to Palestine, where the LRDG came seeking volunteers and, partly because Micky had wireless experience, he was readily accepted into the ranks of the fledgling desert force.

Micky said, 'We often saw enemy aircraft when we were behind the lines, but would often wave to the pilots hoping they would think we were German too. It usually worked, but there was one occasion when some RAF Blenheims mistook us for enemy vehicles and raked us with cannon fire, blowing up my wireless truck "Aramis". It wasn't their fault because we were so far behind the front line, that any vehicles moving around should have been German.'

Micky saw constant action throughout the desert and in the later campaigns, including Yugoslavia, where dodging the enemy became a daily game of Russian roulette. But he never forgot his father's words of admiration for Lawrence's behind-the-lines attacks on the Turks and their allies in the First World War, destroying railway tracks by blowing out the sand beneath the rails, rendering them useless and impassable and causing desert mayhem on a grand scale.

Sitting ducks! A roving, well-armed patrol well and truly stuck. As always, quick extrication from soft sand was vital to avoid being either spotted or attacked by enemy aircraft or patrols. No one was better at getting out of such tight corners than the LRDG. (IWM HU16489)

It was a sabotage technique similar to those which the LRDG carried out more than thirty years later in the Lawrence tradition, and Micky is proud to have played a not inconsiderable part in what has become known as a legendary British desert force.

TRUE GRIT AND SCOTS COURAGE – AND ROMMEL IN RETREAT

Alastair Timpson recalls one of his bravest men in G Patrol of the LRDG, Thomas Wann, who will always be remembered for his prowess in action and his stoicism, courage and cheerfulness after a catastrophic injury on active service left him paralysed, but with his remarkable spirit undefeated.

I first met Thomas at the Tower of London where we assembled a draft to join the 2nd Battalion, Scots Guards, in Egypt. On the seven-week voyage Thomas took the heavyweight boxing competition. I can still see his serene expression, his agility in spite of his size and the sheer skill with which he went about winning.

Something of this skill in parrying off the onslaught of enemy forces remains in my mind from other episodes. Based at Siwa in May 1942, G Patrol was ordered to destroy enemy traffic on the Tripoli–Benghazi coast road near Sirte. We were to put time bombs on enemy vehicles after slowing them down at dusk and at night. For this task we devised a road-repair outfit. We carried five

A truck provides shade for LRDG men on a desert mission, 1942. (IWM HU71344)

44-gallon drums, red hurricane lamps, wooden poles and a notice 'Achtung Strassenbau' ('Attention Roadworks') all the 600 miles from Siwa. The deviousness was necessary in order to disrupt traffic without stinging the enemy into violent reaction that would probably jeopardise the all-important 'permanent' road-watch near 'Marble Arch'. When we came to our roadblock we found an Italian lorry stuck there. Two small Italians, mistaking us for Germans in the dark, asked for help. While some of us were trying to get their lorry started, I noticed that the Italians had disappeared. 'Where are they?' I asked.

'Wann has them as prisoners, sir.' Thomas had apparently picked them both up, sharply and gently, and put them next to him on the back of our truck. I had to tell him to release them, as they would have been a nuisance. Curiously, they did not seem to resent this rather brusque treatment from their 'German' allies and we parted with handshakes and expressions of 'Grazie Kamerad' in their hybrid Axis language.

At mid-day our five 30-cwt trucks were hiding in the steep-sided runnel in the wadi which led after a mile to where our roadblock was starting to cause a bit of a traffic jam. Some Italian troops with vehicles came over the crest of the hillside 100 yards away and others were coming from other sides. They started shooting – our aerial was up for the time-call to Siwa. It was not difficult to dismount the Vickers K guns to shoot back, but activating the main machine-guns on their mountings meant undoing the camouflage netting and getting up

LRDG Guardsman Wann proudly posing in his jeep shortly before his tragic accient. (IWM HU16655)

on the trucks to load the guns and fire back. The trucks nearest the enemy, towards the top of the wadi, were mine with Thomas Wann as gunner, Duncalfe on the next and Matthews on the next.

Matthews had a bullet through the top of his head as soon as he got up to his gun, killed at once. Wann and Duncalfe got their Vickers cracking away without being hit and so did the others. Gradually our enormous firepower got the better of the enemy. In a lull of the firing, I got our three lower trucks away, with orders to stop a mile or two up another wadi and wait for me. On my orders, Inwood got Duncalfe's truck away, leaving Wann doing nearly all the firing. After some tricky driving to get out of the runnel, we escaped and joined up with the others, who had encountered some more Italians but sent them running.

I also think of Thomas often on one of my earlier patrols when we had stealthily worked our way along the foothills of the Jebel in order to attack traffic on the southern of the two main roads from Benghazi to Barce. We were about 400 miles from Siwa. The battle south of Tobruk, begun on 18 November 1941, was raging to and fro. We could see the road that afternoon and I was planning to attack the next evening but Thomas had a stomach ache, which had got much worse after rumbling for a day or two, and he was running a high temperature. The medical orderly and I sent signals to Siwa, with the necessary skill of Signalman Barber, describing the symptoms. Dick Lawson diagnosed the trouble as acute appendicitis. I asked whether I should go on with the attack, which would have much reduced Thomas's chance of survival, but Colonel Guy ordered me to return quickly to Siwa.

That evening, driving south-east between Mechili and Msus, we saw hundreds of headlights approaching from the east. We stopped on some rough ground. Enemy transport and tanks were passing behind us and in front and more were coming on. I realized it must be Rommel in retreat.

The nine o'clock news from London only spoke of the battle for the relief of Tobruk still being fought out. We rigged up the aerial to inform Siwa of the news, the scoop of a journalist's dreams, but to no avail. It was one of the few times that we could not get through, mainly because of the very heavy volume of radio traffic on the air at such a critical time.

We continued south through most of the night. By dawn, near Trig el Abd, we were still not clear of Rommel's forces and passed right through a laager of tanks. Some crews were starting to get their engines going but they did not appear to bother with us. Once south of Trig el Abd, the desert was ours again.

When Thomas and I suffered our accident in the Kalansho Sand Sea, the one which paralysed him, we were again on our way to Barce, a fateful destination for him, but how lucky we were to have Dick Lawson with us. Thomas would have died then had he not been there and my conscience, as driver of the jeep, would have had a sharper, though shorter, soreness to bear. We were also lucky that Tony Browne was in Cairo to navigate the Hudson to 'Big Cairne' after the RAF had failed to find us for two days.

Another of the recollections of Thomas is of our hospital in Cairo, the 15th Scottish. One of the nurses used to come into my ward and say, 'What an incredible man your companion is! He keeps everyone else in his ward cheerful, although he is in a much worse way than them.'

Back at Easton House, Edinburgh, Thomas offered me a cigarette from a case I had given him with the LRDG badge on one side and the Scots Guards on the other. I said, 'I always feel dreadful about my responsibility for what happened to you.'

He replied, 'You should not worry, Sir; I never regret having gone with you to the LRDG.'

A MODEST HERO – TITCH CAVE

Titch Cave wasn't the only LRDG man to be decorated in the Second World War, by a long way, but the words of the *London Gazette* that survive and tell of his bravery in winning the Military Medal eloquently describe the essential qualities which made up a true stalwart of the unit – character, good humour, skilled in his tasks and, when the chips are down . . .

'The King has been pleased to award the Military Medal to the following in recognition of gallant and distinguished service in the Middle East – to

No. 555726 Trooper Holloway Cave, Royal Armoured Corps Yeomanry (parent unit) of Rode Common, near Bath.'

The announcement went on to say: 'During an attack on an Italian fort at El Ezzeiat, Trooper Cave displayed great courage in operating his machine-gun from his vehicle in a very exposed position under heavy enemy fire.

'Two days later, during a night raid on enemy transport on the coastal road near Bomba, he shot one driver and killed a further five men with hand grenades.

'Throughout this and other patrols, he has shown great determination and a constant desire to engage the enemy.'

THE INDIAN SQUADRON OF THE LRDG

Few people know that an additional unit of 350 volunteers was raised from the British and Indian Armies to operate in an Indian Long Range Squadron of the LRDG behind the lines, from the winter of 1941.

Commander was Major Sam McCoy and the squadron patrolled behind the lines from Siwa, Kufra and Hon throughout 1942. It was with General Leclerc during his epic march north from the Fezzan and carried out attacks on enemy transport on routes to the south of Tripoli. In 1943 General Montgomery released the squadron from the LRDG because it was unlikely to find further scope for its activities in the country the 8th Army was now entering, namely Northern Tunisia.

After the squadron was released by Monty after Mareth, it was sent to India. Patrol commanders Captains Boyd and Nangle left to return to their parent Indian regiments. Signals Sergeant Darky Haslam left and Sheffield was believed to have gone back to the special ops base. Taffy Owens, navigator, and Sergeant Ripley, from Ripon, were among the other veterans who were found alternative tasks.

Captains Birdwood and Hudson also returned to their Indian regiments. Wireless ops Jack Cox and Ally Brain were repatriated from Ferozepore. From Zahidan, navigators Colly Collins (Liverpool), Tod Lever (Manchester), Fred Smurthwaite (Bishop Auckland) and Signals Sergeant 'Jargesab' George left for other duties. Other officers included Captains Cantley, Rand and Fitzgerald.

FLYING FRIGHTS

LRDG legend W.B. Kennedy Shaw describes with pin-sharp clarity the exciting side of travelling by service air transport in the middle of a desert war . . .

On 24 November 1941 Jalo was taken by Oasis Force, a mixed column including South African armoured cars and Indian infantry commanded by

LRDG personnel inspect an overturned RAF Lysander aircraft at Melfa, Western Desert, May 1942. (IWM HU25283)

Brigadier Reid. HQ LRDG at that time was at Siwa and Lieutenant Colonel Prendergast detailed me to go to Jaghbub, get a lift from the RAF and go on to Jalo to discuss with Force Commander the possibility of LRDG patrols operating westwards from there.

We took off from Siwa in a Lysander, but landed again almost immediately as the engine failed. Fortunately, we were within reach of the landing ground. I transferred to a 15-cwt and eventually reached Jaghbub after having got stuck in a salt marsh on the way.

The next morning I left for Jalo in a Blenheim. We flew over the northern edge of the Sand Sea and on the way passed over an aircraft that had crashed on the top of one of the 400-foot high dunes. I was told that a search aircraft had seen the footmarks of the crew leading away from the machine but nothing more.

When we got to Jalo I met the brigadier and after lunch returned to Jaghbub. On the way we stopped at LG 125, a (famous covert) landing strip right out in the desert, north of the Sand Sea, to drop a pilot who had been shot down in the fighting over Jalo.

In the afternoon we took off from Jaghbub for the Blenheim's home strip near Army HQ, which was where some of the passengers and I wanted to go. After a short time in the air we suddenly plunged headlong towards the ground.

Intelligence Officer Bill Kennedy Shaw using theodolite at Ain Chetmir, February 1942. (IWM HU25143)

I thought we were about to crash, but after we had flattened out I learnt that the pilot had spotted two MEs (enemy aircraft), from which he had taken evasive action. Later, the rear gunner said they were not MEs after all, but Spitfires. Then we ran into a thunderstorm, and then the navigator fell asleep! As a result of all this we were well and truly lost, so the pilot decided to go due north to the coast – he could hardly miss the Mediterranean – and then turn east or west and land at Sidi Barrani.

We found Sidi Barrani all right but the ground was flooded from the recent storms and it was impossible to land. However, the pilot now knew where he was and set off for his own airstrip some miles south of the coast. It had been dusk when we got to Sidi Barrani, and it was dark when we reached the home airstrip – too dark to land without a flare path. The procedure for getting the boys on the ground to put out a flare path was to fire Very lights in a correct sequence, e.g. red, green, red.

Unfortunately, the navigator had forgotten to bring with him, or had lost, the paper with the day's signals so we flew round letting go a succession of coloured lights which would have done credit to 5 November until our stock was exhausted, but we didn't strike lucky. The pilot then decided to make a 'wheels up' landing in the desert. I knew how hummocky the ground was around there and did not think much of this idea.

The rear gunner and the passengers, two others and myself, were told to sit on the floor facing aft with our backs against the bulkheads. This, we were told, was the best position for the expected shock. The pilot flew round for some time to use up his spare fuel then came down low and switched on his landing lights. They shone on a row of telegraph poles. Judging that they must run along a desert track, he quickly slammed down his wheels and made a perfect landing.

Fifty yards from where we stopped was a tent with two men who belonged to the airstrip. We spent a quiet night with them, took off in the morning and in two minutes were down on the landing ground to receive an amused account of the clot who had flown round the night before giving his own private firework display!

I was very glad to be collected the next day by Trevor Barker in the LRDG Waco and taken peacefully back to Siwa.

History Made

THE MARETH LEFT HOOK –
A HISTORIC LRDG MISSION THAT SAVED THOUSANDS OF LIVES

As the desert war reached its climax, the 8th Army stormed forward from its great victory at El Alamein to link up with its American allies invading from Algeria in the west to smash the Axis forces in a giant pincer movement. But the Afrika Korps and Italians still had a venomous sting in the tail in the shape of the formidable Mareth Line defences, 22 miles of lethal anti-tank ditches, defended in depth with mines, artillery, machine-guns, barbed wire and strong points of steel and concrete. It was a battle situation akin to the bloody horrors of the First World War and the expected casualty figures were appalling.

The French had originally built the huge defensive position between the Matmata Hills and the sea to stop the Italians if they attacked Tunisia from Libya.

An historic photograph. The LRDG became the first 8th Army patrol to cross the Tunisian border on 13 January 1943, enabling British and American armies to link up for the first time. A proud feat. (IWM HU16497)

Now the remaining Axis armies in North Africa – minus a sick Rommel who had been recalled to Germany – determined to make the victorious advancing British pay dearly in a desperate last stand.

The 8th Army had no apparent choice but to launch a main frontal attack on the Mareth Line, but the consequences would have been disastrous. Fortunately for thousands of soldiers and their victorious commander General Montgomery, the LRDG was on hand to do what was considered the impossible by finding a way to get around the enemy position in a sweeping 350-mile outflanking manoeuvre, as former New Zealand Association secretary the late Jack Davis recorded in his diary.

Davis's diary covers the months from October 1942 to April 1943, when he was navigator to the Kiwi's T1 Patrol. Jack gives a detailed account of patrols near the Tunisian border, a road watch (when the LRDG men hid camouflaged near main road routes, noting and radioing back enemy vehicle movements and strength) and a destroying patrol when it laid mines and wrecked several enemy vehicles. On Christmas Day they blew up two ammunition trucks on their way to Tripoli and the patrol made its way to Zella.

But then came the most important job of their army careers when they were detailed to carry out a covert recce of the lethal Mareth Line defences to search for a way through the escarpment. This first patrol to cross into Tunisia was commanded by Nick Wilder and, by 16 January 1943, Nick and his New Zealanders were south of Medenine. They ran into very bad going and so moved

Monty with Gen Freyberg VC and New Zealand LRDG patrol. (IWM HU25000)

An LRDG truck stuck in soft sand. (IWM HU25177)

further to the south, where they discovered the pass by which the New Zealand Division was to carry out its magnificent left hook round the Mareth Line two months later, the route becoming known throughout the Army and to military history as Wilder's Gap. They succeeded, utilizing all their hard-won desert experience to discover the previously unknown pass. This enabled the combat forces to funnel through decisively, thus rendering the key Mareth defences untenable. The crucial NZ LRDG patrol, on this occasion under Captain Tinker, guided the division to a resounding victory.

Montgomery wrote in his memoirs: 'The French told me that any outflanking movement through this sand sea was impossible.' But a route *was* found by the LRDG and countless lives were saved.

A delighted General Freyberg congratulated the victorious New Zealand Divison on its 'Balaclava Charge'. But the real victors of the key battle were the skilled and modest heroes of the New Zealand LRDG . . .

CHAPTER 3

True Grit

Those who fought their way through some of the hardest campaigns in the Second World War describe the mesmerizing power of loyalty which the Scorpion badge inspired.

War, like life, is full of choices – some good; some bad; some regretted at leisure. However, one choice that binds LRDG veterans together to this day is the conviction that they each made a momentous decision in joining the special wartime unit, which was to become so much a part of their lives: a way of life, in fact.

Although the LRDG was only in existence for just five action-packed years, its intense comradeship and enviable reputation quickly became so evident that now, sixty years later, it has welded into a unique, historic and proud part of the fighting tradition of the British Army.

Especially in the desert, the men lived in close-knit groups on raiding and reconnaissance parties for weeks, often months, at a time. They fought, ate, bivouacked and sometimes died together.

It was no coincidence that so many of the LRDG veterans who were captured in the various theatres of war almost invariably escaped, often in the most desperate circumstances, risking torture, especially from some of the brutal rival factions in the Balkans, and sometimes even death.

When captured, it was difficult in the extreme for their enemies to curb the restless, dedicated, but free spirits that the LRDG had become.

Some of the LRDG veterans describe here just what it was that inspired them to volunteer . . .

Why We Volunteered

ARCHIE GIBSON MM

I realize now when I look back on some of my past experiences that some unknown influence often seemed to guide me in the right direction.

My three particular friends in the Guards were fellow drivers Jock Findlay, Tam Pratt and Archie Murray. They had all volunteered for the LRDG. Some months before, an officer had arrived, interviewed them and moved them to the

Citadel all in the space of a forenoon. I was out on a job that day and was very unhappy to find three empty beds next to mine when I got back to the Kasr el Nil Barracks. I visited them at the Citadel and felt extremely lonely when they drove through the archway bound for a new adventure.

The battalion moved back to the Western Desert shortly after this. My truck was my home, my private headquarters. I drove it, ate in it, slept in it or close to it if it was loaded. My last two days with the Scots Guards and the start of a new life happened this way.

Disaster struck as I was driving along with bare feet and dressed only in a pair of KD shorts. The first shell landed behind me, followed quickly by a flash of orange and black 10 yards in front. I nipped out just in time to see my 'home' erupt in flames. My bedding roll, a beautiful set of German spanners and half a bottle of Dewars White Label whisky, a farewell present from Theo Jennings on my last leave in Cairo, were destroyed. A German armoured car with a crew of three arrived to review their handiwork. We all moved back a bit when the ammunition started to explode. I was then bundled into the car. It was a very tight squeeze with four of us crammed inside.

When we were some miles away from the tell-tale column of smoke from my household effects, we stopped and had an excellent brew of coffee; later we had a meal. Conversation was limited. '*Rommel zer gut general*,' I said. '*Ja*,' they agreed, and I think they were trying to tell me that Rommel would soon be in Cairo. I left it at that. We had just cleaned the mess tins with sand and were preparing to move off when a troop of 11th Hussars appeared through the heat haze and a burst of machine-gun fire came dangerously close. The unter-officer opened the door, said '*Raus*' and off they went at high speed. I lay down in the sand, offering the smallest possible target. The 11th Hussars treated me like a prisoner. I told them my story over and over again and eventually used a few choice army words to relieve my exasperation. That did the trick. They realized that no German could have such a command of British soldier language.

I was given a shirt and a blanket and conveyed to their camp. Next day their ration truck delivered me to our HQ. I told the MT (motor transport) corporal that I had lost my wheels. Then he said the magic words, 'We have had an application for a driver/mechanic from the LRDG. Are you interested?'

I certainly was and that afternoon I was on my way to Cairo in high spirits. We were bombed and strafed on the coast road but eventually arrived at Abbassia Barracks. A hot bath and a joyous reunion with my friends followed. I was on top of the world. I finally got off to sleep about 1 a.m. to be rudely awakened by the blast of a bomb that blew a great hole in the wall beside Jock Findlay's bed. Jock was blasted out of bed and lay in a heap of blankets in the middle of the room. Five taxi drivers who were sleeping in their cabs outside the wall were killed. Jock was undamaged but could not find his girlfriend's photograph that had been pinned to the wall.

On another occasion, that photograph nearly cost him his life. His truck was hit and Pratt circled round to pick him up. 'Must get Janet's photograph,' said Jock, heading back to his truck. The enemy shots were getting close but Jock grabbed his pack and made it to safety in the nick of time. He had a charmed life. He had to abandon another truck coming away from the Barce airfield raid. He walked for three days before being befriended by the Bedouin and lived quite happily with them, learning their language and their customs, until we picked him up four weeks later. There he stood, surrounded by goats and sheep, a tall, bearded figure in Arab gear with a big, beaming smile on his face. 'What took you so long?' he said.

Jock survived the war and we were to be together again in 1946 trundling buses around the countryside. I never did find out what happened to Janet, but he later had a fine wife called Betty and a son who became a police inspector. Strange that Jock should have fathered a policeman after all the damage he inflicted on the Military Police in the Middle East!

BLONDIE DUNCALFE

It was simply the quest for *esprit de corps*, which I learnt about at an early age. My father served in the Scots Guards from 1903 to 1911 and then from 1914 to 1918. He was wounded on three occasions and was finally gassed. The many questions I asked him and his replies, made it apparent how he treasured the great comradeship he had experienced, how, during that war where conditions were so terrible and appalling, it was through the bond which existed between them that they gained the strength and fortitude to keep going.

When I was seventeen I added a year to my age and also joined the Scots Guards, where I found that, apart from square bashing, learning regimental history, etc., particular emphasis was placed on *esprit de corps*.

After leaving the depot, I was also to find great comradeship in the battalion and it became a key part of life. In the latter part of 1941, I lost some of my close friends when we attacked the enemy front line. These were lads I had lived and shared all thoughts and feelings with, I knew all about their families, their joys and sorrows and, with their premature departure, I felt as though part of my life had gone also.

At about this time they were asking for volunteers for G Patrol and, hearing that some folk forfeited their rank to join the LRDG, I thought the comradeship in such a unit would be good. I wondered what I had let myself in for, but soon realized this was the ultimate dream of any soldier.

The fact that each and every man was disciplined allowed him to be somewhat undisciplined, for each one could be relied on to do all that was required and expected of him and a little extra if necessary.

Each one was made to feel that he was a cog in the wheel in everything that was undertaken. Here was the perfection of *esprit de corps*, where comradeship existed between all ranks, where we were privileged to be members of a team, of a wonderful unit, a family of brothers to be always united. We shared risks and dangers, joys and excitement, tragedies and successes – always with the strength of our *esprit de corps* . . .

RON HILL

I had always been fascinated by stories of the desert since reading T.E. Lawrence's *Seven Pillars of Wisdom* (different desert, different war). But I had also picked up copies of Bagnold's *Libyan Sands* and Wilson MacArthur's *Road to the Nile* while on leave in Cairo, which reinforced my interest. Perhaps the book that influenced me most was Rosita Forbes's account of her journey from Benghazi to Kufra in the 1920s, the first woman to make the journey – disguised as a man – and one of the first Europeans since the German, Rohlfs, had discovered the oasis around 1879.

Though I had seen a great deal of the desert with the Gloucestershire Hussars from Amiriya to Agedabia, this was mostly of the coastal strip and across the bulges where the great tank battles had been fought.

I had enjoyed life in the desert, its unique beauty, the marvellous stars and its many changes of mood, and relished the possibility of seeing more of it. The opportunity to join the LRDG came at the absolutely ideal psychological moment. I had returned from a spell in hospital in Nathaniya, in what was then Palestine, to find the regiment in disarray – tankless and having suffered heavy casualties at El Alamit. It was now enduring the ignominy of being in quarantine from an epidemic of diphtheria.

Rumour was rife and it was generally believed the regiment would be broken up, so the arrival of a recruitment team from the LRDG created great interest. The team was headed by Jake Easonsmith, who explained, as perhaps only Jake could, what the Group did and how it operated – how it was not a Commando unit and he didn't want any 'death or glory boys'.

I have always been grateful to Jake for selecting me. Certainly, I saw a lot more desert and am only sorry I wasn't able to stay on with the unit until the end.

JOHN SHUTE

I have never listened to old soldiers' advice and always volunteered for everything. It was through volunteering for what turned out to be a staff officer's con trick that I found myself languishing in the deserts of Iraq in 1943. So, when a call came for volunteers for the LRDG, I – with several hundred other bored young men – put my name down and wondered whether I could possibly measure up to the exacting tests to which I expected to be subjected.

The day for the interview came and Bob Maxwell appeared looking avuncular and kindly. He saw us about ten at a time, as there was such a milling crowd of volunteers, and told us a little about the LRDG and its work and asked us if we still wanted to join, to which we all replied fervently in the affirmative. My God, I thought, is that it? No chance to display my sterling qualities! There must be a catch somewhere or he'll never select anybody.

That night I went to the officers' club hopefully and, sure enough, there was Bob propping up the bar, surrounded by an eager crowd of applicants trying desperately to impress him. I hung around and had a few pints and somehow, late on in the evening, I found myself talking to Bob. I don't know what we talked about but at last he said, 'Look here, are you serious about this?'

I said, 'Oh yes.'

'Well,' he said, 'we can't talk here with all these creeps. Let's go to the loo.'

So we went to the loo and had an earnest and alcoholic conversation about life's values and the importance of vital military matters. Very many drinks later I staggered home and crashed out in my tent.

My method of dealing with a hangover in those days was – like a condemned man – to eat a hearty breakfast, but luckily Bob didn't know this. So I was tucking into bacon and eggs when Bob, looking frail, came into the mess tent and sat down. 'Have some breakfast,' I said with an air of cheerful well being.

'Just coffee,' Bob murmured and said no more, but I could see he was impressed. I was selected.

So I am convinced that my ability to disguise a hangover was one of the reasons why I succeeded in working my way into such an illustrious band of warriors! I must say that it has been put to the test on quite a few occasions since then with such stalwart and immortal characters as Leo, Alec, Mickey, Gilly, Trevor, David and Stormy and other friends too numerous to name.

BILL JOHNSON

Embarked on the *Orion* troop ship October 1940. The convoy was quite a big one, destination Egypt. First stop was Freetown to take on water but 50 miles away we had a mishap. The *Revenge* battleship which was escorting us crossed our bow during the night and hit and badly damaged the *Orion*.

The ship was sinking slowly. We were standing by our action stations. Some had lifeboats, mine was a raft. Just my luck as I couldn't swim.

They had some very good water pumps, though. It took three hours to rectify the situation and then we continued our journey. The ship was doing a rumba all the way to Port Tufic. Everybody was sick, even the sailors. When we disembarked, I could hardly stand up. I couldn't face any food and felt awful.

Then we went to TK transit camp for two days. I was posted to Number 4 Command Base Workshops, Abbassia. Next morning we were on parade at 6 a.m. inspected with a storm lamp by a Sergeant Major, then it was a half-mile walk to the workshop. Twelve and fourteen hours' hard graft a day; a week on B vehicles; a week on armoured cars and tanks; a week on heavy guns. Between the six-week boat trip and the long working hours, I felt terrible.

After five weeks a notice was posted on the orders notice board: 'MV fitters wanted for the LRDG.' Twenty-seven of us applied. Only two were picked out to go – me and a Canadian, Jim Spencer.

After an interview with the OC Workshop, questions on fault finding, etc., I got back to my tent – there were eight of us in a tent. I said, 'I'm being posted to the LRDG.' Then they started putting the boot in.

One chap said, 'That's the cloak and dagger mob. You're certain to be shot up.'

'I'll take my chances,' I said, 'Anything is better than that red hot oven of a workshop for twelve and fourteen hours.'

I enjoyed every minute of my stay with the LRDG. The only one thing I feared was being attacked by a first-class Jerry Stuka pilot. He could pick us off like flies as there is no hiding place in the open desert.

JOE CRYER

When the question was put to me recently, 'What made you want to join the LRDG?' I did not need to think too hard to recall my feelings in early 1942 when the possibility arose that I might indeed get the opportunity to do so. The same question was asked of me when being interviewed by the then Captain David Lloyd Owen when he was seeking reinforcements for the LRDG from the 1st Cavalry Division in Palestine.

The answer now is the same as it was then, though perhaps expressed in different terms: 'I wanted to get in on the act.'

To explain a little further. Firstly, I had arrived with my regiment in Palestine in February 1940, an enthusiastic nineteen-year-old and since then, apart from a bit of a fracas in Syria in June 1941, had been serving in what were virtually peacetime conditions. During this time the war in the Western Desert had got well under way, but what was more pertinent to me personally was the fact that my family, mother, father and two young sisters, had seen more of the war than I had, plus my paternal grandparents had been killed in the November 1940 blitz on the city of Bristol. So, although I was happy enough in my regiment, I was very much dissatisfied with the role it had to play.

Secondly, during 1941, word filtered back from the men who had already got in about the special work of the LRDG. The more I heard, the more I wanted to be part of it. Then in February 1942, my prayers were answered. I was accepted. I was in.

In the succeeding years I was not disappointed. I felt I was doing something worthwhile and was completely fulfilled in my job. There was also something else. General Lloyd Owen, in *The Desert My Dwelling Place*, writes about the paradox of the extraordinary 'ordinary men' when seeking men for his unit. Although I did not think about it in those terms then, I began to realize what he meant in this brotherhood I was now proud to be a part of.

KEN LAWRENCE

I arrived in Kenya from New Zealand in late August 1939. I joined KAR [King's African Rifles] on 4 September 1939, then the East Africa Survey Group, mapping the Northern Frontier District of Kenya to Abyssinia and the Italian Somali borders. Later I was with the attacking force under General Godwin Austen until the Italians in Somaliland were subdued.

I was then called back to HQ in Nairobi where Colonel Hotine, Director of Surveys, East Africa, asked me if I would like to go to the Middle East to join a bunch of buccaneers known as the LRDG to map a part of the Libyan Desert. By this time, in early 1941, Kenya was a dead end, the war had finished there and I was excited with the prospect of going to the Middle East to carry out an operational mapping project. Of course, at this time, I knew practically nothing of the activities of the LRDG, but the expectancy of mapping in the great desert was exciting and adventurous, to say the least.

I then flew, by British Overseas Sunderland flying boat, from Mombassa to Cairo. On arrival I went to GHQME, and was interviewed by Colonel Ralph Bagnold. I don't remember much of this questioning session, but I do remember him talking about the barchan sand dunes. He said they depicted organic life. The barchan is a sand mass, crescent shaped, rolling over the desert floor in the direction of the prevailing wind. The big ones were at least a mile from horn to horn and their rate of movement I guessed at about 1 metre a year. The most remarkable thing was, at the horn of the dune I inspected, there was a tiny barchan about 4 inches across, an exact facsimile of its parent, which I suspected one day would grow into a large dune – hence, supporting organic life.

My initiation into desert travel came after a few days when I travelled with a New Zealand patrol returning to Kufra after leave in Cairo. My impressions of that first LRDG journey were that the men in the patrol were very friendly and happy. There was efficiency in all operations – signals, truck maintenance, navigation, with respect for the officers.

I was particularly interested in the Bagnold sun compass, which was to play a large part in my future mapping. Captain Plugs Ashdown of REME converted a standard issue compass to one with a sighting vane which could rotate so that one could take bearings on to features while on the move. This saved a lot of time and trouble.

After a few months, and now able to see how the LRDG organisation worked, I was amazed at the sheer efficiency of the unit. A patrol was given its marching orders – a detailed briefing by the Intelligence Officer, Bill Kennedy Shaw, and some wise words from the CO. In the meantime, the Patrol Sergeant loaded up with the necessary water, petrol, rations, ammunition, spare tyres and mechanical spares, the Medical Orderly checked his first aid kit, the navigator his maps and equipment, and the wireless operator his orders and codes.

All this attention to detail was impressed on my mind and this not only helped me in future tasks with the LRDG but also in life after the war.

I was always proud to be a member of such a distinguished unit and my times with the Group were some of the happiest and most exciting years of my life.

BEWARE THE LRDG – THE 'SUICIDE SQUAD'

Bill Smith's father was a Territorial infantryman during the First World War. He landed in France in 1915, went through the hell of the Somme, Passchendaele and many a lesser scrap, and was wounded three times. Though never concealing from his son the horrors of war, he was eloquent about the comradeship of the front line, and Bill greatly admired him and all the 'poor bloody infantry' that had served Britain so well. When world war tore Europe apart again, Bill wanted to do his bit as faithfully as his father had, but for three years was thwarted by a guardian angel, or so it seemed . . . until he became one of the LRDG's crack radio operators.

On 3 September 1939, armed with a Certificate A from my school OTC, I applied for an infantry officer cadetship along with former school mates. I failed two medicals because of a rapid pulse, but months of patient investigation produced a diagnosis of Tachycardia, a harmless condition.

By then I was due for call-up and was so frustrated that I was ready to take any job in the Army. This time I passed A1 and opted for my father's old regiment, only to be told, to my disgust, there were no vacancies for infantry. I was assigned to the Royal Signals.

I took to wireless operating like a duck to water but still hankered after the infantry. In June 1940 I volunteered for the Commandos but, like my colleagues, I heard nothing. I think a shortage of wireless operators ruled us out.

After training I was posted to 18th Division, already earmarked for overseas, but only HQ and No. 1 Company of the Divisional Signals sailed, as a draft, for the Middle East. The division followed six months later and was diverted to the Far East. Every man in it was either killed or became a prisoner of the Japanese. That time I saw no reason to protest to my guardian angel.

My lot reached Egypt in June 1941. In October the division moved into besieged Tobruk in readiness for the November break-out. Afflicted with desert sores, I was left behind in hospital. On discharge, I begged to be sent to join my friends in Tobruk. Basewallah bloody-mindedness sent me to Port Tewfik. I was sustained by my enjoyment of wireless operating, by working with Regulars and by the normal comradeship of the Army. But I did not feel I was doing much for the war effort.

By great good luck I happened to be in Cairo when vacancies in LRDG were advertised. My sergeant did his best to dissuade me. He sincerely believed I was courting certain death. 'They're a suicide squad, Smudge,' he said. But what I had heard about the LRDG suggested that suicide was reserved for the enemy, so I did my utmost to calm the good sergeant's fears. When finally I left, he displayed on the side of a truck the most gruesome unarmed combat poster he could find [which didn't deter Bill in the slightest].

I was interviewed by Tim Heywood, beautifully turned out and radiating confidence, efficiency and purpose. He handed me over to Wilf Hughes for an operating test. Wilf apologized for having no buzzer. Did I mind reading key clicks? To get into the LRDG I'd have had a go at reading his mind! So Wilf rattled his key on one filing cabinet and I took down the message on another. Thus I became a member of that unique military family called LRDG and now, in the winter of my life, I warm my hands on the memory of the years when I soldiered happily ever after.

THE ENGLISH PATIENT – FACT, NOT FICTION

The Oscar-winning film *The English Patient*, though a fictional and highly romanticized story, was based on a contemporary of the founder of the LRDG, Brigadier Ralph Bagnold. 'Count' Laszlo de Almasy was well known among desert travellers between the wars, a Hungarian who threw in his lot with the Germans, though they never made the fullest use of his experience.

Almasy's most famous wartime exploit was to travel from Tripoli to the Nile to deliver two German spies who were to operate from Cairo. By LRDG standards, the feat and the journey were little more than routine and in any case the deciphering experts at Bletchley Park had rumbled them before they had even started and followed them all the way. The gate was left open for them in the hope that they would identify bigger fish in the enemy espionage network in Egypt, but the two spies turned out to be a couple of fools and were eventually arrested while living it up on a houseboat on the Nile.

Almasy has always been a glamorous, somewhat shadowy figure and so little is really known about him that the film makers had to rely on a novel by Michael Ondaatje, joint Booker Prize winner 1992, to create an intriguing film which became such a major success.

THE DAY THE LRDG RESCUED RICHARD DIMBLEBY
FROM THE DESERT

Ace mechanic Bill Johnson tells of an unusual vehicle recovery he made 10 miles from Siwa in August 1941, involving the fearless war correspondent and later legendary television broadcaster Richard Dimbleby, who was making his mark on the desert war in more ways than one . . .

It was a well-known fact that a camel train did its usual trip from Cairo to Siwa oasis bringing provisions for the local Arabs and returning to Cairo with a cargo of dates packed in our throw-away 4-gallon flimsy petrol cans. In August 1941 one of these camel trains arrived in Siwa and the head Arab in charge brought us a note. It said two men were stranded in a Chevrolet pick-up with a broken front spring and could they have help? So I was sent out with spring, a full toolbox and a canvas chatti full of water. I was no navigator, so I was told, 'Follow the tracks and tyre marks for about 10 miles.'

Siwa lies in a hollow and to get out you have to drive up a long slope. I reached the top and there were no tracks or tyre marks because the night before there had been a bad sandstorm and it had covered everything up. I drove in what I thought was the direction of Cairo and clocked 10 miles on my speedo before I stopped and stood up in the truck. I looked all round and couldn't see any pick-up. I placed a stone on a newspaper so I could find my way back and then forked right and clocked another 1½ miles. In the distance I saw a black object that materialized as the broken-down pick-up.

The two men with it turned out to be Richard Dimbleby and his driver, who told me they had been stuck there for two days. Needless to say, they soon emptied my water chatti and within the hour I'd fitted the spring and got them mobile.

Many years later, looking at the television one night, Jonathan Dimbleby, Richard's son, was a guest on *This Is Your Life*. I wrote and told him this tale and he replied as follows:

I did know about the event to which you refer as there is mention of it in my father's diaries which I used extensively when writing *Richard Dimbleby*, a biography published in 1975.

He had many exciting adventures of this kind, one of the worst of them being when he elected to drive the correspondents' car from Mersa Matruh to Cairo. As Alan Moorhead, the famous writer, recorded: 'We all slept and so did Dimbleby.' The result, he drove off the road breaking a newly-built bridge in the process and causing the Sappers to erect a little sign saying:

Spot the LRDG truck! This vehicle has been made invisible to enemy planes and patrols by being cunningly hidden in a wadi using desert scrub. (IWM HU24973)

'This bridge built January 1941. Destroyed January 1941 by War Correspondents' activity!'

BAGNOLD'S SUN COMPASS BRAINWAVE

Brigadier Bagnold, who was the LRDG's founder and leader for the first eighteen months of the unit's colourful existence, perfected the sun compass, which became a vital part of the unit's pioneering equipment in the Western Desert. The sun compass meant that shadow sitings and bearings could be taken from vehicles while on the move, an important safety consideration where attack by aircraft and speed of use were concerned and a tremendous advantage over magnetic versions, which had to be used at a standstill. The last thing a mobile unit hundreds of miles behind enemy lines wanted was to be caught cold and uncamouflaged out in the open, where fighter-bombers could wreak havoc among the unarmoured and stripped-down-for-lightness Chevrolets and Ford trucks.

Other sun compasses used by the Army could not hold a candle to Bagnold's version. As Major General David Lloyd Owen explains in his book *Providence Their Guide*, the LRDG's compasses showed the true bearing of the course followed at any particular moment, whereas other types only ensured that if the sun's shadow fell on the correct time graduation, the truck was following a set course. If the vehicle or unit then had to change course for any reason, a common occurrence, the truck had to be halted and the compass reset, wasting valuable time. Major General Lloyd Owen cannot understand to this day why the Army did not adopt the Bagnold sun compass for all units.

A simple method of dead reckoning was used by the navigators, who were key members of every LRDG unit, noting speedometer readings and sun bearings to give a reliable knowledge of position. For true accuracy, a theodolite was used to get an astrofix on stars at night.

The job of the navigator was a tough one, requiring considerable ability and powers of concentration. They could seldom relax while on the move or even for considerable periods at night. Yet, as Major General Lloyd Owen recalls, the thought of getting lost never struck him as a possibility – such was the expertise of the LRDG men, widely acknowledged as among the best navigators in all the fighting land forces.

Similarly, the wireless operators were highly trained specialists, using equipment that was robust, simple to use and reliable. No spoken word was ever transmitted; instead, the operators relied on sky wave signalling or key operating. This and simple, regularly changed ciphers meant the LRDG's radio communications were not compromised. The radios, No. 11 high-powered sets, could not be operated on the move, however, and required considerable setting up of aerials and equipment. Like the navigators, radio operators were often kept up at night, transmitting and receiving vital messages.

Each patrol member, every one a volunteer, knew their tasks precisely – and those of the others – interlinking to produce an unshakeable conviction that the patrol was far more important than any individual in it.

ON A WING AND A SAFETY PIN . . .

Patrol fitters worked miracles to keep LRDG trucks mobile in the vast, unforgiving desert. Many hundreds of miles from the nearest spares depot, the ace mechanics had to use what came to hand when tool boxes ran low – resulting in some bizarre but highly effective repairs, as Bill Johnson relates . . .

In the desert all patrol fitters had to carry a variety of spares before setting off on a trip. These included clutches, carbs, water pumps, fan belts, plugs, coils, distributors, etc.

There was one driver in my patrol who persisted in tuning and tampering with his engine. Every night when we stopped he had the bonnet up. He wanted his truck to go faster and he made no secret that it was in case we got chased.

A truck receives vital repairs during the desert campaign. (IWM HU25166)

One night I saw him sifting through a lot of sand under his truck. He had been making an adjustment to the ignition points and had lost the rotor arm. He moved the truck back and dug up sand everywhere, but no way could he find it. Eventually, he came to me and asked if I had one. I had three distributors but not one with a rotor arm. That made him very sick.

Next thing, the Skipper came to me and said we weren't leaving a truck behind and I'd have to think of something. From my thoughts emerged an idea involving a cork from a beer bottle and a safety pin from the first aid kit. With a razor blade I fashioned the cork and with a pair of pliers I bent the safety pin. The engine leapt into life. The driver was very pleased and became a reformed character. His truck kept up with the rest, chased or not, and he gave me his rum ration for a week!

THE MOTHER OF A SANDSTORM THAT SPOILED LUNCH

In the early summer of 1942 Y1 Patrol's hut stood on the sandy southern slopes of the depression that formed the oasis of Siwa. The LRDG often ran into sandstorms; it was part of the way of life for the patrols as they criss-crossed the vast expanses of the desert. But the sandstorm that headed straight for these men on this day was a bit special. Titch Cave was one of those present and Arthur Arger took a photograph of the awe-inspiring

A classic study of an LRDG patrol sheltering from a sandstorm between Cairo and Siwa, March 1942. (IWM HU24964)

phenomenon, which is now in the archives of the Imperial War Museum. Titch takes up the story:

Having just returned from a patrol, it was suggested that a meal centred around some fresh roast meat was something that would be greatly welcome; for desert wallopers well know that although our ration scale was generous, fresh meat was conspicuous by its absence. So a whip round was organized and a sheep bought and butchered.

The mutton was carefully cooked, while we all waited in anticipation, and after being carved was just about ready to be served when an excited voice from outside shouted, '——— me! Come and look at this.'

We all dashed out not knowing quite what to expect and there, all across the northern horizon, was a huge rolling cloud which must have been over 100 feet high. We watched in awe, our dinner forgotten, as the cloud rolled down over the northern cliffs and advanced towards us across the oasis. The air was quite still as the cloud approached, then, when it was closer, the wind began to rise, the temperature dropped and it was upon us, filling the air and every nook and cranny of our hut with dust and sand.

It was the father and mother of a sandstorm which was beyond the experience of even the oldest members of our patrol. Of course, our dinner was ruined, but I would not have missed the spectacle of the awesome sandstorm that ruined it.

A Rhodesian patrol wearing sand goggles. (IWM HU16509)

'It was a towering, solid wall,' said Arthur. 'We'd never seen *anything* like that one.'

TAKING THE PLUNGE – IN CLEOPATRA'S POOL

LRDG Association secretary Jim Patch recalls the indescribable joy of taking a bath in a cool, luxuriant oasis after weeks of patrolling in the desert during which washing facilities were non-existent barring the occasional roll in the sand! Though historic archaeological treasures abounded at the famous Siwa oasis, these went largely unnoticed as all the tired and grimy soldiers wanted to do was to dive into the inviting depths, as Jim explains:

Those of us who were privileged to visit the Siwa oasis during the desert war used to gaze upon the ruins of the temple of Jupiter–Ammon with only mild interest. My recollection is of some tumbledown walls with paintings on them, which still retained a few vestiges of colour. There were a few boulders and broken bits of wall scattered about but nearby was Cleopatra's Pool, which was of much greater interest to us than the ruins of the temple. Returning from patrol, it was a joy to dive from the perimeter wall naked into its refreshing depths and enjoy the luxury of wallowing in all that water after weeks on the move without even enough water for washing.

How the pool got there and who built the wall round it, nobody bothered to ask. And the origins of the temple raised even fewer questions in our young minds. Now the archaeologists have moved in and they say they may have discovered the burial place of Alexander the Great there.

The Times reported the discovery. The temple, it seems, was built by the Pharaoh Amasis about 570 BC and the resident oracle became famous for predicting things. Alexander heard about this and, taking time off from empire building and laying the foundation stone of Alexandria, came for a consultation with the oracle. He was rewarded by being addressed as the Son of Jupiter (also known as Zeus) and being told that he would conquer the world. The temple was built by an Egyptian and dedicated to the Egyptian Sun God Ammon. But Alexander was a Macedonian with Greek connections and after he had consulted the oracle the Greeks took a hand and identified Ammon as their own chief god Zeus. Thus the place became known as the shrine of Jupiter–Ammon.

Recent excitement started when the archaeologists, who are Greek, found two limestone plaques that purport to show that Alexander is buried in Siwa. They are said to tell, in Greek, how Ptolemy, one of Alexander's generals, brought his master's body to Siwa and buried him there.

Scholars are in two minds whether to believe all this. They say there is good evidence that Alexander was buried in Alexandria but they also say he may have

Relaxing patrol members enjoy the cool luxury of Weston Salt Lake at Kufra oasis. (IWM HU71336)

Even the LRDG had to be paid – David
Lloyd Owen doling out wages at Kufra.
(IWM HU25282)

been buried in Siwa first then moved to Alexandria. There is a story that his body was laid in a gold coffin which was stolen by a Roman emperor and replaced by a glass one, but nobody has been able to prove it.

Original Kiwi LRDG veteran Frank Jopling recorded in his diary similar vivid memories of an oasis at Zighan, about 120 miles north of Kufra, where an observation post was maintained as part of the defence of Kufra, during the time that the unit had to do garrison duties to ensure the safety of the main base at the oasis. Frank, who died in 1987, records:

10th June 1941. We set off again at 6.30 a.m. and arrive at Zighan where we are now at 8.45 a.m. S Patrol, who are Rhodesians, have made this into a wonderful place. There is no population and only one or two palm trees. All you have to do is scrape a hole with your hands and you can get a nice cool drink of water. It is marvellous to see nothing but sandy waste all round you and yet an abundance of water only a foot underground.

However, the Rhodesians have made full use of this and have dug a swimming pool which is very cold, far colder than the one at Kufra. The lookout site is on top of a palm tree and they tell me they are going to put a swivel chair up there! What next? They got some timber from the landing ground we passed which, by the way, is where W Patrol captured the trucks on the first trip of the LRP.

The cook house and mess room is built round a palm tree and is a better kitchen than you see on some farms in NZ. They have made a stove out of a benzene drum and sand and benzene tins filled with sand. They have made a small refrigerator with a small biscuit tin inside a large one. The big one has a lot of holes in it and between the tins is filled with charcoal which is kept wet and the evaporation keeps the inside tin as cool as a refrigerator. They have a wine, or should I say rum, cellar underground and they have built a big oven at the back and they tell me that they use biscuits for firewood!

Bartering tinned salmon for fresh eggs and vegetables at Kufra oasis. (IWM HU25294)

THE SPECIAL GENIUS OF COLONEL SIR DAVID STIRLING, DSO OBE

Sir David Stirling died on 4 November 1990 at the end of a momentous and truly adventurous life, but the unique force he created, the world-famous Special Air Service, has carried on to preserve the essence of his audacious spirit and imagination. The following extracts are taken from the obituary written by the chairman of the LRDG Major General Association, Major General David Lloyd Owen for the SAS Magazine, *Mars & Minerva*. There is no better epitaph.

I will never forget the first time I met David Stirling. It was in the rather cheerless light of early dawn a hundred or so miles behind enemy lines in the Western Desert on 20 November 1941. I was then commanding a Yeomanry Patrol of the LRDG, which had been positioned to report on enemy movement before and during the Eighth Army's offensive across the Egyptian frontier. David, together with Paddy Mayne and fifty-five men, had been dropped four nights previously with the intention of destroying as many aircraft as possible on the enemy airfields at Tmimi and Gazala. It was a bold conception.

The legend of the failure of that first and only parachute operation carried out by the SAS in those days is now part of the Regiment's history. But what is, perhaps, not so well known is that the working relationship between the SAS and the LRDG stemmed from that moment [more than] fifty years ago.

Lt Col David Stirling DSO, founder of the Special Air Service and leader of many early desert raids, who was transported to and from enemy airfields and other targets by the expertly navigated truck patrols of the LRDG. This study was taken shortly before his capture in Tunisia in 1943. (IWM E21340)

It resulted in a unique partnership which achieved such brilliant success inspired by David Stirling's genius for piracy behind the enemy lines.

He never forgot the help that our patrols were able to give his newly formed SAS. It was in recognition of this that a few years ago he decreed that members of the LRDG Association should be looked after, if ever they were in need, by the SAS Regiment charitable funds. We have been immensely grateful for this.

So those of us who are still alive remember him with special affection. We can but mourn the passing of one of the undoubted architects of victory in the Western Desert and we also remember the founder of a Regiment in the British Army, which is unsurpassed in its role today.

We, in the LRDG Association, salute the memory of a quite remarkable leader. His flair, commanding presence, boldness and conspicuous success always earned our profound admiration.

Perhaps the most extraordinary of all his characteristics was his ability to bounce back again after the most dismal failures; and then he would aim for ever more, and apparently impossible, targets.

Yet when this self-effacing giant of a man was captured in Tunisia in early 1943 he was only twenty-six. He was known throughout the Allied armies for the sheer daring of his exploits and for his skill at overcoming the objections to his ideas from unimaginative staff officers.

His name will surely live for evermore.

SAS LEGEND – PADDY MAYNE

The hard-bitten veterans of the LRDG fought alongside some of the toughest soldiers of the Second World War, but none came any braver, or more deadly, than Paddy Mayne, DSO and three bars.

Major Mayne was a giant of a man, well over 6 feet tall with prodigious strength and instinctive tactical awareness in the field, one of the most decorated soldiers of the Second World War. He always led from the front and took on the enemy personally at every opportunity, no matter what the odds, with Tommy gun, Bren, grenades or machine-gun.

In the desert war, he notched up a huge tally of enemy aircraft destroyed by Lewes bombs and Vickers K fire on numerous enemy airfields – even ripping out the control panel on one aircraft when he had run out of explosives to render it useless!

Mayne, Stirling and their fellow SAS raiders destroyed nearly 400 of the enemy's best aircraft, and put the vital coastal railway out of action for thirteen of the twenty days immediately preceding the crucial Alamein battle.

After Stirling was captured by the Germans during a risky scouting mission of the Mareth Line flank near the Gabes Gap in Tunisia, in January 1943, Mayne took over command of the SAS, becoming Lieutenant Colonel and leading his men to further glory in Sicily, Italy, France, Belgium, Holland and right into the heart of Germany itself. He later led a force of liberation into Norway at the end of the war.

Bravest of the brave. SAS Lt Col Paddy Mayne DSO and three bars, one of the most decorated soldiers of the Second World War. This larger-than-life Irish warrior first achieved fame on his devastating early desert raids on airfields and other enemy installations thanks to the navigational skills of the LRDG, who took Mayne, Stirling and their men to and from their targets. Mayne later led the Special Raiding Squadron/1st SAS to further glory in Sicily, Italy, France, Belgium, Holland and on to final victory in Germany. (IWM MH24415)

The incredible exploits of the larger-than-life Irishman are reckoned by many to have been worth at least one VC. However, if Mayne had one flaw, it was his quicksilver temper and contempt for red tape, which infuriated the high command on more than one occasion. This could have swung the balance in him not gaining the highest award for valour which experts agree he so richly deserved.

But those who witnessed the fearless Mayne in action, eyes flashing, gun blazing, will never forget the sight.

Major Roy Farran, a close friend of Paddy's, told me he was one of the finest soldiers he ever met. 'Brave as a lion, fearless when his blood was up. A great soldier and his men would follow him anywhere.'

Sadly, Paddy, who survived countless hand-to-hand fights throughout five years of war, was killed in a car crash near his home in Newtonards, Northern Ireland, just ten years after the end of the war.

SIR FITZROY MACLEAN – A SPECIAL FORCE HERO

Sir Fitzroy Maclean had an amazing career in the wartime SAS and later daringly parachuted into Yugoslavia as Winston Churchill's personal representative to Tito. It was he who persuaded Churchill to back Tito and not Mihaelovic in that country's desperate fight against the Germans in the powder keg that was the Balkans.

But to LRDG and SAS men Maclean is best remembered for his starring role in the first foray into Benghazi in the Western Desert in May 1942, with David Stirling and other SAS desperados, including Churchill's son Randolph. After being escorted by two LRDG trucks as far as the Barce–Benghazi road, they bluffed their way through roadblocks into Benghazi, driving boldly through the enemy-occupied streets in Stirling's 'Battle Wagon', which was a Ford station wagon thinly disguised as a German staff car. Unfortunately, due to the earlier rough going, the car wheels started to produce a high-pitched scream because of

They didn't know what Blitzed them! SAS commander David Stirling behind the wheel of his famous battle wagon or 'Blitz Buggy', a powerful, converted Ford V8 staff car that was armed with concealed Vickers K machine-guns and driven into Benghazi disguised as an enemy vehicle on a daring raid to blow up ships in the harbour. This photo of the raiding party was taken at a secret rendezvous with the LRDG on the return leg. Rose, at rear in beret, sits alongside Reg Seekings, with Johnny Cooper in front next to Stirling. (IWM HU69884)

David Stirling, in officer's cap centre right, together with SAS and G Patrol LRDG comrades and his famous 'Blitz Buggy' on the way back from the Benghazi raid. Left to right: Archie Gibson MM, LRDG; Reg Seekings, SAS; Jack Crossley, LRDG; Johnny Cooper, SAS; Stirling; 'Scotty' Scott, LRDG (behind Stirling); Rose; Guardsman Archie Murray, LRDG. The man standing on the vehicle is Guardsman 'Ginger' Blaney, LRDG. (IWM HU69650)

bent track rods, drawing unwelcome extra attention from numerous enemy soldiers in the area.

In the course of the raid, fluent linguist Maclean, tired of being constantly challenged by Italian sentries at various roadblocks, sent for the guard commander and tore him a strip off for not demanding to see their papers as they could be 'British saboteurs carrying high explosives!' (As indeed they were.) Incredibly, the party got through unmolested, laughing uproariously at Fitzroy's cheeky improvisation.

The audacious mission was frustrated from its main aim of blowing up harbour shipping by sheer bad luck in various forms, but Maclean's courageous and inspired humiliation of the enemy guards remains one of the best, most daring and humorous stories of the desert war.

Incidentally, just before Sir Fitzroy died in June 1996, his family revealed it was widely accepted that the cloak and dagger diplomat, soldier and super-patriot who had packed an incredible amount of action and adventure into his lifetime was the original role model for James Bond, 007 himself . . .

FORTUNE MADE FROM GAZELLE HANDBAGS

Gazelle provided more than fresh meat when shot on patrols in the desert. Some enterprising LRDG men kept the skins, which they cured on the backs of the trucks in the searing heat, to be sold at mission's end in Cairo for a small fortune, benefiting all the patrol members. Bill Johnson explains:

I was with a Rhodesian patrol. We were sick of bully and biscuits, so we used to shoot gazelle and eat them. The drill was to shoot only stags as the does might be in kindle and the meat tainted. The first time I saw it done I thought I'd never eat it, but I learnt to love it.

The drill was: first shoot a stag, drop the tailboard of the truck and with a sharp machete, chop it up into joints. Then we would dig a shallow slit trench, soak the sand with petrol, place over a well-polished sand tray and set fire to the petrol. We put the joints on the sand tray and the blue flames would come through the holes. The joints were basted with 10-pound tins of Australian butter and all the innards and the skin buried.

But I never buried the skins. I kept them all on my truck and the men in the patrol used to play merry hell with me as they attracted thousands of flies until I had dried them all off! Some months later, we had a week's leave in Cairo. We parked up the trucks in Abbassia Barracks so I said to my driver: 'Get in, we're going to get rid of those gazelle skins.'

We found a handbag factory and, after a lot of bartering, I finished up with £150 cash, a sheikh's ransom, which was divided among the patrol. The lad that did the butcher's job was named Trevor Boswell. He was from a circus family in Cape Town and his wife appeared on TV here in England in the 1960s – Eve Boswell the dancer-singer.

THE FITTERS WENT BANANAS!

Fitter Bill Johnson and LRDG colleagues like him often had to repair trucks in the desert with incredible ingenuity and imagination, using highly unorthodox materials and methods. Many lives literally depended on the fitters keeping vehicles moving, no matter what the difficulties and shortage of spares. Repairs hundreds of miles from base often meant that the mechanics made parts from whatever was handy at the time – from parts of petrol tins to safety pins borrowed from the first aid kit! But on one occasion, Bill surpassed himself using nothing more than a few bananas begged from local Bedouin to complete a crucial major repair . . .

There is no Relay or get-you-home service in the desert. Furthermore, no one realizes the vastness of the desert until they have travelled it. It's very hot but very cold at night, very quiet and even frightening at times.

A crashed truck in Jefren after Tripoli raid. (IWM HU25039)

My role as patrol fitter was to keep the wheels turning — by make-do and mend. I also had to look after a point five Vickers machine-gun.

Starting from Siwa oasis, destination Benghazi to do a road watch, the fitter's truck position was in the last truck to pick up the cripples as they broke down. We had travelled many days trouble free apart from a burst tyre and a burnt out clutch. I was just congratulating myself on what an easy trip it had been when all of a sudden the truck in front of us went up in the air at least four feet.

We thought he had hit a coffin mine at first and as we drew alongside, we saw the occupants were sitting in the truck, shaken and dazed.

'What happened?' we enquired. The driver said he thought he'd hit a rock. I got down to see if he'd ripped off the exhaust system and noticed oil pouring from the gearbox. By the time the patrol skipper came to see what was wrong, I could see the gearbox had been cracked badly and we couldn't travel above another 20 miles otherwise it would seize up solid. We did 20 miles, pulled up, brewed up, had some bully stew and the patrol got off to kip.

The following morning, just breaking daylight, I heard a voice and saw in the distance a Bedouin driving his flock of sheep and goats. I woke up my mate who could speak good Arabic. I told him to get the Arab to sell us some bananas in exchange for tea and flour.

Sure enough, we got our bananas. I removed the top of the gearbox and stuffed it with the skins. This enabled us to continue our journey and we did almost 900 miles before a replacement gearbox was fitted at base!

HOW HARRY SECOMBE NEARLY GOT THE BULLET!

Bill Johnson was reading an old TV magazine when he found an article headed: 'The night a lone Secombe faced the enemy'. Former Goon Michael Bentine told the hilarious story about Harry Secombe being sent out as a dispatch rider and getting lost in the desert. What Harry didn't know at the time was that he and his noisy motorbike were spotted by an LRDG patrol, which included Bill, and Harry was very nearly taken for a German and shot! Considering he was behind enemy lines at the time and at the mercy of any lurking Afrika Korps or Italian, Harry was fortunate to have been discovered by a crew who asked questions first before shooting. Bill's side of the story goes like this:

In June 1942 we, S1 Patrol, had been on a mission. Suddenly John Olivey, the patrol skipper, ordered us to stop and switch off our engines. Far away in the distance a black speck was seen and the noise of a motor bike heard. They all thought it was a German. I said, 'That's not a Jerry, they use BMW bikes. That's an English bike. It's either a BSA or a Matchless, I can tell by the exhaust noise.' I was a keen motor bike enthusiast before the war.

The dispatch rider reached us and our skipper said to him, 'What are you doing here? Do you realize you're behind the enemy lines? You'll get shot up.'

He admitted he was lost and asked, 'Why won't *you* get shot up?' We convinced him it was our job, put his bike in the back of a truck and took him back to his unit – Royal Artillery battery, 25 pounders.

The lost dispatch rider turned out to be Harry Secombe.

Bill wrote to Harry long after the war and sent him a Scorpion tie, mentioning that he was one of the LRDG patrol who had found him lost. Harry replied that Bill's letter had brought back many memories and that he had related the incident many times.

But it was so very nearly a case of here today, goon tomorrow . . .

FEARED MORE THAN ANY FOE – THE DEADLY DEVIL'S BREW

Roy 'Blondie' Duncalfe's worst nightmare was alcohol induced, at dead of night, in the middle of nowhere in the dark and silent desert. If you find it hard to believe that a tough LRDG man could be spooked by an inert object about 4 inches long, you've obviously never heard of the deadly Devil's Brew, a mind-blowingly potent 'cocktail' created exclusively by the fertile imaginations of the LRDG patrolmen. To gain some insight into the extraordinary ingredients which went into the concoction that kept the desert veterans, including Blondie Duncalfe, glowingly warm on cold, lonely nights, read on . . .

I always said that providing you could see who, or what, you were attacking or being attacked by, then things weren't so bad. One of my most hair-raising experiences was after a session on the Devil's Brew at Siwa. Devil's Brew was an LRDG speciality, consisting of jars of strong Navy rum emptied into a very large dixie, with tins of fruit, lime juice powder, eggs, *toothpaste*, etc., boiled up during the daytime and allowed to cool ready for the evening session.

I realized I needed to go to the toilet and retired to do so, releasing my lanyard from around my waist and placing it around my neck. My slacks dropped about my ankles and I sat there meditating and dreaming. Suddenly, I was aware by the light of the moon of something moving towards my slacks. Aware of all the creepy-crawly things that frequent the sand, I eased myself off the seat and in a crouched position with my slacks still around my ankles, I started off at speed into the desert.

Unfortunately, this thing kept following me and it wasn't until I had covered 20 or 30 yards that I realized what it was – my jack-knife on the end of my lanyard!

NEVER OUT OF THE WOODS

Y Patrol veteran and ex-cavalryman Arthur Arger fondly remembers atmospheric sunsets and velvety evenings in the desert, enhanced by the precious ration of Woods rum which was carried in stone jars by every LRDG patrol as a vital morale-boost to their basic rations. Arthur remembered, with a wistful smile: 'Woods rum was like rocket fuel, well over 100 per cent proof, though we only got one tot at night after a hot, thirsty day's work. I used to mix mine with powdered lime and rest it in a dish on top of one of the wheels of my truck and let the desert wind gently cool it, before pouring it into a tin mug. I can taste it now, it was like nectar.'

At the same time, the late Captain Tony Hunter, another Y Patrol stalwart, used to get out his well-thumbed copy of the *Rubaiyat of Omar Khayyam* and quote long passages to his comrade. 'The scenery was breathtaking, the desert awe-inspiring. It felt perfectly right,' Arthur added. 'He carried the book everywhere he went. It was his philosophy of life.'

Sadly, Captain Hunter was killed when he parachuted into Yugoslavia later in the war on a dangerous mission to work behind enemy lines with the Partisans. His heroism will never be forgotten.

THE HUMBLE JERRYCAN – SO VITAL TO DESERT WARFARE

All LRDG and 8th Army veterans recall the transformation the arrival of the jerrycan made to the transport of petrol in the North African campaign. No matter how many tanks, lorries or aeroplanes either side had, none of them would work without fuel, and the transport of this vital liquid in the heat and harsh and remote desert terrain was a real headache – until this truly superb and typically efficient piece of German equipment came into Allied hands.

The design came out of Hitler's devilishly thorough preparations for war. A close examination of the container reveals brilliant features, which are not at once apparent.

The weight, loaded, is about as much as an average man can conveniently handle to re-fuel a vehicle. Also, when dealing with the can in an awkward storage position on a vehicle, it can be lifted without difficulty. Yet, in an open place, a man can easily carry two. The three handles enable the can to be passed from man to man in bucket-brigade fashion. The air chamber at the top keeps a filled can afloat if dropped in water. The spout is secured with a leak-proof snap closure which props open for pouring, and an air tube from spout to air space makes for smooth pouring.

The two sides of the can are welded together to give a safe join and the can is lined with a material which enables it to be used either for petrol or water. Finally, its shape is ideal for storage.

Loss of petrol between supply base and consumer because of the hated, flimsy, square petrol tins used initially by the British was said by General Auckinleck to be a disastrous 30 per cent. It was certainly disconcerting for LRDG members when re-fuelling a vehicle out on patrol hundreds of miles from anywhere, to find can after can half empty.

Not surprisingly, the LRDG was among the first units to be issued with jerrycans for general use.

Jim Patch has a vivid recollection of transferring petrol from the old flimsies into jerrycans in a large, enclosed building in Kufra:

Before long the place was full of fumes and we were soon all high as kites, singing while we worked and rolling about drunk as owls. I think it was the first and only time any of us had got plastered in the line of duty!

Then came those terrible American substitute jerrycans with screw tops. They were the same size and shape as proper jerrycans but the lack of a spout and an air passage made them impossible to pour from without extensive spillage. Not only was the spout and clip fastener absent from these cans, but they were not lined to contain either petrol or water and the sides were joined with rolled seams, an unsafe method to use on a petrol container.

The name jerrycan came about when the Germans invaded Norway in 1940 and the can came to the notice of the British. An American engineer, Paul Pleiss, came to London later that year and was consulted about the design. To the everlasting glory of British good sense, the manufacture of exact copies was ordered.

However, to the everlasting shame of British organization, two years later the British Army, about to fight for its very existence at El Alamein, had to rely on captured jerrycans for the safe transport of petrol for its fighting vehicles. It was not until early 1943 that 2 million British-made jerrycans arrived in North Africa and a year later they were being made in the Middle East.

Millions of the cans continued to roll off the production lines and it is said that by the end of the war in Europe there were 21 million of them.

OMO KALEEF – THE LRDG'S SECRET LISTENING WEAPON

Gazelle, as has been revealed, were often sighted by patrols out in the wide open spaces of the desert and could make a decent meal of fresh stew if the pursuing soldiers were canny enough not to goad the graceful but speedy animals into a panic-stricken flight, and good enough shots to bag a kill on the run. Once startled, the tiny herds would bolt off at terrific speed and would often not stop until they dropped from exhaustion. Bill Johnson tells the story of one baby gazelle that was adopted by two veterans and became 'one of the boys'.

On one trip, we were five days away from Siwa. We had travelled many miles and were in the middle of nowhere. It was mad hot and bright sunshine; mid-summer so that at noon there was no shadow from the needle of our sun compass. In the distance there was a herd of gazelle, about fifteen or twenty of them. I don't think I have ever seen so many in one group. As we approached, the noise from our trucks frightened them off and they ran away at a very fast speed.

When we reached the spot we discovered they had left behind a baby stag. It couldn't have been above ten days old. One chap said, 'Leave it here, the mother will return for it.'

But my mate and I said, 'No, we'll keep it for a pet.' Everyone thought we'd gone mad, but we kept him anyway.

The gazelle travelled with us on our truck. We made a collar and, when we pulled up at night after a full day's travel, we tied him to the truck with a length of rope in case he wandered off. My mate rummaged through the truck and found an empty beer bottle. I went in my toolbox and got a rubber gaiter from the clutch stave cylinder and that made its teat. His bottle feed consisted of diluted tinned milk and two crushed Horlicks tablets from an escape kit.

The following day we gave him a name and christened him 'Omo Kaleef'. He became very tame and had very good hearing. One day my mate said suddenly, 'Omo has heard something.' He had got from under the truck and stood upright with his head up towards the sky. We couldn't hear a thing, but seconds later a lone Jerry bomber flew over very high. On our journey back to base we took Omo off the bottle and he went on the same menu as us – bully stew. He loved it.

Back at Siwa it was decided we should have seven days' leave. We made our way to Cairo, three of us on our truck. We got almost into the centre and decided we would have a glass of ice cool beer and pulled up at the roadside at the Spitfire Bar. We were at a table almost on the pavement complete with beards, Arab headdresses, shorts and chaplis. We had Omo with us on a lead like a dog.

The troops were on leave in Cairo sight-seeing and within minutes we had gathered in a crowd. Seconds later, the table was full of beer. There was a clicking of cameras and a barrage of questions. 'Where did you get him from?' Everyone wanted to stroke him. We were just enjoying all this when two redcaps blasted up in a jeep.

'You're causing an obstruction. You'll have to move on,' they barked. So we were forced to ask them the directions to the Zoological Gardens.

We arrived at the zoo and reluctantly handed over Omo Kaleef. The zookeeper was over the moon with him. 'How did you get his coat to shine like that?' he asked.

'Bully stew', we replied proudly.

'I'll breed from him,' he said.

So Omo Kaleef was RTU'd back to his original 'unit' after a brief but spectacular LRDG career!

THE SACRED DESERT DUMP . . .

LRDG veteran Archie Gibson has often told a quirky anecdote, courtesy of Major Chris Fitzgerald, a neighbour of his in Crieff, Scotland.

In late 1947, 3 Commando Brigade, Royal Marines, had arrived in Malta from the Far East. Each of the three Commandos were based at Tartuma Barracks in

North Africa in order to train in desert conditions as a marked change from the jungle conditions with which they were familiar. Frank Harrington, Intelligence Section 2 i/c, decided to use some of their time in practising navigational skills and so a party duly set off, LRDG style, to spend ten to twelve days away from base.

On return, one of the sergeants told how late one afternoon, when carrying out that night's duty navigation, he had set as his objective a large mound of sand far away in the distance. The soldiers were surprised on reaching the mound to discover an enormous stock of compo rations and other items, pre-dumped for use by the LRDG during the Second World War – and still intact.

When the NCO went into Tripoli district HQ to report his strange find, he was told that though unusual, the 'treasure trove' was not unique as such stores were still – several years after the end of hostilities – seldom stolen. The reason was that the Bedouin in the area still held the LRDG in such high esteem that their dumps were sacrosanct!

NICKNAMES

As in many fighting units, nicknames were widespread in the LRDG and some of the stories behind the nicknames are worth relating.

Bill Anderson, for instance, was known as 'Swede'. In his school days they called him 'Willie' and he hated it. Then came the 2nd Battalion Scots Guards and Egypt and that's where he met Archie Gibson. Archie, always a great talker, learned that Bill's dad was a Norwegian sailing ship man and immediately called him Swede and it stuck.

Archie was known as 'Flash'. He was a dispatch rider in the Scots Guards, and one day the orderly sergeant, finding Archie lying in bed after reveille, whipped the blankets off and said, 'There he lies, Flash Gibson, the demon biker' and that stuck too.

Joe (real name Ron) Cryer told a sad tale with a happy ending of his first annual camp with the North Somerset Yeomanry [NSY]. He went to the tent earmarked for his section only to find it full and a card school going on. He was told in the most un-refined army language to go away. Feeling crestfallen, as a new boy, he tried the next tent. There, a friendly character he'd never seen before said, 'Come in here, Joe, there's room enough', and Joe it was ever since, not only in the NSY but also in the LRDG and the SAS.

Ron Hill told a story about a detachment of Y Patrol in a gully on Leros overlooking a potential landing beach and waiting for the invasion. They didn't move about much for fear of being spotted by enemy planes and passed the time telling yarns. Spud Murphy came up with one about a chap who went into a restaurant and said, 'Steak and kidley pie, please.' The waiter replied with a

Members of various LRDG patrols display classic – and unorthodox – Arab head-dress gear at Abbassia barracks, Cairo, March 1942. (LRDG)

sneer, 'I suppose sir means kidney,' to which the man said, 'I said kidley, diddle I?' After that, Sid Broderick, a railwayman in civvy street, told how he planned to achieve his ambition, and that of all youngsters at the time, of becoming an engine driver. Apparently, you had to get in the right stream. It was no good being a porter or a parcel man. You had to be an oiler and greaser, progressing to wheel tapper and fireman before being considered for driver. It was a colourful tale that had everyone in fits and, following Spud's story, Sid immediately became Sidley.

Here are some more wacky names which Association members remember well:

Wink Adams, Jesus Armstrong, Stinker Arnold, Tanky Babb, Baggers Bagnold, Ali Barber, Shorty Barrett, Snowy Berry, Taffy Bevan, Torchy Biddle, One Shot Browning, Bullshit Burgess, Lofty Carr, Bomski Cashin, Titch Cave, Flog-Nob Crichton Stuart, Stormy Stormonth Darling, Jungle Davis, Darky Devine, Happy Dorrington, Blondie Duncalfe, Toity Du Toit, Bull Ferrier, Buster Gibb, 'Maggie' Gibbs, Stalky Gifford, Geordy Greason,

LRDG officers on leave in Alexandria, April 1943. (IWM HU25305)

Snooky Greenhill, Grannie Greenwood, Boozy Gunn, Nobby Hall, Foo Harper, Harry of Y, Will Hay, Fiddler Hill, Basher Inwood, Jacko Jackson, Jankers Johns, Wacker Jones, Kipper Kaplan, Kip Kiley, Louie Leach, Jigger Lee, Chippy Loveday, Tobruk Lowenthal, Daisy Mackay, Dead Loss McKay, Blondie McKinnon, Spider McNeilage, Zucky Mann, Jessie Matthews, Rufus Montagu, Spud Murphy, Olly Ollerenshaw, Pedler Palmer, Potty Potgeiter, Tam Pratt, Taffy Rees, Pongo Reid, Buster Roberts, Scottie Scott, Ginger Sharratt, Carry On Simms, Tiny Simpson, Tashy Smith, Stuka Stokes, Timoshenko Timpson, Edgar Wallace, Lofty Westlake, Gook Williams, Tug Wilson, Pooky Wood

Many veterans recall that One Shot Browning got his name from his uncanny ability to hit anything with a rifle at seemingly any range. Many was the occasion when his comrades benefited from wildlife bagged for the pot in the Western Desert. Some of the other nicknames are of more obvious derivation, while others are intricately obscure – but all are an essential part of the rich folklore of the LRDG.

Meanwhile, time for some leave . . .

CHAPTER 4

The Cedars of Lebanon

The LRDG was now ordered to abandon its beloved trucks and reorganize into small foot patrols capable of maintaining communications up to 100 miles behind enemy lines. Training took place in the Lebanon, where men were expected to carry packs of up to 70 lb on their backs, taking enough food with them for around ten days.

Pack mules were also to be used where necessary, along with jeeps for reconnaissance, though these would not be as heavily armed as those of the SAS.

The desert veterans were ordered to familiarize themselves with operating in mountain terrain and so were also taught to ski, billeted in a hotel 6,000 feet above sea level, situated amid mountains of towering grandeur in a breathtaking setting high above Beirut.

German and Greek were taught and the men had to work up to a high peak of fitness for their arduous new tasks, with exercises covering scores of miles in the most difficult conditions.

The heat of Alexandria was obviously not conducive to this type of training regime and so the unit made its base at The Cedars in the mountains of Lebanon, where Jimmy Riddell, of Olympic ski fame, was running a school to train soldiers in mountain craft, along with Griffith Pugh, who was acting as Medical Officer. Pugh had been with Sir John Hunt on the attempt to conquer Everest before the war, a dream that had also inspired David Stirling in his pre-war climbing days.

There was much talk of a seaborne landing on the island of Rhodes, which in the end came to nothing. It was also thought that in order to cover the sort of distances now being envisaged for missions, parachuting should be added to the LRDG repertoire, and so volunteers were called for to learn this then perilous technique. Only six out of 130 asked to be excused and four of these changed their minds and completed their allotted jumps in the end.

Then came a 'Most Secret and Officer Only' order received by David Lloyd Owen, as commander of B Squadron LRDG, involving a likely move into Kos and Samos to 'stiffen resistance of the Italian garrison and local guerrillas to German control of the islands'. The orders only vaguely referred to possible operations in Rhodes, however.

As many of those involved at the time and historians have since reflected, the blunder in failing to take Rhodes, the largest and most important of the

Jimmy Riddell, former Olympic skier, instructing the LRDG in the Alpine arts at the Cedars of Lebanon, May 1943. (IWM HU25311)

Ski instruction in Lebanon, ready for mountain warfare, May 1943. (IWM HU25088)

Dodecanese islands, and to gain control of its vital airfields was to cost the Allies dear if Turkey could not be persuaded to come in on their side.

Turkey was not persuaded and the decision *did* cost the LRDG and British and Commonwealth forces dearly.

In the meantime, the LRDG took stock, recharged their batteries and trained hard in a glorious, famous and unforgettable setting . . .

TRAINING IN THE MOUNTAINS OF LEBANON

When the LRDG, acknowledged masters of desert navigation and hit-and-run fighting, left North Africa and its beloved trucks in the summer of 1943 bound for the breathtaking Cedars of Lebanon to retrain for mountain warfare, many privately thought the conversion would never work, that the new type of fighting would be too different and demanding, or that the best days of the unit were behind it.

But the amazing versatility and hardiness of the desert veterans were to prove all doubters wrong, as Bill Smith remembers, prompted by the memories of

A fit-looking LRDG soldier with a pack weighing 70 lb-plus, a common burden for LRDG soldiers during patrols in the Dodecanese campaign. (IWM HU25275)

another well-known LRDG character and unit doctor, Doc Lawson. As the enemy were to find to their cost, the roasting, strenuous days and freezing nights, and the sheer hard graft in the thin mountain air meant the LRDG men emerged fitter and tougher than they had ever been in their lives. Bill said:

No one who was there will ever forget the magnificent setting of the Cedars, the crescent of mountains running from north through east to south, towering above the hotel and the cedar trees, with a steep drop of a thousand feet to the west and the village of Bsharri.

At the end of the desert war, the New Zealand Government insisted on the repatriation of 1st, 2nd and 3rd Echelons, roughly the brigade groups which made up the original New Zealand Division. To their great credit, many of our men decided to stay with the unit, but many new recruits had to be found. My own patrol lost 50 per cent. Consequently, A Squadron began mountain training much later than B, and to the best of my recollection, were restricted to two months.

At the time we took it for granted that we would do what was required of us. Looking back, it is astonishing that we achieved so much in such a short time, both in physical and mental adaptation to a new environment and in testing and learning to use so many new items of equipment. But LRDG planning was, as ever, on the top line. As I remember it, we got everything right first time, apart from the packs, which had to be strengthened.

I suppose we were among the first British troops to wear the thick pullovers which are now universal in the services, string vests and ski caps. My South African reinforced boots saw me through the mountain training, the Aegean campaign and the rest of the war, and endured much hard gardening before they expired in the fifties. A few chaps tried out hand-made boots with Commando soles, now common but then a novelty.

I recall with relish how easy it was to hit quite a small target at 800 yards with a sniper's rifle. We had an uproarious two days, in more ways than one, on explosives with the legendary Captain Bill Cumper of the SAS, whose act blended expertise and Cockney humour in equal measure.

The radar [homing] beacon 'Eureka' and the new pack radio sets and miniature battery-charging engines were of special interest to us radio operators. Three men from each patrol did a course on rock climbing at the Mountain Warfare School and afterwards helped Ashley Greenwood to teach the rest of us to abseil down a rock face. We used a simple rope, not the fancy equipment the Marines use nowadays. Fred Whittaker, our patrol sergeant, was a good psychologist. He knew that the only Pom in the patrol would manage to lean backwards into space with passable nonchalance if fifteen New Zealanders were watching; and that those same Kiwis would allow no Pom to beat them by so much as a hair's breadth!

So when he caught my eye and said, 'You first Smudge', I knew the score. To my surprise, I enjoyed it and I was one up in the end, for after the first men were down, Ashley decided everyone should have a safety rope attached.

Doc Lawson and others would recall the dehydrated minced meat, the smell of which suggested it was well able to crawl over the mountains on its own! The patrol had to be reassured that Doc had passed it as fit for human consumption, but we could not forbear to murmur, as we stowed it in our packs that, 'The old Doc must be losing his flaming touch.' It is only fair to add that he was proved right.

The French-built roads through the mountains were few and appalling, being narrow, rough and crumbly at the edge. There were no safety barriers whatever, despite the many sheer drops of hundreds of feet. We suffered a number of serious accidents, one of which I witnessed. I was attached to Stan Eastwood's patrol at short notice, his radio operator being absent for some reason. We set out on a jeep exercise to the Turkish border. As we descended the switchback before Tripoli, one jeep came out of a hairpin bend too near the edge and somersaulted down the slope to the road below, a complete wreck. Jenky, the patrol sergeant, had been able to jump clear but Tex Riley, the driver, accompanied the jeep for the first half of its descent. We looked up to see him sitting on a rock, white and shaken but unharmed. We reckoned he had been protected by the .5 Browning on the back, which had taken the main shock of each bounce.

Some of us lived for a while near the cedar grove in tents, which proved an irresistible attraction for the local Arabs. These gentry, who lived at 4,500 feet on the far side of the mountains, made quite a hobby of climbing 4,000 feet, descending 2,500 feet and crossing several miles of rough ground in darkness to whip kit from under our tent walls, carrying it home by the same route. Willie Watson, who slept opposite me, drew blood from a 'klifti' hand with his sheath knife one night, but by the time we got outside the tent, the thieves had vanished. In order to stop these thefts, we had to sweep the mountain sides all night with a searchlight and direct a burst of .5 Browning at anything that moved. Flocks of animals were impounded to compel the return of the stolen property, but I don't think we got it all.

An exercise I particularly remember lasted ten days, one day of which was devoted to resting, overhauling equipment, weapon training and receiving a night parachute drop with the aid of 'Eureka'. We started somewhere near Damascus and covered 100 miles by the map, but the numerous ups and downs must have added a significant distance. In the course of the exercise we climbed the highest mountain in Lebanon. We called it 'That big bastard at the back of the Col'. My atlas gives it the name Qurnet es Sauda, 3,086 metres, 10,125 feet.

Our final climb on the last afternoon was about 4,500 feet up a narrow shoulder with no room for traversing and an unbroken gradient at or near the maximum for the human foot. We did it in two hours less one five-minute halt. Although our packs were apparently a bit lighter than theirs, I suppose we could fairly compare ourselves with the yomping Marines of the Falklands War.

My patrol, R1, was accompanied by R2, who were somewhat reluctant muleteers. One of their animals was even more reluctant and was therefore nicknamed '*Stana Shwaya*', little slowcoach in Arabic. When we had discovered the full range of his villainy and knew him for the bad bargain he was, he became 'Stana Swizzle!' One drawback with mules, was that once loaded, they had to keep going non-stop for four hours and then off-load for two hours. So we, the PBI (Poor Bloody Infantry), had to forego some of our hourly halts and spend longer over the midday meal than we liked.

Just before we were summoned to the Aegean, Bob Haddow joined the patrol. He played the guitar and knew all of the many verses of *The Ball of Kirriemuir*. During the night dash to Haifa, we stood and sang in the back of our 3-tonner. We sang popular songs, soldiers' songs, Maori songs, but always we came back to *The Ball of Kirriemuir*.

Finding no ships at Haifa, we went 20 miles north to a hutted camp by the coast road at Nahariya, where we spent two days cleaning our weapons, training with them and filling Bren magazines. On the first night some of our chaps were alleged to have caused an affray in a cafe in the village. The culprits were not identified and no confessions were forthcoming. So Jake Easonsmith had the whole of A Squadron on parade and took the line that we all must suffer for the sins of the few. He sentenced us to a 7-mile cross-country run over the rough but flat ground at the back of the camp, which was at sea level.

Spirits were high and we treated it as something of a lark. We had ample breath for lively conversation as we ran, and all finished in a bunch, not blowing the snuff off the proverbial sixpence. Thus we discovered, rather earlier than the world's leading athletes, the value of altitude training.

A PRESCRIPTION FOR FITNESS

The unit's Medical Officer, Doc Lawson, had the awesome responsibility of ensuring the LRDG's safe transition from fighting in roasting temperatures at sea level in the Western Desert to that of mountain patrols and raiders in the dizzy heights of Yugoslavia, Italy and elsewhere. The fact that the versatile veterans made the change so effectively is in no small part due to his medical skills and sound advice which gave the troops the best chance of acclimatizing successfully in a gradual, well-planned but increasingly tough, training regime. The superb fitness of the patrolmen also stood them in good stead when many were later captured in the Leros debacle and in other theatres and made their escape, in many cases over considerable distances, back to Allied lines. Doc Lawson explains:

The wind of change first blew about us in January 1943 at Hon [in Libya] when Colonel Prendergast told us our desert role would soon be over and that we should return to Alexandria for leave and later train for a new job. 'Those with a beard like the doctor's, or worse,' he said, 'must shave them off' and the rest could trim and keep theirs.

So it was that, clean shaven, I arrived in Alexandria for leave, spending some very good days with Bob Melot's Belgian friends who set out to give us a really pleasant change and a taste of social and family life among them. [Melot was a Belgian patriot who spoke Arabic fluently and worked with the LRDG and SAS helping British Intelligence in the desert, later also operating with the SAS behind the German lines in France after D-Day.]

While there, I learned that we were to be trained to do a similar job to a desert one but in the mountains of the Balkans working with the Partisans. To start the training some of us were to learn Greek and some German, and this was the first step in what was to be for me a remarkable transformation. What I had to do on the medical side was to find out the best way to change completely motorized patrols into small groups of mountaineers carrying everything they needed from the start to the finish of the objective.

We were to train at the Cedars of Lebanon 6,000 feet above Beirut and to be billeted at the Cedars Hotel, near which was a small grove of the original Cedars of Lebanon. In peacetime, it was a ski resort and the mountains went up a further 3,000 feet.

I was advised the patrols should be picked from resourceful, older men who liked hills and solitary conditions and who had no arthritis or chest diseases. We were, of course, already self-selected so this was no worry. Even with the best men I was warned that it took three weeks for the body to adjust to high altitudes by making more red blood cells and increasing the absorbing surfaces of the lungs.

Having got the right men, there was then the question of training. This had to be done slowly. The danger at that height was that over-exertion before adaptation could bring on a dilated heart and also a severe depression from accumulated fatigue, which took a long time to get over. The mountain warfare people suggested a five-month period of training.

The first three weeks was camp routine with one-, two- or three-hour climbs or walks and lectures on the country, the people, on moving as inconspicuously as possible, bivouacking and cooking. At four weeks, light packs of 15 lb were taken on four hour climbs on one or two days and at night up to 17 miles with 30-lb packs, with practice in night-time camping, cooking, map reading and

A spectacular vista greets LRDG patrol members in a meal break during arduous training in the Syrian Mountains in 1943. (IWM HU25069)

weapon training. In the fourth month, more ambitious schemes took place away from base of five days with 45-lb packs and visits by observers from HQ to watch from vantage points and make useful suggestions.

The fifth and final month found us doing 80 to 100 miles with packs of between 60 and 80 lb, and practising with aircraft supply drops of rations and any other gear needed. By this time camp routine, guards, camouflage and feeding were so much of a routine that these activities took as little of the patrol's working time as possible.

Everest-type packs were used to carry the loads. Some were adapted with the frames made to carry wireless sets or batteries and this meant that these men's gear and rations had to be shared among the others.

At the Cedars, we tried mules and they could carry 120 to 160 lb, but they had their disadvantages, the first being that where you could get the men to the starting point of a trip in a truck it was extremely difficult to get mules there without them damaging themselves or each other. They also made the patrols more easily visible and had to stick to tracks and carry their own fodder, 7 lb a day. If they were not adequately fed, they soon lost condition and the local mountaineer's advice was that if possible you got local animals at the start of your trip rather than the Army's.

Rations were made up of packs for so many men for a day and the calorie value was 4,500 to 5,000 daily and had to be chosen for the highest food value in the smallest volume and weight.

At Becharre before a ten-day trip to Damascus, July 1943. (IWM HU25048)

Comrades in arms Spud Murphy and Jack Harris in an armed jeep in Syria, June 1943. (IWM HU250071)

At the Cedars the patrol started with one officer and eleven men but this proved too cumbersome and was cut to seven men. In the Balkans, they reverted to ten men. Of these there was one officer, one sergeant, one Royal Corps of Signals and two regimental signals and two general duty men, one of whom was trained as a medical orderly. All were later trained in first aid and all were able to fight.

I have photographs of the patrols in beautiful weather in the hills above and around the Cedars with their mules winding their way up through green, bushy areas with stone walls not unlike the Pennines and up into the bare rocks and gullies above.

Then, quite suddenly, we were moved away to the Castello Rosso (now Megisti), then Kalymnos and Leros, where we hardly moved from the gun batteries of the Italians, our new allies. However, when the island fell, a number of LRDG did escape and it was no doubt due in part to their fitness training that they were able to make their way to Turkey and then by various routes to rejoin the unit. When you read in *Providence Their Guide* of the achievements and exploits of the Balkan patrols, it is hard to believe some of these soldiers were the same men who only a year before had been completely dependent on transport over very long distances to achieve their results on the Road Watch, which involved days of patient near-immobility.

It says a lot for body and mind's adaptability that these men within so short a time achieved such successful results in so different climates and by such very different means.'

CHAPTER 5

The Dodecanese Disaster

Winston Churchill was undeniably obsessed with the idea of invading the 'soft underbelly' of Europe in both world wars. The First World War leader was a key player as First Lord of the Admiralty in the costly and complete failure of the landings on the Gallipoli peninsula against Turkish forces in the Dardenelles in 1915–16. In the Second World War, he was the driving force behind another, lesser-known but equally ill-fated campaign to strike through the supposedly easy southern route. This, it was reasoned, would beat the German war machine by bringing neutral Turkey into the war, this time on the side of the Allies. Churchill gambled that the so-called Dodecanese Campaign would bring in Turkey's forty-six divisions in a powerful, combined thrust through the Balkans, possibly even making the D-Day Normandy landings unnecessary.

The LRDG's role in this confused and ill-prepared scheme was never really made clear. As the then LRDG second in overall command David Lloyd Owen said, 'Thus began the Aegean Campaign of September, October and November 1943. It was tragically vague throughout and many fine lives were lost in a cause which few of us ever fully understood.'

As early as November 1942, plans had been made for landings on Rhodes, Kos and Leros, as a preliminary to the grand strategy. However, President Roosevelt and Gen Eisenhower were not impressed by the scheme for many reasons, both political and military, and refused to divert long range fighters from the all-important Sicily/Italy operation.

Germany, meanwhile, was grimly determined to deny the islands to the Allies as she saw them as vital to the defence of her supplies of chrome ore for armoured steel and bauxite for aluminium, and to safeguard her import of antimony and copper from Greece and Turkey. It was also vital to the Germans to deny airfields to the Allies, which might threaten the crucial Romanian oil fields.

Italy surrendered on 8 September 1943 and Germany struck swiftly. The Italian garrison on Kephellenia was ferociously attacked and surrendered after seven days. All Italian officers offering resistance were shot on Hitler's special orders and over 4,000 men of the garrison were killed.

German occupation of the Aegean islands started on the day of the Italian surrender. Karpathos, Siros, Andros, Tinos, Zea and Naxos were first. On 9/10 September, Earl Jellicoe, the courageous commander of the Special Boat

Squadron (SBS), parachuted into Rhodes in a bold attempt to persuade the Italian commander to co-operate and hold the island for the British, but two days later all 40,000 Italian troops on the island surrendered to the Germans.

However, in spite of this hostile situation, the British Operation Accolade, as it was code-named, went ahead. Troops including elements of the LRDG, SBS, Durham Light Infantry, Royal Irish Fusiliers and Royal West Kents were landed on Leros, Kos and Samos. Two Spitfire squadrons and a squadron of the RAF Regiment were established on Kos.

On 23 September, the British destroyer *Eclipse* intercepted a German convoy with Italian prisoners from Rhodes and sank two transports and a torpedo boat. This led to the German decision to land on Kos and Leros to eliminate them as British air and naval bases. Air attacks sank the destroyers *Queen Olga* and *Intrepid* in Portolago harbour, Leros, on 26 September and by 29 September bombing had rendered the airfield on Kos inoperable. Kos was invaded on 3 October and by the next day the British had been taken prisoner. Finally, 65 British were killed and 1,388 taken prisoner. One hundred and two Italian officers, including the CO, were executed.

The Italian garrison on Kalymnos surrendered to the Germans on the threat of more air attacks, providing many hiding places for the German Navy in the narrow bays. The invasion of Leros was delayed when a troop convoy was surprised by the Royal Navy and ships sunk with the loss of 659 men.

But the Royal Navy also suffered terrible losses. In addition to the *Queen Olga* and the *Intrepid*, ships sunk included the destroyers *Panther*, *Harworth*, *Eclipse* and *Dulverton*, the anti-aircraft cruiser *Carlisle* was damaged beyond repair, the destroyer *Adrias* forced to beach in Turkey and the destroyer *Rockwood* damaged by remote-controlled glider bombs.

German forces continued to gather. Reinforcements continued to increase the British forces on Leros. There were 5,000 Italians on the island, but only half were armed. They manned the 6-inch guns, which were on almost all the mountaintops, and the smaller guns defending bays and harbours.

The Germans had complete control of the air when the invasion started on 12 November. There was vicious ebb and flow as the enemies confronted one another and positions changed hands in contest after deadly contest. Attack followed bitter counter-attack in the fragmented and hard-fought battle. On 16 November, Brandenburgers broke into the British headquarters where the harassed CO was surprised by a grenade and automatic fire and taken prisoner. He decided to surrender the island and the news was taken to all parts by German and British officers travelling by jeep. Only the LRDG and SBS refused to give up and continued fighting until they could escape from the island. Around 3,200 British and 5,350 Italians were taken prisoner. Another 357 British were killed. The Germans suffered 246 killed plus 659 killed at sea and 162 missing.

Many British escaped to Turkey and lived to fight again; among them were a large number of LRDG and SBS men. But the cost had been high – around 100 LRDG casualties, missing and taken prisoner out of a force of around 400, including many experienced and irreplaceable desert veterans. Among them, sadly, was the LRDG's charismatic Commanding Officer Jake Easonsmith, killed while leading his men typically from the front into the little village of Leros. He fell to a sniper's bullet as he approached the houses where the Germans were hiding.

LRDG who died in the campaign and are buried at the war cemetery on Leros include:

J. Easonsmith	H.L. Mallett
J.T. Bowler	L. Oelofse
S. Federman	A.J. Penhall
K. Foley	A. Redfern
P. Wheeldon	

STARING DOWN A GUN BARREL ON THE LEVITHA COMMANDO RAID

Ron Hill, a member of the 2nd Royal Gloucestershire Hussars who fought in the bloody battles along the desert coast in North Africa, later joined the select ranks of the LRDG. The following hair-raising action is typical of the missions carried out by the elite LRDG men and has never been published before. It includes Ron's risky escape after being taken prisoner, along with Desert Group colleague Jim Patch, and their amazing 'private war' against the Nazis in occupied Macedonia.

I joined the LRDG in company with Keith Mann, Wilf Drabble and John Hews. This was a completely different kind of war; long, lone patrols into the desert proper as far south as the oasis of Kufra and always behind the enemy lines.

When the desert war was over, the LRDG, though keeping its name, was reorganized and retrained for operations into Europe. While at Ramat David on a parachute course, the unit was ordered at a moment's notice to the Dodecanese, following the capitulation of Italy. The Dodecanese was one of the minor tragedies of the war when the failure to capture Rhodes sealed the fate of the British garrisons on the various Greek islands and culminated in the debacle of Leros, where a whole British infantry brigade was put in the bag (including many LRDG veterans).

But I had already been captured on a Commando-type raid on the island of Levitha. And this was how it happened.

LRDG veterans Jimmy Patch and Ron Hill with a partisan in the Balkans, 1944. The duo had escaped from a prisoner of war train following capture on the Aegean island of Levitha in October 1943. The determined comrades then carried on a private war by joining up with partisans in Yugoslavia, including this sinister-looking Macedonian fighter called Krsto, who was the group's official executioner of traitors and collaborators. His 'score' of victims at the time, in August 1944, was eighty-four – and rising! (IWM HU25272)

The day – 23 October 1943 – started badly. In the morning we held a strenuous training session with the assault boats. These were heavy collapsible craft of canvas and timber but had been spattered with shrapnel on the unprotected deck of the destroyer that had brought them in to Leros and it was hard work doing the repairs and the landing exercises at the same time. We were resting on a stone wall – five minutes for a drag at a fag – wet, tired and getting hungry, when along the road in a cloud of dust bowled a jeep laden with brass hats, naturally inspiring the usual ribald comments! In a few moments it returned, fast, in reverse, and out poured a choleric, red-faced brigadier.

Slaying the unfortunate sergeant in charge, he wanted to know whether we ever saluted our officers and dressed us down as though we were day-old recruits on a barrack square, ending with the words, ominous and prophetic, 'So you think yourselves tough, do you? I'll bloody well give you something to be tough about . . .'

Within 24 hours, five of us were dead, several wounded and the rest prisoner. In fairness, I don't think this was solely the result of the brigadier's outburst, but the raid on Levitha, which followed, was a hasty, ill-conceived and totally disastrous expedition.

Without reconnaissance, two half patrols were to do a night raid on Levitha, destroy the radar station and German guard, hold the island for the day and be picked up by ML (seaborne craft) the following night.

I was assigned to A Squadron NZ Patrol, which was to land on the south-east part of the hourglass-shaped island and complete a pincer movement with the B Squadron Patrol on the northern part, trapping the enemy in the waist of the hourglass.

Even the journey over from Leros was hazardous: the sea was very rough for the Aegean and many of the troops were seasick. The embarking into the turning and tossing folboats, down the scramble mats from the ML in pitch blackness, was almost suicidal, particularly when the NZ sergeant slipped on the scramble mat and fell head first into the laden boat, almost capsizing it, water pouring over the freeboard. For one awful moment I had visions of going to the bottom of the Aegean, laden down as I was with a Tommy gun and spare magazines, two pouches of hand grenades, to say nothing of my heavy, German rock-climbing boots. Somehow we staggered ashore through the surf and heavy swell, dragged the folboat into hiding among the rocks, scaled the cliffs and our invasion was on.

In the meanwhile, the ML had landed the other party and begun to give covering fire by shelling the enemy HQ, which succeeded only in waking up the enemy to the prospect that something was on. Thereafter, Germans seemed to materialize from nowhere all over the island. We found out afterwards that Levitha was being used as a base for the forthcoming attack on Leros. Our progress to join up with the B Squadron Patrol was thwarted by several dug-in positions, which resulted in two of our New Zealanders receiving nasty wounds from stick grenades, although we captured a German machine-gun and one light mortar in the process of clearing up.

While finding some cover for the wounded, I nearly became a casualty myself. Entering a dug-out previously over-run and understood to be cleared, I snatched a blanket from off one of the make-shift bunks to find myself face-to-face with a very live German! At the same time someone grabbed my ankle from a lower bunk and it took a sharp kick in the face to make him let go. My first adversary then fired at me at point-blank range, but it was starlight dark and the shot missed as I made a hurried exit, clutching the blanket. It was then necessary to flush out the Germans with hand grenades and Tommy gun fire, during which two of the Germans were badly wounded.

By the time daylight was breaking we had thirty-five prisoners, but our position was untenable and deteriorating all the time. The enemy were pressing forward relentlessly and as soon as the light improved sea planes took off from the anchorage and over-flew our positions, to be followed later on and for the rest of the day by Stuka attacks. Inevitably, ammunition began to run out so that towards the end we were using captured guns and their ammunition. Our wounded, too, were in a bad way. The only hope was to last out until dark and endeavour to make our way to the boat and try to rendezvous with the ML.

Two troopers were sent to reconnoitre the position regarding the folboat but they did not return and did not appear later as POWs. Presumably they were killed.

At dusk, the Medical Orderly, on his own initiative, arranged to surrender the wounded to the Germans under a white flag as we could do no more for them. I helped to carry the badly wounded New Zealanders down to a boat waiting in the inlet and here a German NCO took them over. The Medical Orderly surrendered at the same time. I hadn't agreed to this myself so gave the German my best military salute, turned smartly round and began the long slog back up the hill.

I must confess the hairs on the back of my neck stood up in dreaded anticipation, but no shots came as I plodded on towards our own people. As I drew near I noticed little 'fire flies' darting past and it took me some time to realize I was being fired on by some other Germans on the higher ground. I was too engrossed in trying to work out what to do next.

By the time I re-joined the patrol, the officer in charge had decided to surrender to avoid further bloodshed. Our ammunition was expended and we were now being bombarded by rifle grenades. It was too late to take any evasive action, especially under the full view of our prisoners. I gathered together the now useless weaponry and the captured German guns and threw them over the cliffs into the sea.

So ended the Battle of Levitha.

From then on it was the routine of search and interrogation by field officers and then we were put into the POW cage in Athens, to which we had been flown by flying boat. Our wits were stretched to prevent the enemy finding our escape kits. In Athens, by dodging about in the various queues and groups and ostensibly larking about, some of us were able to get by with our silk escape maps, miniature compasses, hacksaw blades and the like intact and undiscovered.

Eventually, the move to Germany was under way – thirty men and one bucket to a cattle truck – a pretty horrid experience. Fortunately, Jim Patch and I were able to escape from the cattle truck as it went through a tunnel near Veles, north of the Greek border. We had spent several days loosening the barbed wire over the ventilation spaces with our escape equipment. Taking advantage of the dark, wet night, we wriggled through the little aperture and dropped on to the track. I remember quite clearly lying on the ballast recovering from the fall (parachute training came in very handy) watching the rear light of the train growing smaller and smaller until it disappeared round the bend.

A feeling of utter loneliness came over me and I asked myself whatever was I doing in the middle of occupied Europe when everyone I knew and all the comforts of food and shelter were on the train . . . but this dispelled as I heard

Jim approaching. The intention was to walk south-west across southern Yugoslavia and Albania and, eventually, to get to Italy and rejoin the Desert Group. In the event, after five days' walking, we met up with a company of Chetniks (supporters of King Peter and General Mihailovic) and continued our private war caught up in the bewildering pattern of Balkan conflict, with the German and Bulgar occupation troops chasing us around as a sideline.

Eventually we reached the relative comfort of a British military mission, continuing the war in a more organised manner, arranging support drops to resistance groups, rescuing shot-down airmen and, above all, persuading the various resistance groups to combine and fight the Germans *and not each other*. And there we remained, as members of the mission, until we were brought out when Macedonia was liberated in 1945.

JIM AND RON'S GREAT ESCAPE, PART TWO

After taking their lives in their hands in the perilous jump from the train, Jim Patch and Ron Hill saw how the bloodthirsty Chetnik resistance fighters of Macedonia operated at first hand, 'somewhere just south of Skopje'. This is Jim's version of those dangerous days.

We made off towards the Adriatic coast with high hopes and a lot of enthusiasm. The fact that we had the whole width of Albania to cross before getting anywhere near the Adriatic did not seem at all daunting. It was pouring with rain and very cold. We knew there would be mountains to cross but we knew all about mountains: hadn't we just spent a whole summer running up and down the mountains of Lebanon? (Training for mountain warfare.)

What was unfortunate was that, in jumping off the train, Ron had twisted a muscle in his thigh. He had also taken a couple of chips out of his flesh lower down on his leg. Moreover, Ron's pack had rolled on to the railway track and had been damaged by the wheels.

The pack itself was not damaged, which was good because it contained the remains of a Red Cross parcel we had been given in Athens, but there was a blanket rolled up and tied to the pack and the wheels had run over one end of the roll. (We each had one of these blankets, issued by Jerry, very small, being designed for diminutive Italian soldiers.) When Ron unrolled his blanket, it had rows of large holes in it like one of those patterns you can make by cutting folded paper.

Ron's twisted muscle made it difficult for him to climb hills and the one field dressing we had between us was hardly adequate for the nasty open wounds on his leg. We decided to walk only by night and to avoid all human contact for fear of betrayal and re-capture. We were still in Yugoslavia and the country was more difficult than it had been in Lebanon. After two nights' stumbling and groping along in the dark we gave it up and decided we could make better progress by day. We thought that if we kept our eyes open we could spot people before they spotted us and stay out of sight.

One day we were climbing up and up for hours. It was raining as usual but it didn't seem to matter any more because we were long since soaked to the skin. We couldn't see much because of the rain and we seemed to be in the clouds. Then suddenly the rain stopped and we found ourselves in bright sun. A few more minutes brought us to the top of the hill. Below us were clouds, stretching away into the distance for miles in the brilliant sunshine. There was no land in sight. We were on the highest peak as far as the eye could see and had climbed to that height by accident in our blind progress. Later we learned that the mountain was called *Solunska Glava* (Salonika Head) and it was 8,250 feet high. This had its effect on Ron. The raw places on his leg were looking angry and, after another night out, we thought it was time we took the risk and sought help from the natives.

In the next valley there was a village. We walked boldly into it. The villagers were collecting water from the stream. They seemed to recognize our Britishness at once, which was astonishing because we were both bearded and had appeared in their midst out of the hills like ghosts. We filled our water bottles and walked, strolled almost, towards some houses but were met by an anxious character who waved his arms about and made it clear that we were in danger. We didn't need telling twice but disappeared quickly into the scrub on the hillside to our left. Ron said that he distinctly saw a number of figures in military uniforms round the houses we were making for before being warned.

Twenty-five years later, we went back to the village – Belitsa by name. They told us that the man who warned us off had been called Jordan Svetkovski. The soldiers seen by Ron were Bulgars. If they had taken us there can be no doubt that torture and a slow death would have followed. As it was, they took poor Svetkovski and shot him. Ron and I have that man's death on our consciences, but at that time we were not to know about this. We marched on until evening and found a small, thatched hut, which was inhabited. A young man and an old man were there. They took some persuading, but finally they agreed to let us stay the night.

The hut, known as a *koliba*, was just about as primitive a human habitation as you could imagine. There was a partition in the middle with the men on one side and a cow on the other. The walls were of wattle and daub. A fire on the earth floor provided warmth and the means of cooking. The smoke found its way up through the thatch. There was no table, chair or cupboard. There were a couple of rush mats for sleeping on. There were two tiny stools about a foot high; each one cleverly cut from the trunk of a pine tree where side branches came out at the right angle to form legs. A cooking pot swung above the fire suspended by a chain from one of the roof timbers.

We were fed and told to lie by the fire and get some sleep, which we gratefully did, this being our first dry night after constant rain.

Some hours later we were woken up by a man with a rifle demanding 'Documenti'. We showed him our pay books which Jerry, fortunately, had not taken from us. He thumbed through, first one, then the other. Finally, he produced a Bulgarian bank note with the printer's name in small lettering along the bottom. It said, 'Thomas de la Rue, Angleterre'.

The man's name was Stojan. After some difficulty we managed to persuade him that we really were British in spite of the absence of the magic word 'Angleterre' from our pay books. In sign language we told him our story and he was convinced. Dawn being nigh, he took us away to a more secure location across the River Treska and up to a deserted hill-top village, where he installed us in a room full of dried bean stalks and told us not to move.

Later, we were taken to meet some more resistance fighters at another isolated *koliba* and thence to a large and comfortable cave where the main band of Chetniks, the King's men, were gathered. They became our friends. There was the Colonel, Rorkanspit, Temelko, Rat-catcher, Ragged-pants, Gaitski, Leban, Miro, Anton, Zhivko, Ivan the Terrible and many others. One chap was called Asic, which is pronounced, believe it or not, Arse-itch. They were trained soldiers of the Royal Yugoslav Army whose General was Drazha Mihailovic. With them we passed good times and bad, starvation and plenty, relaxation and violent action, in that sad and troubled corner of Europe, until liberation.

THE DARING ASHLEY GREENWOOD

These are the highlights of Ashley Greenwood's activities during the battle for Leros and its aftermath. The confused debacle threw up many fascinating tales of British bravery under adversity and Ashley's story is based mainly on an account which he later wrote in Turkey for the British Consul in Smyrna, partly as a guide as to how to move around undetected in German-occupied islands.

During the battle Ashley drove a jeep by day and night, supplying forward patrols with ammunition and rations, often under fire and having some narrow escapes, particularly when hunting parachutists on foot.

After the surrender, George Jellicoe walked away from the surrender conference and organized a caique to take his men (SBS) to Turkey. Ashley, who was with them, took his jeep to pick up John Olivey and Dudley Folland and their patrols to take them to where the caique was moored but John declined to come and Dudley elected to walk because the jeep was fully loaded with ten men on board.

The caique had already put out when the jeep party arrived, but it came back for them so they pushed the jeep off the jetty into the sea and set sail. Dudley arrived late and was captured.

In Turkey, George Jellicoe dropped a broad hint that someone should go back to Leros to collect any men who might still be on the loose and Ashley volunteered at once, departing in a high-speed launch commanded by Lieutenant Commander Frank Ramseyer of the Levant Schooner Flotilla. He landed at S. Nicola Bay about 0100 hr on 21 November 1943 with a Greek agent whose name is recorded only as S. A chapel near their landing spot was decided upon as a rendezvous for any escapees who might be gathered in, then Ashley and S parted company.

Being confident there were no Germans in these off-road parts, Ashley began to shout up and down

Ashley Greenwood disguised as a partisan in Turkey after his brave escape from the Leros disaster, November 1943. (IWM HU25273)

the wadis in case there were any evaders hiding there. About 0400 hr he entered a Greek house where he was given a drink and enquired, with negative result, whether they knew of any British hiding up nearby. A walk along the coast then brought him to a spot on the south-east slope of Mount Calogero, where he kept a watch on a guarded storehouse by a road junction until 1600 hr.

Returning after dark to the chapel, Ashley met S, who had produced a lot of Greeks and two British soldiers. One of these was Keith Balsili from the SBS who had found a cave, which was usefully placed because it gave a view of the chapel.

They watched, listened and flashed torches for the high-speed launch for six nights but it failed to return. Meanwhile, the number of British at the chapel rose to fifteen. German patrols visited the bay most days. They were very slipshod, and badly dressed and equipped. Movement at night was fairly safe provided it was kept to the hills, the Germans being reluctant to venture away from the roads.

Ashley soon began to go out by day in civilian clothes, trying to arrange a get-away because he thought it unlikely that the launch would now turn up. Whenever possible he joined a convoy of Greeks with mules, though their nervous whisperings and furtive actions when Germans were about posed the risk of giving him away. There was a lot of indiscriminate firing at sheep and goats and if the persecution complex that an escapee so easily gets was not controlled, it was easy to imagine that this was connected with oneself. In fact, the Germans did not seem interested in hunting escapees.

After eight days, Ashley had been joined by Peter Mold of the LRDG. He had bad dysentery and was still in battle-dress so they bandaged him up to look like a casualty. This enabled him to walk all over the island, a privilege given to all patients at the Alinda hospital.

When it became clear that no rescue boat from Turkey was going to arrive, some other arrangement had to be made. No large boats were available, so Ashley, with four others including the Greek agent S, decided to get away in a rowing boat. A boat was found in S. Nicola Bay. S was to bring some food and a piece of wood to make a spar for a sail, but they waited for him in vain. The next day it was discovered that he had been arrested and his bag of food confiscated. He was only kept in overnight, but then the news came that the Germans were about to occupy the chapel which was the escape rendezvous, the secret having been given away by an informer. The escape boat was, of course, near the chapel and within sight of it. Keith Balsili and Ashley managed to warn most of the potential escapees of the Germans' occupation of the chapel but two of them arrived and were re-captured.

A Greek known as Z then arranged to take the party to Blefuti Bay where there were said to be more boats, but on the way they were stopped by a sentry. The party managed to get away but Z was called over by the sentry and, when he was released, failed to find the party.

They did not know the way to the boats without Z so they went to their cave (which overlooked the chapel) for some food. Z then showed up and gave them directions to Blefuti Bay. On the way they were hailed by some Germans from a storehouse for reasons which were not made clear and a shouted conversation took place in broken Greek until Z appeared on a bicycle and diverted the Germans with cigarettes and mandarins. Two of the party were then conscripted by some other Germans for loading motor cycles on to a lorry. The Germans treated them very well. Indeed, one of them, whose hand was bound up, was not allowed to work and finally the two were thanked and sent on their way with a cigarette apiece.

When finally the party got to the boats they found that all had holes in them so Z was sent off to fetch a maestro (craftsman) to repair them. People living nearby said that every night about six o'clock, five Germans arrived at some huts only 100 yards from the boats and spent the night. Unable to wait for the maestro, the party borrowed tools from the locals, scrounged some wood and did a repair job on one of the boats. The job was so well done that it needed only minor adjustments by the maestro when he arrived soon after. They stole the Germans' blankets, only just resisting the temptation to leave a note of thanks, and at 5.30 p.m. paddled the boat to a spot out of sight from the huts. They had lost touch with S, but he later got back to Turkey.

At 6 p.m. they quietly put to sea. Progress was not easy because they had only two paddles and one long oar and there was some bother with rowlocks and thole pins, which made it necessary to paddle most of the way. They reached the island of Lisso at 9.30 p.m. and made an excellent landing in a bay near the south of the island. They made for the nearest house where they were greeted with, 'Hello, boys, come right in!'

From then onward they were well looked after and, contacting a British agent Ashley knew of on Lisso, they got away to Bodrum in Turkey the next evening.

GUY PRENDERGAST'S HEROIC STORY

This is a shortened form of the report written by Brigadier Prendergast in December 1943 about his part in the battle for Leros and his subsequent escape from the island. Its staccato tone superbly portrays the danger-fraught

Guy Prendergast DSO (LRDG CO; right) and Jake Easonsmith DSO, MC (2nd i/c and future CO) discuss the unfolding desert campaign earlier in the war. (IWM HU25158)

desperation of those critical days, when escaping soldiers stubbornly refused to surrender in the face of appallingly difficult odds . . .

Raiding Forces Aegean was formed on 15 October 1943 in order to control the operations of LRDG and SBS in the Aegean, and Guy Prendergast was promoted to full colonel to take command. He handed over command of the LRDG to Major Easonsmith on the same day. He set up his headquarters in the LRDG cave on Mount Meraviglia above Leros town near the cave where Brigadier Tilney, the overall commander on the island, had his headquarters.

The invasion started on 12 November. On the evening of the following day, the Colonel went on a personal reconnaissance to find out whether the enemy parachutists on the Rachi feature were trying to join up with the force established in the Castello which dominated the town. He worked his way through the town being sniped at from the Castello and, on turning a corner, came face to face with a German parachutist who was talking to a couple of Greek women. The soldiers fired at one another and both retreated. It seemed that the two enemy forces were indeed trying to join up.

On the night of 14/15 November elements of the Royal West Kent Regiment were landed by destroyer near Portolago. The Colonel met their CO, Lieutenant Colonel Tarleton, whom he used to know in the Sudanese Defence Force. Having landed, they were heavily bombed but no casualties occurred and the Regiment then moved off to attack the enemy on Mount Rachi.

During the night of 15/16 November, Jake Easonsmith was sent by the Brigadier on a similar recce to that which Guy Prendergast had carried out two nights earlier. He was ordered to make as much noise as possible with grenades etc., to make the enemy think they were being attacked in strength. Sadly, during this operation, Major Easonsmith was killed by a sniper's deadly snapshot.

The Colonel then resumed command of the LRDG. He went to the top of Meraviglia and found it a very uncomfortable spot as it was under mortar fire and fire from the Castello. There were at least six Stukas permanently looking for targets and periodically JU 88s would drop anti-personnel bombs. Germans were seen ascending the hill and, after exchanging a few shots with these, the Colonel descended to the main HQ cave and told the Brigadier there must be a counter-attack to stop the advance. But the situation was so desperate, there were no men available to make this and the Brigadier ordered his own HQ and the LRDG HQ to evacuate their caves and retire to Portolago.

The LRDG personnel destroyed their radios and retired but the Colonel, worried that the Brigadier could not continue to direct the battle without his radio, went to the command cave with Sergeant Hughes and found Captain Rochford, RIF, one signalman and a few very shaken Italians. The signalman managed to raise the

Brigadier in Portolago and the Colonel spoke to him. The Brigadier said he was about to return to the cave and ordered the Colonel to run the battle as best he could in the meantime. When the Brigadier arrived, the Colonel bravely began to make his way to Portolago to raise a force to counter-attack the enemy.

About twenty minutes into his journey he looked back and saw a large number of Germans on the top of Meraviglia and what appeared to be the whole of the HQ staff lined up. The Colonel continued into Portolago but he was still attempting to assemble enough men for a counter-attack when the Brigadier drove up in a jeep with Captain Baker, RN, and two German officers, saying he had been forced to surrender the island.

The Colonel continued to search for LRDG men and found Dick Croucher and Ron Tinker who said the main body of LRDG, under Richard Lawson, MO, had gone off towards Patella, one of a few selected places where the Navy had been briefed to call for escapers should the island fall. Patella was, however, a populated area and it was thought the enemy would soon search there. So the Colonel decided that it would be better if he and his party (now joined by Captain Craig, the Brigade Intelligence Officer, and a private from the King's Own Regiment) made their way to another escape point on the east coast of Mount Tortore, where there was a cave. He himself decided to go to Mount Scumbarda to find out what had happened to Lieutenant White and his patrol, which had been doing very useful work there. Before leaving, he tried to contact any other LRDG men from the large crowd of rather demoralized troops in Portolago but failed to find any.

The Colonel advised as many officers as he could find from other units to try to re-organize their men to make for one or other of the escape points, but everybody appeared too exhausted to want to do anything but sleep. He then continued to Scumbarda, where he found Private Lennox in the cave which the patrol had been using. Lennox had been attempting to find a boat which was known to be nearby, but it had been destroyed by a bomb and, when he returned to where he had left the patrol, they had gone.

The two determined men then loaded rucksacks with rations and blankets but, while they were doing so, some Italians came into the cave. They stole the Colonel's field glasses, which he had put down, then produced revolvers and a Tommy gun and said they were taking them prisoner. The Colonel demanded to see their commanding officer and they were then taken to an underground control room for the coastal gun, but the officers there were all drunk and threatened to hand them over to the Germans. The two decided to run for it.

They got away after two attempts, had a bathe and made their way to Mount Tortore, where they found the cave with Captains Croucher, Tinker and Craig and the private from the King's Own. They found some cans of water on the way and with these and the rations in the rucksacks they eked out an existence for three days. During this time three of the party made a desperate attempt to swim to Kalymnos via two smaller islands but had to give up because of rough seas.

With rations and water almost gone, the Colonel set off late on 20 November for Serocampo Bay to look for a boat or find food. He undertook this task personally because only he had rubber-soled footwear and could walk quietly. He found two boats, both with holes in them, then walked into the village for help in mending one of the boats. Some Germans were singing and playing an accordion in one of the houses but in the house next door the Colonel found some Greeks who, fearfully, agreed to repair a boat the next day and leave it by the water's edge with oars and a rudder.

On arrival back at the cave about dawn he was told that during the night a craft had hove to just off the rendezvous for about two hours. Because the Colonel was not there the decision was taken not to flash a signal.

With the newly found and, hopefully, repaired rowing boat they decided they would attempt their escape the next night but, when the time came, the sea was too rough. They went to the beach as usual and about midnight heard a craft approaching the coast. It hove to about half a mile out and, with much trepidation, the decision was taken to flash a signal.

Presently, a small boat appeared and the occupant hailed in a language unknown to the waiting party. They shouted their names and, hesitantly, the boat approached and the occupant was identified as friendly. The party got on board and were taken to the waiting craft. It was an Air Sea Rescue launch, which had landed a Greek three nights previously who was to attempt to find escaped British personnel. The craft had approached the coast the previous night to pick up this man but he had not appeared. The hesitation on the part of the small boat was because the party had flashed the wrong letter and did not give the counter-signal arranged with the Greek.

The nightmare chain of events finally ended when they were taken to Bodrum and met Major Jellicoe of the SBS and Lieutenant Commander Ramseyer of the Levant Schooner Flotilla, who were helping in the rescue of escapees.

THE BOMB THAT 'KILLED' DON'S BEST FRIEND

Following the death of comrade John Mackay, Don Coventry was reminded of the following hairsbreadth escape which happened to the LRDG veterans during the desperate, ill-fated battle on the Clidi Heights, Leros.

On our arrival at Leros from Kalymnos after the battle of Kos had taken place, we were welcomed there in the early hours of the morning by a Stuka raid on Leros harbour and had to dash for cover. S1 Patrol was then sent to man Clidi Heights to bolster the Italian gunners manning four 6-inch naval guns.

During our stay there we were bombed and strafed intermittently until Captain Olivey had a tin helmet placed on top of a flagstaff and assured the patrol that, while we had faith, we would be safe from attack!

This worked well for about a month until one day Captain Olivey was called to HQ and Lance Corporal Coventry was left in charge. Coventry, with Mackay from Y Patrol, was on guard next to one of the big naval guns when eight Junkers 88s attacked from the Turkish coast. Coventry continues the tale:

Having faith, we remained at our post. 'The Junkers dived and dropped their bombs, which missed. They then turned and came back out of the afternoon sun and did another run.

I was watching through the binoculars and a bomb seemed to be coming straight down the lens. I shouted to Mackay to take cover and we jumped over the dannet wire and slid down the slope into a cave where our wireless operators were. The bomb scored a direct hit on the naval gun, chopped the barrel clean off and tilted the gun out of the ground. The explosion set fire to the gun's magazine.

At this time, unknown to us, Flossie Kevin was coming along to have a chat and, being a bit hard of hearing, saw us leap over the wire, so he crouched down on a ledge below the naval gun where we found him afterwards, covered in stones and earth but, miraculously, alive. He was temporarily totally deaf and shocked from the explosion.

With all this, I had forgotten my .303 rifle leaning against the naval gun and all I found of it afterwards was the breach and bolt.

When Captain Olivey returned I was in serious trouble, as not only had I lost faith in the helmet on the flagstaff, but I had abandoned my 'best friend' leaning against the naval gun!

THE HEIGHT OF COURAGE – DON COVENTRY'S DCM

The following classic first-hand report of the ferocious Battle for Clidi Heights retells how Don Coventry won the Distinguished Conduct Medal.

It is the only authentic, detailed account of the action in existence and, as such, richly deserves a proud place in the fighting annals of the LRDG. Don's widow, Elsie, found the report among Don's papers shortly after he died and she recalled that Tommy Haddon asked him to record his crucial part in the encounter which ran from 12 to 17 November 1943, on the blood-soaked island of Leros.

The battle for Clidi Heights started on Monday, 12 November 1943 about sunrise and ended at 0900 hr on 17 November.

I was with S1 Patrol under the command of Captain John Olivey and we were supporting the Italian gun teams manning the three 6-inch naval batteries. The other naval gun had been knocked out in an earlier raid.

The Germans mounted a naval attack of troop landing craft supported by four destroyers which came in from the Turkish coast. We watched their approach until they came within range, at which point our naval batteries opened fire drawing an immediate response from the destroyers. One landing craft was destroyed by our fire as it neared the shore. The remaining landing craft then were protected by a hill as they approached the shore, which rendered our firepower useless, except in regard to the destroyers, and these continued to bombard our position.

Our first casualty was Rifleman Oelofse, a Rhodesian, who received a direct hit from a mortar on his position in the forward trenches.

After landing, the enemy deployed with mortars and machine-guns on the high ground which had protected their landing from our batteries. The battle then continued right through the day, with the enemy advancing under air support, totally lacking on our side because the RAF base on Kos had been captured during the battle for that island.

At approximately 1500 hr on 12 November, an enemy air fleet of some thirty troop carriers came in below Clidi Heights and dropped parachutists, which resulted in cutting the island in half. During this engagement, Captain Alan Redfern was killed.

The intense bombing of Clidi Heights resulted in another naval gun being dug out by a bomb from a Stuka.

On the same afternoon, while Andy Bennett and I were manning a Bren gun in a rock sangar, Andy received gravel chips in his face and he was replaced by Sergeant Cito Calder-Potts. As it got dark we were engaged in savage hand-to-hand fighting, tossing grenades at the enemy until our supply ran out. Cito was wounded in the leg by a grenade in this engagement.

We were then ordered to evacuate Clidi. We withdrew to a position on a ridge some 400 metres distant. We held this position all day, during which very little activity took place. On the morning of 14 November, the Italian anti-aircraft batteries and other high point batteries shelled Clidi Heights and an attack was put in by the Buffs Regiment, who recaptured Clidi and seized a number of prisoners. Ken Foley, our Medic, was wounded at this time and later died from his wounds. We moved back to hold the position on Clidi, where we were still being subjected to mortar and machine-gun fire from the ridge.

The Buffs were ordered to attack this ridge, being led by one LRDG member to each section of Buffs, because we were familiar with the area. As we were advancing up this ridge we were under heavy machine-gun fire and fighter attack from the air, which aborted our attack and we withdrew. Todman, a Rhodesian, was wounded and sadly later died from his wounds.

The Buffs were then withdrawn and we remained on Clidi Heights, coming under sporadic fire for all of Thursday, 15 November. About 1700 hr, we were again engaged in hand-to-hand fighting and about this time we were reinforced by a platoon of Irish Fusiliers, who brought grenade supplies. A Major commanding the Irish Fusiliers then attempted a fixed bayonet charge, which was short lived and resulted in the Major and two Fusiliers being killed. The Fusiliers were then withdrawn from Clidi Heights and the battle quietened for the night.

On the morning of Friday the 16th, Captain Olivey climbed on to the top of a pill box to survey the area and had the binoculars literally shot out of his hands. Fortunately, his only injury was to his face from splinters of the smashed binoculars. The rest of the day passed fairly quietly. At 1700 hr the island of Leros surrendered and we could see white flags on all the heights. Captain Olivey then deployed us into position for the night, which passed quietly. At this stage all the Italians had left, except for one officer who remained with us during the battle.

Early on the morning of the 17th, while it was still dark, we were sent by Captain Olivey, using a door as a stretcher, to bring in all the dead from both sides for transportation. Captain Olivey then immobilized one of the two remaining naval guns and Rifleman van Rensberg immobilized the other. At 0845 hr Captain Olivey called us together and confirmed that the island had surrendered. He told us to hide out all day then to make our way to an RV (rendezvous) point, where he would meet with us that night. There were fifteen of us and, as Captain Olivey failed to turn up for two nights, we agreed to split up and make our own way.

Skinny Evans, van Rensberg and myself from Rhodesia, Signalman Watson, who was in S1 Patrol, and three New Zealanders, Munroe, Macleod and Ellis, were taken off six nights later by an aircraft rescue launch. Jack Rupping got off in a fishing boat seventeen days later. The rest ended up as POWs.

THE AMAZING JOHN OLIVEY, MC AND BAR

This abridged version of John Olivey's own account of his daring escapes as a prisoner of war is taken from papers liberated by Bill Cooke when Rhodesia became Zimbabwe. Olivey's gripping story starts on Leros about the time of the island's surrender.

I decided to hold Point 320 until such time as I could from my vantage point get an appreciation. By 0800 hr it was clear from the singing of German songs from the village and from the large number of enemy seaplanes in the bay that the island had surrendered.

The courageous John Olivey, MC and Bar. (IWM HU25274)

I ordered my corporals to inform their sections that their men should withdraw as quickly and quietly as possible and make for the broken and rocky country to the north. The patrol moved out unnoticed, while I remained in position for a further hour. In the meantime the enemy, driving sheep before them, suddenly arrived at Point 320. I disguised myself as a dead body and the German soldiers passed by down the road, concluding that the position was deserted. I moved into hiding some hundred yards below the fort.

When darkness fell, I decided to return to the fort with the idea of destroying one large naval gun to the east which I felt was not sufficiently destroyed. I had laid the charges on the gun and in the magazine but was without matches. I returned to the fort where I knew I had concealed a box. I was surprised to find the fort occupied by two Germans, who took me for one of their officers. I was forced to shoot them both, but the noise attracted others and I had to make a hasty withdrawal. I was followed down the valley to very rocky country.

I hid in the rocks until none of the enemy appeared to be present but every time I moved, the flock of sheep which could be heard around me became most active. It became obvious the enemy were using sheep bells to cover their moves. By moving quickly down the hill and disguising my whereabouts by throwing stones and immediately hiding, I was able to make the searchers pass by. Three groups of about ten men passed me. By early morning they had moved well down the valley and I decided to cut across country to the RV (rendezvous) given to my patrol. It was daylight by the time I arrived there and I was not surprised to find no one. I was tremendously tired and very thirsty. I could find no water cans in the place where we had left them so proceeded to the Italian barracks near the road. Here I found some bread, bacon fat and water. A bed with sheets proved too great a temptation and I climbed in. As a light sleeper, I considered that I should have plenty of time to get out of the back window if anyone approached.

I woke to find two German officers and some men at the foot of my bed. One spoke English fluently and we discussed the battle at some length. I was put in a jeep and taken to a central collection position. Unfortunately, I still had my LRDG shoulder titles, cap badge, MC ribbon, beret and identification card, all of which were recorded against my rank and name. I went upstairs for a wash and removed my shoulder titles, badges of rank, ribbon and beret, and appeared with the other ranks and with them was marched to the docks. I contacted the Medical Officer and men of the LRDG who were POWs and informed them that I had now become Private Harvey (my married sister's name) of the Sherwood Foresters (my parent unit). This information was never taken from me by the Germans.

I slept on the docks and early next morning escaped from there with a party of Italians going out for water. Unfortunately, I bumped into a patrol in the hills which was looking for an escaped officer, and I was again marched back to buildings east of the harbour where POWs were now installed.

Next morning, I walked out again accompanied by many shouts and clicking of rifle bolts. A German private who followed me was far too frightened to do anything about taking me back. When I told him I was not going back he ran off for assistance although he was armed. I then hid in a cottage nearby but by bad luck I was discovered there in the evening by a party of Germans on the scrounge and was again taken back to camp.

A ship of about 6,000 tons was provided to take all British POWs to Athens. On this ship were about 1,500 other ranks and we were joined by about twenty officers. Captain Lawson MC, Medical Officer, LRDG and a Church of England Padre, performed great service for the troops. They were the only officers who organized any comfort.

On arriving at Piraeus, we were met by a battery of cameras. The troops, now on top of their form, replied with a 'V' sign every time a camera was produced! We were marched off at about 1500 hr on an overcast afternoon. The guards were noticeable for either their old age or their youth. Buttons were missing from their uniforms and the troops got a lot of amusement at the guards' expense.

The march through Athens was more like a victory march than an escort of POWs. The route was lined by Greeks, who threw oranges, apples and cigarettes. The Germans tried to intercept these gifts. Some women were in tears but the Tommies jested with them and cap badges etc. were thrown to the girls.

It was dark by the time we got into the city proper and the streets were crowded. A number of Germans could be seen in the crowd, armed soldiers carrying rifles. It seemed unlikely that one would get far in the streets of Athens.

The column turned right after crossing a small river and we now were marching through a back street. It was quite dark and we crossed some unoccupied ground with a cemetery to the north. The Acropolis could be seen on its hill to the south. At this stage, after about 10 kilometres' marching, the column had become straggly so that the guards were unevenly spaced. The guard next to me had dropped a little behind and, taking advantage of a side street on a bend of the road, I ran down it.

I believe the guard followed a little way but he had no hope of seeing me in the dark, as I lay under a wall. I turned into the first house I saw. A few moments later two Greek women followed me, having seen me escape. They removed me from this house, which they said contained Germans, and took me to the house next door, where lived a tinsmith and his Maltese wife and three children. I explained that I wished to exchange my uniform for some civilian clothes. A pair of very patched trousers and a jacket were produced at once. A neighbour who called, having seen the fun, immediately took off his shirt.

I explained that I was a British officer and, having acquired the clothes, I offered to leave. The family was obviously nervous. But they were more than kind, and I found myself sitting down sharing their interrupted meal.

I slept the night in the room shared by all the family and early next morning I was taken back through Athens by my host, who was called Costa. I was taken to his tinsmith shop which was underground and contained the usual tinsmith's tools and bits of scrap iron. I stayed there for a week.

During this week, I began the long and difficult business of getting out of Athens and back to British forces. I was treated with suspicion, as I had no papers to prove I was Captain Olivey. Many English-speaking people came to see me. I was moved between houses, flats and shops and, after being passed through several hands, I met by arrangement in the street a Mr Fotakis, who seemed to have some authority but the movement from house to house continued and people were talking in terms of months before my departure.

In a basement flat of two rooms and kitchen and bathroom which was very small and cold, food became a problem. There had been some misunderstanding and I was lost to the organization for five days before Christmas. Then Fotakis turned up again and there was food. Quite a big sum in gold changed hands and it became obvious to me that I was of great financial advantage to the family.

On 5 January, after several abortive attempts, I was taken to meet a Greek American called Major T. He was, I gathered, head of the secret organization known as M04. I was then passed to a 2nd Lieutenant Elias Georgopoulos who took me to his uncle's house, where I was made very comfortable with a room to myself and sufficient good food.

After a month, I was desperate for something to read and also for exercise through not being allowed out of the house. Because of this and because M04 could not be produced, I showed some bad manners and as a result Major T came to see me. I was then allowed to send a wireless signal to HQ Cairo but no reply was received. I was told that because of the absence of a reply I could not be returned.

I gathered that my February board and lodging had been paid for in gold.

I sent an urgent note to Major T that I could no longer live without exercise and would make a break for it myself if he would not assist. My feet had frozen badly during the winter through no exercise but were now healing, as the weather was warmer.

A caique was found and ten sovereigns were handed to Georgopoulos, with whom I was to travel. I had to sign a statement for Major T that, as he did not know the caique I was to travel in, he was in no way responsible.

We left Athens on 27 March and went to Port Orafti, where we stayed for ten days in hiding. Eventually, we set sail on a very small caique with ninety-five refugees. In Turkish waters engine trouble developed and the caique was eventually wrecked. We landed in Turkey with the loss of one Greek life.

Finally, I arrived in Cairo on 25 April 1944. My capture had taken place on 18 November 1943 . . .

M1 PATROL'S ESCAPE FROM ASTYPALEA

Ken Lawrence pays tribute to the remarkable bravery of George Metaxas, who hid and kept M1 Patrol members fed and supplied for thirty-seven days at the fall of Leros, enabling them to escape to neutral Turkey and to rejoin the LRDG. George, who died in Astypalea (a Greek island) on 17 June 1990, aged ninety, was universally known as George Metaxas. Kalis was added to his family name to distinguish him from another man of the same name. His sons have taken the name Kalis.

M1 Patrol was dispatched from Leros to Astypalea as soon as it arrived from Kastellorizon. The object was to observe and report to Group on Leros, aircraft and shipping movements, and to liaise with the officer commanding the Italian troops, about two Company strength.

When German bombers were pounding Leros, the enemy landed by seaplane at the south end of the island and paratroops in the north. M1 were in the middle where they were strafed while having breakfast. The patrol broke into two parties of five to make their way independently to a rendezvous at the north-western end of the island. Unfortunately, one party was captured by the enemy and the other, more cautious and travelling only by night, failed to make the RV because of the very rough and rocky country.

This party took shelter in a small crypt at dawn and lit a fire to keep out the cold. The smoke was seen by two Greeks, who took the party to a cave high up from the sea on a steep rocky face on the west side of the island. This was the patrol's first contact with George Metaxas, whose house was about a mile from the cave.

For thirty-seven days George and his family supplied the patrol with splendid food, fresh bread, sweet potatoes baked with honey, and meat stews and roast kid. They brought tobacco leaf, finely chopped by hand, cigarette papers and matches. What more could the soldiers have asked for, living in luxury in a comfortable cave?

The food had to be carried over a mile of rough terrain. George's little daughter, about eleven, would bring the food in the morning and George in the evening. The family had to work hard to feed five additional hungry mouths. Possibly some of the food was donated by other island families; they were a very close community.

The Germans twice visited George's isolated home and interrogated him and his wife Maroula as to the whereabouts of the British soldiers, but nothing was given away. Greek friends retrieved the wireless set from the bushes where it had been hidden and somehow found a charged battery. The radio operator spent a couple of days trying to get through to Leros. No one knew what had happened there. But it was all a wasted effort.

After a couple of weeks when things had become a little quieter, the question was raised with George about the possibility of finding a small caique for escaping to Turkey. During the third week George arranged a meeting with a trader, Pepino, who said a caique was on its way. In the fourth week a small caique arrived and was moored in a concealed inlet a mile south of Astypalea town. The next thing, Pepino said, was to find a crew and obtain supplies. Three nights later, the crew had been organized but there was no flour to make bread. The patrol thought they would never get away.

However, on day thirty-six, George arrived at the cave with food and good news. All was ready to sail the following night providing the wind was suitable. The little ship had no motor.

A rough walk of 3 miles to the other side of the island and we embarked on the very small caique – 15 feet long with a beam of 5 feet, skippered by George Metaxas, two Greek crew, myself, Les Wilton, Louis Leach and two others. George cast off at midnight and, under a stiff breeze, set forth to the small island of Sirna, about 25 miles to the south-east, where we tied up before dawn. After lunch with a farmer, sole occupant of the island, the party set off at sunset towards the east and the Turkish coast. After a couple of hours the wind increased to almost gale force, but the captain and crew were experts at small boat sailing and by dawn the Turkish coast was only a few miles away and the wind had dropped. George said, 'It was a rough night, but God was with us.'

After a few miles, the boat pulled into a jetty and the party were greeted by a platoon of armed Turks. The patrol and the Greeks were now POWs. They were the guests of the Turks for four days, then were put on a large caique and taken to Bodrum, where they were transferred to a British caique, a headquarters of MI9, another clandestine organization, where everybody tucked into unlimited supplies of bully beef and biscuits. The next day we sailed by caique to Cyprus.

It was there that the patrol and their Greek saviours were separated. George Metaxas went to work for MI9 in Turkey for the remainder of the war and the other two joined the Greek Brigade. The residue of M1 left by caique for Haifa to rejoin the Unit.

George Metaxas was a fine man, determined, cool in action, honest and sincere in all his undertakings. The patrol never forgot his great kindness and bravery in keeping them alive for so many long days on the island and helping to arrange their escape to Turkey and their safe deliverance there.

CHAPTER 6

Cloak and Dagger in the Balkans

In the latter stages of the war, the men of the LRDG had to emulate the veterans of 1st and 2nd SAS and learn how to parachute into action. It was, at first, an alien art, but in most cases the versatile and adaptable desert veterans mastered the basics. There were no reserve chutes in those days and if anything went wrong, your first jump could be your last, but there was no shortage of volunteers among the battle-hardened veterans of the unit. The wide open expanses of the desert were left far behind, with not a little regret, and the LRDG travelled into even more dangerous areas of operation such as the Aegean, Yugoslavia and Italy.

The qualities of stealth, navigation and radio reconnaissance were still a very important part of the objectives that the LRDG was trying to achieve. But now the veterans had to contend with Partisan allies, of varying degrees of fighting ability and trustworthiness, and an enemy who was now fighting desperately for his own existence as the tide of war began to turn at last.

Bill Smith gives an eyewitness account of those hazardous, yet exciting, days when reserve parachutes were a pipedream and a 'chute failure meant certain death . . .

GLORY, GLORY, WHAT A HORRIBLE WAY TO DIE

Being young and keen, I had done a bit of volunteering before I joined the LRDG. With these attempts I had no luck, a major difficulty being that the Army was short of wireless operators and averse to transferring them. But one pastime I would never have considered was parachuting. I thought it beyond me. About August 1943, though, when we learned that parachuting was to figure in the LRDG's repertoire, my view changed. Having a pessimistic streak, I naturally thought of the worst possible case. Yet, while a 'Roman candle' ('chute failure) and other hazards loomed as nasty possibilities, RTU (Return To Unit) was a *certainty* if I chose not to go ahead.

The Aegean campaign then intervened and soon afterwards I went into hospital with a badly poisoned leg. By the time I returned, the parachute training at Ramat David had ended and the unit was preparing to move to Italy. So, with some others, I did my course at Gioia del Colle, between Bari and

Men of LRDG at San Nicandro, Italy. (IWM HU25120)

Taranto. Our instructor was Titch Lightfoot, a former steeplechase jockey and all that a parachute instructor should be. He imparted his wisdom with humour and unfailing encouragement and was not afraid to admit to butterflies in his own stomach before the event, even after 150 jumps. Under him, the ground training was both highly effective and enjoyable.

All our jumps were to be in the afternoon and I decided to set up a routine to keep the butterflies at bay in the long interval between lunch and the arrival of the airfield truck. Every jumping day after lunch I went to the ablutions, stripped, washed in cold water and gave myself a hard towelling. Returning to the hut, I re-tied firmly my boots and short puttees, then lay on my bunk and read *The Warden* by Anthony Trollope. I gave every word of Trollope's my undivided attention, so that nothing existed for me except the trivial goings on in mid-Victorian Barchester. I had never read Trollope before and I have never read him since. But whenever anyone says he was a great novelist I concur heartily, for he served me well in my hour of need.

Having given us first-class ground training, the RAF then proceeded to damn nearly kill the lot of us before we had jumped at all! The first jump was to be slow pairs from a Wellington. At take-off we had to stand forward, in near

LRDG at San Nicandro, Italy. (IWM HU25131)

darkness, between bulkheads of some sort. As the plane approached take-off speed, it began to bucket about violently and clouds of dust showered upon us. No connoisseur of take-offs, I merely formed the opinion that metal strip runways were not all they were cracked up to be! A squadron leader who was jumping with us was standing next to me and through the din, I heard him suck in his breath sharply as he grabbed for a handhold on the bulkhead. I interpreted his reaction as that of a professional of the runway.

Then we were airborne. As we moved aft, I noticed the dispatcher was looking very pale and wondered why.

We learned afterwards that the pilot had temporarily lost control of the plane, which left the runway and headed for a line of parked American Fortress bombers. The pilot had taken the only option open to him, yanked back on the stick and cleared the Fortresses by inches.

From a sitting position, sideways to the aperture, I swung my legs into the void, pushed off with just enough force to achieve an upright stance in the centre, and through I went. When I opened my eyes, there was that beautiful canopy spreading out above me. Then came the brief, delightful interlude when I seemed to be suspended motionless in the sky. I had time for a few experiments, turning and some lateral movement, then the ground came up slowly at first, then faster and faster. A megaphone bellowed from below: 'Keep those legs and feet together'; a quick check that my position and intended roll were in accordance with the wind and then the landing, which was the least of my worries.

Of the second jump, fast pairs from a Wellington, my only recollection is of trudging away from the dropping zone with my rolled 'chute, looking round and seeing an unfortunate jumper descending with one leg vertical above his head, caught in the rigging lines. If you were not upright when leaving the plane, the slipstream could thrust you into a somersault, which coincided with the extraction of the 'chute. Maintaining the position of attention was then paramount, for any stray limb would become entangled and landing on one leg inevitably caused a fracture.

Jumps three and four were done in one afternoon from a Hudson. The Hudson's door was small and all but the shortest of men had to duck through it and straighten immediately. If you came up too soon the top of your parachute pack caught the top of the door and you were checked momentarily in mid-leap. It was disconcerting and it happened to me on the third jump.

For the last three jumps, we changed to the DC3 Dakota, an ideal plane for parachuting, with a big door and room for twenty men. Combining with another stick we totalled eighteen. Jumps five and six were uneventful. Then came the last jump.

Titch Lightfoot said, 'I want a really good stick this time. I want to see you coming out fast, like a string of sausages.'

At 'Go' we all moved through the plane at a lively shuffle. Lofty Issard went through the door and I followed closely, possibly too closely. To this day I don't really know what went wrong, but a split second after my exit I felt a sharp blow on the back and my left arm went numb. I think I must have been swept either into the side of the plane or on to Lofty's taut strop.

The rest of the stick were drifting away fast. To follow them I had to pull on my left-hand lift webs. I could not raise my left arm and reached across with my right. I couldn't get sufficient pull so I turned left and tried again with the front lift webs. That was better and I made some progress but not enough to close the gap. I had spoiled the stick and felt miserable about it. I was concerned that they might fail me, but all was well. Later, Doc Parsons diagnosed a fissure fracture of the shoulder blade. It healed quite fast and soon ceased to trouble me.

Finally, it seems appropriate to recall the song which, night after night, raised the roof of the Parachute Training School canteen. To the tune of *John Brown's Body*, it had a lurid candour, which stimulated masculine bravado but was less than fair to those unsung heroines and perfectionists, the parachute packers. It went like this:

'Are you ready, paratrooper?' said the sergeant, looking up.
The paratrooper feebly answered, the dispatcher hooked him up.
But when he hit the atmosphere his chute became unstuck.
And he ain't gonna jump no more . . .

Glory, glory, what a horrible way to die!
Glory, glory, paratrooper.
Glory, glory, what a horrible way to die!
And he ain't gonna jump no more.

There was blood upon the lift webs, blood upon the chute.
They brushed his intestines from the paratrooper's boot.
They poured him from his harness and they scraped him from his suit.
And he ain't gonna jump no more . . .

WELL OVER A HUNDRED ENEMY CRAFT SUNK BY THE DEADLY LRDG TRAP

Ken Lawrence gives a brief but revealing account of the secret, simple, but deadly method used by LRDG to transmit the location of enemy shipping on the Adriatic coast. The method, an LRDG invention known only to a limited number of people, was later used extensively in forward areas in close collaboration between Army and RAF units.

In Bari, Southern Italy the LRDG invented a method of directing rocket-carrying Hurricanes and Spitfires to shipping targets on the Yugoslav coast.

These were always well camouflaged and difficult to locate by fast, low-flying aircraft. Balkan Air Force [BAF] stationed at Bari aerodrome had a complete photographic air coverage of the Yugoslav coast, so we devised a method of co-ordinating a particular point on a numbered photograph by means of a square of celluloid, inscribed with grid lines and superimposed on the photo, copies of which were in the possession of the patrol commander, HQ Bari and the Balkan Air Force. Both HQ BAF and the LRDG were in the same building.

We would receive a signal from the patrol like this: 'Photo number 10996 3E Lighters at A45 627'. In minutes, the aircraft would be away from Bari following the co-ordinates and the results known within the hour.

When I went to discuss this idea with BAF, they were most cooperative and, in fact, they actually made the grid squares.

It worked well for us and also for the Desert Air Force, who made thousands of sorties to aid the advancing armies.

INTO THE GREEK FACTORY OF DANGER RODE THE VALIANT LRDG MEN

When Eric Bamford and Harry Chatfield smashed their way out of a cattle truck on the train taking them to a forbidding POW camp in Germany, after being captured in the Aegean, little did they realize that they would soon be emulating the great Greek hero Odysseus in hiding among a flock of sheep to avoid capture by their arch enemies, or riding off mounted on spirited stallions to carry out a clandestine spying mission at a Nazi-run factory! Harry tells their exhilarating, previously untold story.

The day Eric Bamford and I jumped the train in Greece began the strangest experience of my life. After making our escape, we decided to go for higher ground, to avoid capture as we thought, and walked into a German outpost within minutes! We heard the Germans shouting and they switched on a searchlight. We dropped to the ground and luckily there was a nearby flock of sheep into which we managed to crawl. Some of the sheep were wearing bells around their necks and the noise from them seemed to satisfy the Germans, who switched off the searchlight. We managed to creep away, deciding after that to travel by day and rest by night.

Our intention was to go north over the mountains to Salonika. The next day we set forth and soon came across a farmer who was working alone in a field. He seemed terrified and we tried to tell him who we were. Eventually, he led us to his village, which was actually a stronghold of the resistance and very soon we were surrounded by armed guerrillas.

They were extremely suspicious, we found out later that the Germans had tried to infiltrate the resistance by sending spies to join the movement, and eventually we were led into the hills to a village called Gora. Here we met M04 agents Ken Craven, Bob Ford and John Mulgan, who was the leader whom we all called 'The Major'. They were in contact with London by wireless, via Cyprus, and we were eventually cleared by London, who gave us the 'all clear' as LRDG personnel.

As the Greeks could not pronounce my name, I became known as 'Arribul' because of a resemblance to a Greek actor, and Eric became 'Ericus'. We were armed and became part of the resistance band. Working with the agents, we did many jobs for the resistance too numerous to recount, although one in particular is worth a mention. We were ordered to investigate a large works, which was in the valley a few miles away. The Major decided that Ken and I should do the job.

We set out on horseback with a Greek guide in a blinding snowstorm to get to a little village near the works in question. I remember thinking at the time how strange it was that not very long ago I was in the heat of the Western Desert and now I was half frozen on a stallion in a snowstorm!

After having something to eat at the village, Ken and I decided to go in that night and take advantage of the snowstorm. We cut the perimeter wire fence, crept by the guards and entered a large building about the size of a hangar. We found huge turbines and were busy having a look around when the metal door that we came in by was suddenly clanged shut and locked. A voice over the tannoy system said menacingly, 'Come in, gentlemen' and a door at the far end opened.

We had no option but to go through the door, our hearts sinking and expecting to be confronted by armed Germans. However, we were met by a Greek who told us in perfect English that he was the manager of the works, but working under the direction of the Germans. He had spent a few years in England and returned to Greece to take charge of this project. He was allowed to carry on the work under the Germans, who also used the works to repair railway engines. He told us everything we wanted to know and introduced us to his wife and family. They gave us the best meal we ever had in Greece and we had quite a lot to drink.

To our surprise, they told us it was New Year's Eve. We had completely forgotten. The Germans were singing in their quarters only about a hundred yards away, but we cheekily sang *Roll Out The Barrel* and had a few more drinks! We were feeling quite merry and in the early hours of the morning decided to make our departure. Our host gave us two white tablecloths under which we wriggled away, camouflaged in the snow. I often wonder what on earth we would have done if we hadn't been feeling so merry. We made our way back to Gora to report and found that Eric wasn't feeling well. He had contracted hepatitis and I had to keep him on a fat-free diet, which was extremely difficult under the circumstances.

Not long after, we had a call from Cyprus that the LRDG wanted us back and that arrangements were in hand. We were not sorry, as we had just seen two men tortured to death, which was rather sickening. We said goodbye to our friends in M04 and made for our rendezvous village. Here we met some airmen, American and British, who had bailed out.

We were picked up by the resistance and had to stay at this village for some time and Eric was getting worse. I had to scrounge all the food I could find that did not contain fat. I was very worried that he was not going to make it and was very pleased when the order came through for us to go.

Unfortunately, we had quite a long trek over the mountains to get to the coast. It was obvious that Eric could not do this and he was smuggled by cart down the road in the valley. The rest of us went over the mountain and, apart from a minor brush with some wolves, we landed at the coast and were very relieved to find Eric waiting for us. We boarded our boat and set out for Turkey. Some time later we were challenged by a submarine. However, it turned out to be British and we were allowed to continue.

Eventually, we sighted Turkey and stopped about 3 miles off Smyrna where a boat came out to us, after a wait. It was the British Consulate representative who brought us civilian clothes – but no shoes. We then went ashore as civilians. We wore new suits with our old boots and, as we all had beards, we must have looked rather weird. However, we were all taken to a hotel near the waterfront, not far from the German Embassy.

Eric was whisked off to hospital. I was pleased about this, as I knew that he would now be all right. The strange thing was that I never saw Eric again. I was told that I could not visit him or go to any public places such as nightclubs or bars. It wasn't that I was an escaped POW, but because I knew such a lot about M04.

The hotel was very pleasant. We even had sheets, which was a luxury we hadn't had for years. We also had to shave off our rather bushy beards. I remember the Americans were amazed to see me without a beard and remarked how young I was! They must have thought I was a hard-bitten old veteran and we had quite a laugh about it.

After about three weeks of this rather comfortable living, four of us Brits were taken to the British Embassy to see the Consul himself. He told us that we were leaving Turkey the next day. We were all going on a group passport with two civilians, a man and a woman, who were spies and had come in from Russia. Our job was to guard them, make sure they were not approached by anyone and to see that they crossed the frontier all right. We were strictly told not to ask them any questions about themselves.

We shook hands with the Consul and he wished us the best of luck. The next day we all boarded the train and met our two charges. The man looked like a typical businessman, while the woman was a little old lady who looked less like a spy than the man in the moon! We travelled south to Aleppo, where we crossed the frontier into Syria. Here we were met by members of British Intelligence and some American brass hats. The civilians were whisked away by plane within minutes. The Americans were also taken out by air later.

Our little band was certainly diminished. The few of us that were left were given uniforms and documents to report to 2nd Echelon in Cairo for debriefing. We were then put on the train, indomitably British, at Aleppo for the journey to Cairo. It was a weary journey and the only break we had was a few hours' stop in Haifa. We had a walk round the town and I spotted two officers wearing LRDG cap badges. I didn't know them, but it was very nice to meet someone from the unit. They told us there was an LRDG camp outside the town and offered to give us a lift out there, which we gladly accepted. We were met at the camp by Colonel Lloyd Owen, who made us very welcome. I was rather gratified to think that I had made it back to the LRDG, although it had taken quite a few months.

We had a walk round and I was staggered to find that the only other person I knew was Hickey in the medical tent. The rest I didn't know at all. Anyway, they gave us a meal and a lift back to town to catch the train. We were still under orders to report to Cairo and I expected to be back with the LRDG in the near future.

We finally arrived back in Cairo and reported to 2nd Echelon. We had to give an account in detail of our adventures, which took rather a long time. I was then given a list of names of personnel who were posted as missing. I was astounded to see that most of the names were LRDG men who, of course, I knew. I then realized why I didn't know anyone at Haifa. I accounted for most of the names on the list who I knew were prisoners and, sadly, had to report one death. The officer was astounded and, as we chatted, he actually asked me how he could join the LRDG. I don't know if he ever did.

I asked him when I was returning to my unit and it was then that he dropped his bombshell. We were not allowed to rejoin! It transpired that Winston Churchill had recently stated that all escaped POWs must be repatriated. So the two British airmen were flown home and the others were to follow later. I was sent to Heliopolis to await transport, as no troopships were going to England. I felt like a fish out of water. I recall one officer pulling me up for wearing a fountain pen with the clip showing. He said that if I was ever posted to the desert, the clip would shine in the sun and give our position away!

A few weeks later, I was posted to the hospital ship *Oranjes*, which was going to England, as a Medical Orderly. It was ironic that all the others were flown home whereas I was going to work my passage. However, it was a pleasant ship. The only flaw was that I had to work nights in the mental deck. Two of us were locked in with the mental patients. There was an alarm bell, of course, but I found it a rather strange experience.

We landed at Avonmouth, Bristol. Apart from the patients I was the only person to leave the ship. I remember walking down the gangplank in the pouring rain. There was a policeman there who said, laconically, 'Welcome home mate . . .'

PARTISANS, SBS, THE SS AND M1 PATROL:
LOUIE LEACH'S STORY, YUGOSLAVIA 1944

The LRDG's M1 Patrol was detailed to travel to the area south and east of Dubrovnik. The patrol left from Brindisi by motor launch and reached the Yugoslav coast in the early hours. Having found a suitable landing 10 to 15 miles south of Dubrovnik, the patrol moved off inland to a thick wooded area in the foothills of Montenegro. Here it met up with a large party of Tito's Partisans and was invited to share their camp. The offer was accepted. The problem now was to understand each other, but they had plenty of food, mostly British, and the site was ideal for the patrol's purpose. Louie Leach tells the story:

The Partisans never seemed to go anywhere or have any means of communication with their HQ but it was so peaceful here that one of them went to the village at night and used the phone box. The peace and quiet was uncanny. There was no sign of troops, army trucks or heavy weapons anywhere. The local farmers and other civilians just carried out their work as normal. There was no blackout in Dubrovnik and elsewhere. The patrol could move about quite freely.

This left only one target, a railway bridge over the main coast road. So the SBS section arrived with demolition gear and were able to plant explosives more or less at leisure and up it went. It was a good result. The centre of the arch came down almost complete and blocked the road.

We returned to camp to await the next night to return to Italy. The alarm was now up but most of the group was able to make it. But David Skipwith, one SBS chap, Anka (a Serb Partisan girl) and I were caught. David had gone walkabout earlier so I went to find him, but all of us ran into an ambush. I was hit in the arm and not a lot of use. We were taken to Dubrovnik and then to Mostar by truck and again everything along the way was as if no such thing as a war existed. Anka vanished in Dubrovnik. She was a lovely girl, well educated and from a good family I should think. I always thought she had friends in Dubrovnik but never found out.

Arriving at Mostar prison we were separated and I saw no more of David or the others. I was then taken to a room for questioning. There were three SS officers. They were waiting for a passage home before getting cut off by the advance of the Russians. They found it amusing that a unit that was well known to them as desert specialists should be sent to Yugo of all places. It made no sense to them for us to come over and demolish a bridge or anything else for that matter in a country that was more trouble to anyone occupying it.

The unusually humane SS captors told Louie they were not bothered with the threat from Tito and his Partisans as they were keeping to their Montenegro hideout, well supplied by their Allied protectors. Louie continues:

According to them this was in the hands of Randolph Churchill. Our captors were the Domerbrand (they said, lucky for us), who were trained and armed by the Germans, though by now the Huns had got off their mark.

Then there were the Ustashi. These were no more than bandits, brutal and a menace to civilians or anyone else so long as loot was around. They were real villains, responsible for mass murders and vile concentration camps, as I can confirm. There were other lots too but nobody seemed to know what they stood for and they were a nuisance only. (In the forties, Yugoslavia was the same as Bosnia is now; all the various factions at each others' throats, never mind what was going on elsewhere.)

And so the SS left and I was handed back to the Slavs. They took me to a prison camp at Stavenenski Brod, on the borders of Croatia. Here were all civilian prisoners, why I don't know as no one spoke English. It was disgusting and the only things happy were the lice, with the arrival of fresh British meat — me. Take it from me, Bosnia breeds the biggest and hungriest lice in the world.

In 1965 David Skipwith, who sadly died the next year, wrote of returning to the scene of the bridge demolition, which Louie refers to above. Lunching in a local restaurant, he asked the waiter where the prison was, explaining that he had once spent a night inside it with a comrade. The waiter asked, 'Are you the so-and-so who blew the bridge up?' When David admitted complicity the waiter asked if he remembered Anka. David did. As Louie has stated, she was a lovely girl.

The waiter disappeared but returned a moment later with a piece of paper. 'That's her address,' he said. 'She's married to General Sumonja, the Naval Commander-in-Chief in Split.'

Later, on a visit to Split, David was met at the quayside by General Sumonja and Anka and they enjoyed a memorable tea party together. David reported that Anka enquired after Louie, whom she had also never forgotten.

HIDDEN BY THE PARTISANS:
A CLOSE SHAVE IN ISTRIA, YUGOSLAVIA

Len Poole fills in the details of a heart-stopping incident briefly outlined in David Lloyd Owen's masterly book, *Providence Their Guide*. This, in the typically understated parlance of the LRDG veterans, is what happened.

Alf Page and I relieved the previous watch outside the village of Castel Nuovo and went on to the watch position on top of a scrub-covered hill overlooking Arsa. We got out our sleeping bags and settled for the night before commencing the watch next morning.

In the light of a misty dawn we took out the hidden radio left by the last watch and began the usual chores. During a meal of bully, oatmeal slab and compo tea we saw two women approaching our position. I recognized one of them, a young, short, jovial girl of about sixteen whom the patrol knew as Tosca. The old woman with her was in a state of great agitation and we were told that an informer had given our presence away to the Germans, who were mounting a hunt to catch us. To remain where we were was rash and unwise. They also said that search parties were combing the area looking for the patrol.

The news was disquieting but, with a patrol radio schedule due at 7 a.m., I decided to remain where we were until the threat became more clearly defined. I felt it was very important to keep the radio schedule but arranged to meet Tosca at a point half way to a farmhouse occupied by Partisan sympathisers if we were forced to clear out. At 7 a.m. the radio vigil began, but we received no answer to repeated calls.

Half an hour later Tosca returned with more news. A Partisan flushed out by German hunting parties was at the farm with his wife, whose family owned the farm. Tosca could give me no news of the patrol, whose camp area was alive with German troops.

The women departed and once more Alf and I were alone and waiting, packed up, to move when the situation became clearer. A little after 8 a.m., while scanning the harbour of Arsa and adjacent coves, Alf called over to me, 'I can see three Germans and you won't need glasses to see them!' A quick check showed an extended search party coming up one side of our hill, with other parties swinging in to complete the circle over the summit of the ridge connecting us to other high ground. We moved pretty smartly, got down to the ridge, and moved away below the flank out of view of the enemy.

Ten minutes later, we arrived in the cobbled yard of the farm with Tosca as guide. Arrangements were soon made. Tosca led Alf away across some fields along a path hidden between stone walls separating the fields. He was taken to the village 'odbord' or mayor, Joseph, who had already gone underground, literally, down a dry well, covered in and provided with water and food and playing cards for recreation. Alf spent the day there playing endless rounds of cards until late afternoon.

With Alf safely out of the way, another daughter of the house, Amelia, led me into a stone barn and across to a corner where I helped her move several stones at the junction of wall and floor which revealed a recess beneath the floor of the adjoining store room. Into this cramped space I crawled to join two other occupants, Jaco the Partisan and his wife Maria, Amelia's sister.

There I stayed until 3 p.m. while the hunt continued all round. Several times the barn was searched and more than once Amelia and her aged parents interrogated. What I found amusing was the fact that the Germans looking for us took turns with us taking drinks from the water barrel in the barn! The hunt seemed to have died down a bit about 3 p.m. and I, with great reluctance on Amelia's part, persuaded her to let me out to keep the next radio schedule with the patrol. I received no reply to my signals (in African lingua franca known as Kitchen Kaffir for security) and returned to the communal hiding place.

Just after 5 p.m., we heard voices in the barn and Amelia let us all out perspiring freely. Alf and Joseph had arrived and, with the hunt nowhere close at hand, we held a council of war. Jaco and Joseph wanted us to move into more secure quarters in Castel Nuovo and Alf was keen to head back to the patrol. I remember Jaco being highly amused by my decision to return to the observation post. My theory was that the enemy, having thoroughly searched the area of the observation post, were highly unlikely to look for us there. Besides, I did not think it wise to return to the patrol camp completely unaware of the situation there. I was relying on the final radio schedule at 7 p.m. for more information.

So Joseph, Alf and I returned to the top of the hill in the darkening evening and waited for 7 p.m. It came and I called up the patrol. I did so again and again without result and was preparing to close down when a reply came surging through the earphones. The message was brief. 'Come back at once to the patrol and bring the radio. The Germans have been walking all around us and we dare not put up the radio aerial. The hunt parties have moved away.'

But the excitement was not yet over! As we packed up the radio we heard a scrambling among the rocks and a woman's voice calling in Serbo-Croat. It was Joseph's wife and two children and Joseph informed us that a fresh search was being made, and that we should go with him and his family to their cottage in Castel Nuovo where there were no search parties.

I'll never forget that walk. The four adults walked together through the village streets while the two children, Aurelio (about twelve) and his little sister (about nine), skipped and ran laughing and shouting as they darted down side lanes and the road ahead. In their singing they were reporting on whatever other traffic there was about. What a grim game for two young kids.

Alf and I had a cup of ersatz acorn coffee and a few minutes' rest. Alf was just lighting a cigarette when I announced we must leave immediately. Alf thought I was being unreasonable but put out his fag and we left. A short distance outside the village we passed a German checkpoint, an easy matter as it had begun to rain. A few hundred yards further on we passed the turn-off to the village of Carnizza and eventually reached the patrol camp on a headland above the sea.

The last word in our little saga was a couple of days later when Joseph came and said, 'You were lucky the other evening. Ten minutes after you left a German cycle patrol came into the village.'

Alf said, ''ow I forgive you for making me put my fag out! Did you have some intuition?'

There is no answer to this except what David Lloyd Owen said in his book: 'There were few of us who did not also recognise that Providence, in the guise of the benevolent care of God, often watched over us . . .'

SECONDS AWAY FROM DEATH ABOARD ML 359

Bill Smith tells a harrowing tale of a remorseless Nazi air attack while he and his LRDG mates hid, helpless under camouflage, as the unit so often had to do in their cleverly concealed vehicles in the desert. On this occasion, however, the hiding place was a motor launch in the deceptively idyllic Aegean.

On one occasion, eight of us aboard ML [Motor Launch] 359 had to spend a day under camouflage at an island which seemed to be uninhabited. I have never been able to find it on any map.

At first light, we moored to rocks at the western end of a crescent-shaped bay and lost no time in getting on the long grey camouflage net. As the light improved, the island was revealed as a desert of rock with a solitary spit of sand on the far side of the bay. There was no sign of life. At the water's edge, alongside the ML, were two rows of flat stones forming steps about 9 feet long, the only indication that people had ever lived there.

Long afterwards I read that, by stripping the rest of the Mediterranean and withdrawing squadrons from the Russian front, the Germans had assembled between 450 and 500 aircraft in the Aegean. The first of them soon appeared and until the sun went down the sky was never clear for very long. They came from all directions and flew at all heights, from overhead to the far distance. Sometimes two or three flights were in sight at the same time. On that day, I saw more of the Luftwaffe than at any other in the entire war.

There was a weakness in our camouflage. I was told that later types of ML were fitted with telescopic masts. Most of ML 359's mast, including the yard, was exposed and projected above the rocks.

As the sun climbed higher, nearly everyone moved to the rocks or the steps, still under the net. I thought the deck more comfortable and stretched out there trying to doze. I wondered what chance we should have if the Luftwaffe found us. The ML was about 110 feet long, built of wood and petrol fuelled. She had a capacity of 1,000 gallons and I thought she might have perhaps 750 left. There was a magazine and right aft there were depth charges. I thought a near miss would be enough to hole her and probably start a fire.

We could not betray our position by shooting first and had to wait until we were attacked, when it would be too late. I hoped the aircraft would continue to pass to and fro without taking any notice of that funny 'rock' with a mast embedded in it.

The hours dragged on. Suddenly, about mid-afternoon, a formation of six Ju 88s started to take a closer interest. Ominously, they began to circle the island, losing height as they did so. Heading westward, they flew behind the saw-tooth crest, which filled the northern horizon. The sound of their engines faded and they remained out of sight long enough to kindle a spark of hope that they were on their way home with empty bomb racks and were just doing a recce in passing.

Then, abruptly, they re-appeared very low over the western ridge and came diving down the slope straight for us. In all that sterile landscape we were the only conceivable target. They must have seen the mast! For once in my life I could see no way out. I thought I had about ten seconds left. I then discovered the truth of the saying, 'When hope goes, fear goes too'. Once I had accepted that death was certain, all the weariness, tension and fear fell instantly away and I was enveloped in a miraculous peace. My mind seemed to have got off to a flying start for the next world and to rather like the look of it. Yet, oddly enough, part still functioned in the present. As the planes drew nearer I remembered the LRDG dictum that a face is always visible through a camouflage net at close range. Here it seemed totally irrelevant, but somehow training prevailed over personal conviction and, feeling a bit ridiculous, I looked down.

Then they were on us, the deafening roar of their engines vibrating the air . . . and nothing happened. Stunned, I turned and watched them skim across the bay. They pulled up to clear some strange rock spires and levelled out again. The thunder of exploding bombs came to us over the water but we saw no flame or black smoke, nor did we hear any further explosions. The planes flew on and never returned. A faint sandy coloured haze rose slowly above the distant rocks.

The consensus was that Jerry must be losing his touch, to fly clean over us at 50 feet and then drop his bombs where they would do least harm. The euphoria lasted about two hours. Then the dire news came over the ML's radio. Unknown to us, another ML had been lying camouflaged 2 miles or so to the east and she had been the target. Her crew had suffered grievously though, amazingly, some had survived. There must have been another naval vessel in the vicinity, which had gone to her rescue and transmitted the report we had received. ML 359 was told to proceed as ordered.

Illogically, I felt guilty. It was the fortune of war, but it was impossible to dodge the old unanswerable question, 'Why them and not us?' We never spoke about it. Very little was said by anyone. But we all felt the same.

It was as well that, soon afterwards, in the last of the light, we had to get in the camouflage net, cast off and turn our minds to the landing we had to make and the job we had to do.'

SELFLESS COURAGE WON THE SUPREME AWARD

The George Cross, instituted in 1940, is awarded only for acts of the greatest heroism or the most conspicuous gallantry in circumstances of extreme danger. It is worn before all other decorations except the Victoria Cross. Signalman Kenneth Smith won the LRDG's greatest individual award just a few months

Courageous George Cross winner Ken Smith. (LRDG Association)

before the end of the Second World War. A softly spoken, quiet countryman from Lincolnshire and the eldest son of the family, Kenneth Smith had enlisted in the Royal Signals as a regular soldier on 23 January 1939. He became, in the opinion of his comrades, a superb operator and was completely unflappable. His outstandingly cool act of courage, in which he knowingly gave his own life to save helpless civilians, is described below. This tribute is based on the reminiscences of Gilbert Jetley, formerly of the Sharpshooters, and Cyril Smith, formerly of the Kent Yeomanry, RMA.

In late 1944, there were Germans and Fascist-minded Partisans operating in Yugoslavia and there was considerable movement of German shipping in among the islands which abound along the north-east coastline of the Adriatic Sea.

A Yeomanry patrol of the LRDG, consisting of an officer, eight or nine troopers, a signalman and a medical orderly, embarked in a trawler near Manfredonia in Italy and were landed on the small island of Ist. The object was to keep a watch on shipping and to provide a jumping-off ground for raids on enemy-held islands and the mainland. Ist depended upon fishing, with only just enough soil to grow sufficient grapes to produce wine for home consumption. The able-bodied male population had been deported as slave labour.

There were three varieties of Partisan: the Ustashi, fascist supporters; the communists, supported by the Allies; and the Chetniks, who appeared to be nobody's friends. Military activities witnessed by the patrol included an ML being blown out of the sea by an E boat and a traitor being executed by a Partisan firing squad.

The patrol was billeted in three houses – one as the sick bay, one where the Signalman Kenneth Smith and those who helped to carry the radio lived, and one where the remainder were accommodated. The chore horse did not always work and many a long hour was spent on the alternative means of power, a pedal generator. Otherwise, life on Ist was pretty good and sometimes light-hearted. The locals were extremely friendly and their loyalty extended to learning the patriotic songs of the Allies.

This dramatic painting by Peter Archer records the heroic incident when Signals Operator Ken Smith saved a civilian family and comrades from an Ustashi terrorist bomb while observing enemy shipping for the LRDG on the island of Ist, off the Balkans, in January 1945. Knowing he was in mortal danger, Smith picked up a live time bomb and ran as far away as possible from the house where he and his comrades were billeted, and which contained his vital radio set. At the last second, the bomb detonated with a tremendous explosion and he was killed instantly, but everyone else was saved. For his outstanding courage and self-sacrifice Ken Smith received the George Cross. (LRDG Association)

On 10 January 1945, about 10 p.m. on a pitch dark night, Smith and Jock Watson, a trooper of the Yeomanry, were asleep in their house, Sergeant Jetley was a patient in the sick bay and the rest were playing nap in the main billet. A noise woke Watson and he went to the front door. As he opened it, he heard something heavy and metallic clank behind it. He saw it was a large time bomb, which was ticking, and there was a booster of extra explosive alongside in a canister.

Watson ran to the nap school next door, where he had some difficulty in convincing them that he was serious. They returned and woke up Smith, who dressed quickly, and he, Watson and Cyril Smith each picked up the portion of the radio for which they were responsible and made for the open air.

At some point in the chaos Smith must have remembered the family who were asleep in the back room and had to choose between their safety and that of the radio to which he owed a duty. He saw a way to save both. He put down the equipment, picked up the bomb and made for a piece of waste ground between the house and the village church. Before he could get there, there was a tremendous explosion. Smith was blown to pieces, a member of the patrol received thirty-seven wounds from the fragments and a Partisan was killed. No harm came either to the family at the back of the house, or to the precious radio set.

Later events that night proved that but for Smith's actions, they would have been killed because a similar bomb, which was found at the back of the main billet, blew up before it could be dealt with and totally demolished the back of the building. About thirty Ustashi had infiltrated to Ist from a nearby island to complete this deadly handiwork.

Kenneth Smith's valiant deed was not the spur-of-the-moment action of an ignorant man. The whole patrol knew of these lethal time bombs and they also knew that, in addition to being unreliable if touched, many contained mechanisms to explode them immediately if moved. Smith was an extremely gallant soldier who gave his life for his comrades, for defenceless civilians and his allies. There were no braver deeds.

The posthumous award of the George Cross to Signalman Kenneth Smith was announced in the *London Gazette* on 19 October 1945 and his heroism has been a proud part of LRDG tradition ever since.

Deadly Danger at Sea – The Frightening Fury of the Bura

Joe Cryer was a crew member aboard *La Palma*, one of the MLs with which the LRDG used to ferry men and equipment on missions among the intricate seaways of the North Dalmatian islands. The vessels' worst enemy were the heavily armed German E-boats which could blast one of the Motor Fishing Vessels (MFVs; armed with machine-guns but no match for E-boats) to pieces in seconds, given half a chance. But sometimes the elements, in the shape of the notorious Bura wind, were even more lethal, as Joe Cryer explains:

The MFV *La Palma* chugged out of the small harbour at Vis. The sea was choppy and there was a light breeze blowing. Piled high on deck was our cargo – supplies for the patrols operating in the Northern Dalmatian group of islands.

E-boats were active in the area and our plan was to travel through the hours of darkness arriving at Souje Cove on Duigi Otok before dawn. It was a trip we had made several times before without incident and we had come to look on it largely as a routine mission. 'Full ahead,' ordered Alan Denniff, the skipper, as we rounded the headland. In the engine room Danny, the engineer, opened the throttle. The *Palma* shuddered and shook. We worked our way slowly up to our maximum speed of 6 knots. At this time, I was second-in-command of *La Palma*. John Hews, three Partisans (Ben, Tony and Mario) and a couple of others, whom I remember with affection but whose names I cannot recall, made up the rest of the crew. All of us had our allotted tasks and we went unhurriedly about our business.

La Palma forged ahead. Vis faded slowly into the dusk behind us. The sea became a little rougher, the breeze a little stronger. We sensed nothing unusual. We were mercifully unaware that November evening that the Bura was about to pounce.

The Bura is a cold, dry north-easterly wind. It occurs for the most part in winter when atmospheric pressure is high over Central Europe and the Balkans and low over the Mediterranean. It sweeps across the great Central European plain and piles up behind the Adriatic Mountains. Its only escape is through the passes. Its giant breath can derail trains, overturn cars and capsize ships. It's a killer and our course lay across its path.

Without warning the storm began. Within minutes, the wind became a howling banshee. The sea raged. Short steep waves broke over our bows and crashed down on to the compo boxes and other deck cargo. It became pitch dark and the conditions steadily worsened. The seas ran ever higher. *La Palma* plunged violently over towering crests into bottomless troughs.

From the engine room, Danny reported that water was rising faster than the pump could cope with. Then he shouted that the pump had broken down altogether. The level of the water in the engine room began to rise at an alarming rate. Quickly we organized a bucket chain from the engine room up the ladder, from the ladder to the side of the ship. The water had to be kept down. Danny had to have time to repair the pump. Buckets passed swiftly from hand to hand, but the water continued to rise. It was within a foot of the top of our four-cylinder Ansaldo diesel engine: it wouldn't be long before that packed up too.

Although *La Palma* was still pitching madly, she was less buoyant now and more sluggish in the water. The situation was becoming desperate. It was clear that we would have to ditch our cargo to lighten ship and make for the nearest land. The order was given. Box after box of supplies went over the side in rapid succession until at last *La Palma* was able to ride the seas more easily. We turned on to our new course. Instead of pitching, we now rolled. We were still shipping a vast amount of water and quickly re-formed the bucket chain. Baling was more difficult than ever.

Eventually, we reached the German-occupied mainland and anchored in a cove. We didn't know or greatly care whether we had been observed. Sheltered from the storm we baled out all the water and repaired the pump and the following night we sailed back to Vis and on to Manfredonia and Rodi over a placid, windless sea. The nightmare events of the past 24 hours were over.

Before she could put to sea again, *La Palma* had to be fitted with a new stern-post and rudder and have her seams re-caulked. She had been badly mauled and unable to accomplish her mission . . . but she had survived the fury of the Bura!

SEEING THE FUNNY SIDE – X PATROL'S YUGOSLAVIAN EXPLOITS

A fine sense of humour was an essential requirement for men operating behind enemy lines for long periods of time, in circumstances which were tense and hazardous to say the least. In this hilarious and well-written piece, John Shute remembers the very comic essence, ridiculousness and sheer incongruity of war which went hand in hand with the deadly serious side of killing the enemy, achieving the objectives of highly ambitious missions – and hopefully getting back in one piece.

The sea slapped gently against the side of the ML as we climbed down into our frail little craft. With myself and Micky and Alec and Leo and Jonah and a lot of heavy rucksacks and Pedro, the Partisan interpreter . . . who spoke no English . . . it settled well into the water. Silently we dipped our paddles into the sea and strained to get the boat moving against the swell. After some minutes I looked up and saw a row of moon-faces gaping down.

'Will one of you bloody stupid matelots cast us off!' I shouted in a whisper. Stormy leaned down, moustaches quivering.

'There's something straight ahead,' he said. 'Looks like a destroyer. If it is, give it a quick burst and come back.'

'Famous last burst,' somebody muttered and then we were off.

We paddled quietly past a little island, which looked like a destroyer in the moonlight and which should have been somewhere else – or we should. I noticed that my bottom was decidedly wet and observed that with each thrust forward, about a bucketful of water slopped in over the back. Balaclavas do not make efficient balers and it was an interesting speculation whether we would make the shore before the sea made us. It was pleasant and warm in the water and little rivers of phosphorescence glittered down our arms as we struck out for the shore. The little band of brigands in the village perched high up the hillside overlooking the coast was unexpected but welcoming. So too was the steaming dish of macaroni and hot corn bread and rough red wine and mounds of grapes they set before us. Millo, their leader, was a debonair figure in tattered breeches and sandals made from a tyre. Then there was Ilya the commissar, young Marco, the other Ilya, who took a night off once a week to spend with his wife who still lived on the coast, several other cheerful ruffians and two burly females with grenades dangling from their belts! We learned later that all women Partisans had taken a vow of chastity until the enemy was driven out. In most cases, this seemed hardly necessary.

Most important from our point of view was Luka Gregovich, an old man of the mountains, square-jawed and square-bodied, who had been in the Yukon gold rush, so he said, and was able to tell us in colourful and quite unprintable language what it was all about.

Most of our kit lay in the bottom of the bay, but Micky had had a feast of gloomy inspiration before we embarked and had attached spare life-jackets to some of the rucksacks with the result that we had salvaged, among other things, half a radio set. Luckily, it was the transmitting half, enabling us to send out rude messages and get nothing back. This was an ideal arrangement, which we strongly recommended as a regular drill, but without result. So were many of the best ideas of the war ditched.

We had a parachute drop and watched helplessly as a number of parachutes drifted down the hillside to be plundered by appreciative Germans. What they did not get, unfortunately, were two large sacks of dried carrots and these were something we just had to learn to live with!

Marching with the Partisans by night in a long single file reminded me of boy scout expeditions. They scorned our requests for quiet and clattered down the rocky paths in happy abandon. Messages passed up and down the line and could be heard approaching in a crescendo of sibilants. Often they had a quaintly delayed-action effect. We halted and waited . . . and waited. 'Why have we halted?' The message went forward. Then we moved on and came to a road, looked to see all was clear and darted across. With the whole column safely over, the answer came back along the line, 'We are about to cross the road. Take care.'

We sat around the camp fire chatting, when there was a loud explosion. We dived for cover. Luka came scurrying over. 'It wasn't me,' he said. 'It wasn't me.'

'What wasn't you?' we said.

He grinned sheepishly. 'Was a can of beans!' he said.

Luka had a donkey, which he called his female jack-ass, and the donkey carried a large sack into which everything we tried to throw away was stuffed. Luka also had a daughter whose name was Vala.

Lots of lovely bangs in the night and chunks of railway line flew about and water gushed in a flood from a water tank and a signal box disintegrated. Then we marched off into the dawn. We stopped for breakfast by a little village in the mountains. The Partisans gathered in a circle and sang songs of triumph and fired *feus-de-joie*. This enabled the Chetnik patrol to find us and exchange rifle shots and insults from the hillside. As we grovelled in the dust a gentle old lady from the village wandered among us protectively. 'I do hope none of you boys gets hurt,' she said as bullets whistled about her ears.

Food became more and more scarce. Rakia, the home-brewed firewater for breakfast, was an acquired taste. It did nothing to fill the void, but created a pleasant illusion of warmth. Boiled potatoes and honey in an isolated shack in the mountains – this was a feast. We smoked anything we could lay our hands on, mostly homegrown tobacco, very fierce, wrapped in the leaves from corncobs and lighted with flints and dried fungus. It took a lot of patience and perseverance to keep this vice going.

We had a prisoner – a husky young man, but very subdued and deferential, as well he might be with Millo saying he wanted him for his POW camp and pointing to the village graveyard. But he pedalled our battery charger most assiduously and he survived. He even survived when the Germans on the coast took ten hostages and shot them – among them Marco's father, which seems to prove that civilization is not necessarily related to appearances. But the Partisans took no more prisoners.

Somewhere, remote and inland, was a landing strip and a British mission and, as we came nearer to it, life became more organised and hospitality deteriorated. We sat in a row in the Commissar's office, wet and dirty and hungry, and watched him toying petulantly with a plate of what looked like devilled kidneys. We drooled, but said nothing. We would gladly have stuck a knife in him for the kidneys, but still had a proper native reserve when it came to speech. An orderly came in with a bottle and six little glasses. The Commissar pushed his plate aside. 'Ah, Rakia,' he said. We sighed. It was another liquid breakfast!

By a blackened, burnt-out farmhouse, deserted and forlorn, we found a fig tree laden with juicy fruit. Five men disappeared into its branches and when we left it was barren. A miracle in reverse.

We were guests in a house in the mountains along with the goats. A fire in the centre of the earth floor filled the place with smoke, which drifted up and out through the thatch. Leo had scrounged a small bag of flour and was cooking pancakes. A villager had died that afternoon and the mourning party came in and squatted in a circle and started to wail. When Leo tossed a pancake and caught it expertly in the pan, the wailing faltered and died and they watched in silent fascination.

With civilization there were lavatories and we learned the origin of the term 'bog'. Either Yugoslavs as a race had very bad aim or they never had the general idea explained to them. We knew just what was required: *Steady! Aim!! Fire!!!*

For the last 50 miles or so we spoke and thought of little but the enormous and delicious meal which would greet our arrival at the British mission. We speculated and planned a menu. Bacon, eggs, sausages, real bread, butter, tea, steak and kidney pudding, stew – all these unaccustomed delicacies featured in it.

It was about ten one morning when we tottered in and met our host with three shining pips on his shoulders. He eyed us with distaste and wrinkled his nose. 'My God,' he said, when he could find words, 'I'll send for the barber.'

'We're starving,' I said tentatively.

'Breakfast is finished,' said our host. 'Lunch is at one.' We were home!

THE DROP INTO DISASTER – ITALY AND M2 PATROL

Kip Kiley and his comrades from B Squadron of the LRDG's M2 Patrol parachuted into the midst of battle-hardened German paratroopers when a mission behind the lines in Italy went horribly wrong. With typical guts and determination, Kip and some of his comrades made a break for it, hid out and escaped the jaws of death with the help of local Allied sympathizers.

While dressed in 'scarecrow' civvies, Kip was even given a cigarette by a German soldier as they shared a meal, the trooper never once suspecting he was in the company of a British Special Forces soldier! The squadron's ill-fated mission became the basis of a strong bond between the survivors which lasted for many years, along with the sadness for those who did not make it. Kip remembers the mission:

Thirteen is regarded by many as unlucky. The 13th of the month is a date on which it is unwise to tempt the fates. For M2 patrol, caught up in the war, there was no choice . . .

In June 1944 four patrols of B Squadron were to be dropped behind the lines in Italy. Their two-fold objective was to create havoc and to feed back information to Eighth Army HQ.

The eight members of M2 – Skipper Simon Fleming, Sergeant Swanson, Corporal Thumper Murray, Mick Keeley, Parry-Jones, Taffy Lock, Bob Savage

David Lloyd Owen in a jeep at Rodi, Italy, 1944. (IWM HU24252)

and I – boarded a Dakota at Salerno. Our destination was a point some 30 miles south of Sienna. Over Anzio, one engine caught fire and we had to turn back. It was 12 July and the drop was put back 24 hours. All of us had a sense of foreboding about the postponement and although we tried to keep it to ourselves, Bob Savage voiced the general view when he said he had a premonition of serious trouble. How right he was.

The following night we took off again and had an uneventful flight. As we approached the dropping zone we took up action stations and when the green light glowed we jumped. But we were 34 miles off target and came down right in the centre of the HQ of the German 1st Parachute Division. They were waiting for us and opened fire. Skipper Fleming was killed instantly. The rest of us managed to form up but we were unable to get to our equipment, which was dropped separately.

The Germans sent in dogs to flush us out and Bob Savage – poor Bob who had feared the worst – shot one of the dogs and was himself then killed. Swannie, Parry-Jones and I became separated from the others and were surrounded in a cornfield about 400 yards square. While the Germans were calling on us to surrender, Swannie and I made a dash for the shelter of some woods. Parry-Jones gave himself up. For the rest of that night and all the next day we heard the Germans searching for us with their dogs. As we made a break for it in the evening, we came under heavy fire from a patrol and I lost contact with Swannie. I was alone.

Eventually, I managed to get past the enemy patrol and headed south towards our lines. I was carrying nothing but my carbine and ammunition. Not far behind I could hear the Germans following up my trail with the aid of their dogs. In the best Hollywood tradition, I took to the river to cover my tracks. I had been without food for five days when a young Italian farmer stumbled across the place where I was hiding. He took me to his home and hid me in a cubby hole which he hollowed out of a haystack. He also provided me with some civilian clothes, which had seen better days on a scarecrow! A short while later, when we were having a meal, a German soldier came and sat down beside us. Fortunately, there were several men around the table and I did not have to join in the conversation. When the German gave me a cigarette I mumbled my thanks.

In the evening two days later, I crawled past the German positions without being discovered. On reaching the Allied lines, I was challenged by a fierce looking Arab of the French Ghoum Division. It was no fun having a black-bearded warrior pointing his rifle at my stomach and refusing to accept that I was British. I began to wonder if my troubles were over even then. He took me to his French officer who escorted me back to HQ, where I was interrogated. Eventually, I was able to establish my identity.

Back in transit camp in Rome, I learnt that Thumper Murray and Mick Keeley had also evaded capture. I found my way to their tent and entered – dirty, bearded and dressed in my scarecrow clothes. On seeing such a bedraggled civilian enter his tent Thumper rose to the occasion. I was subjected to the choicest selection of his own special vocabulary I had ever heard. But it was music to my ears!

AN LRDG OASIS – ON THE OCEAN WAVES!

THE TRUSTY MV *KUFRA*

The LRDG not only travelled into action by truck, jeep or by the more spectacular, if hazardous, means of parachuting. The Motor Vessel (MV) *Kufra*, named after the famous desert oasis, saw sterling service in the Adriatic transporting the patrol veterans to and from various raids and operations. Her former engineer Tom Payne was better placed than most to remember the vital part she played.

I joined her from the very first, after the LRDG took her over from the Royal Navy, as engineer, and I remained with her until she was finally handed over to the Royal Air Force at Taranto, Italy, after the war.

From a rather haphazard beginning, including a jammed gear lever when leaving the slips after caulking the hull which resulted in much bad language in Molfetta harbour, and rather disastrous trials which resulted in becoming stuck on a sandbar in the same harbour, we were finally ready for operations.

Our first sailing orders instructed us to proceed, with a patrol calling at Vis en route to Ist, Yugoslavia, where the patrol were to relieve the one already on Ist. The clouds were fairly racing across the sky when we cleared Manfredonia harbour and the Navy had warned us of a Force 8 gale. The initial part of the trip, from Manfredonia toward Viestry Point, was fairly sheltered by virtue of our being in the lee of the high rocky coastline. Skipper Dick Croucher had set the course and had given Doc Smart, our medical orderly, the wheel.

After I had carried out my engine checks and seen to it that all was well, I went on deck for a smoke and there

Dick Croucher hoisting the flag of MV *Kufra* at Rodi, Italy. (IWM HU25110)

On board the MV *Kufra*: LRDG veterans go seaborne. (IWM HU25338)

we were turning through 360 degrees with Doc frantically wrestling with the wheel in a vain attempt to keep on course! A call to the skipper and everything was fine until we rounded the point. After this all hell was let loose. Alf Colyer and Paddy Sweeney manned the wheel for the rest of the night and, more by luck than knowledge, managed to keep her headed into the heavy seas.

The *Kufra* was a deep-drafted vessel and built for rough seas, but even so she took a real hammering; her galley was wrecked and she shipped a tremendous amount of water, the store cupboards were burst open and the contents added to the swirling water, equipment from our unfortunate passengers and the evil-smelling diesel oil from the 160 hp 4 Cylinder Deutsche engine – but she made it!

As a former deep sea trawler man, I must say that the crew, who were all, except the Skipper, literally green, did a very good job. To the best of my knowledge they were: Skipper Dick Croucher, wireless operator Alf Colyer, engineer – self, Doc Smart, Paddy Sweeney, Joe Cadwallen, Jock the cook, Bangers King the electrician, and signaller Dave Davis.

After many adventures, during which time our crew became pretty proficient, we finally had to say goodbye to the Old Girl. This was done at Taranto, but not before we had bartered most of the movable gear which, I am sure it will be realized, was our only means of total survival!

Tom was the oldest member of the crew and the one with the most experience and he became a well-loved father figure to all who sailed aboard.

CLOAK AND DAGGER – LRDG STYLE

Geoffrey Arnold, who used to navigate the unit's Waco aircraft in the desert, left the LRDG in 1943 to join SOE and led a very exciting, clandestine life, including active service in Italy. His story is a superb example of the very different sorts of dangerous adventures men got up to after they left the LRDG ranks they had known so well.

On this night, we used a Goatley fold boat and a rubber dinghy. We were to land three agents and take off some escaped POWs. In the event, with our escort, we arrived off the pinpoint at the appointed time and, as the boats were about to be put in the water, an enemy E boat was seen to seaward. Tom Maxted informed Lieutenant Bloomfield RN, in charge of the escort, and turned our craft out to sea, going on auxiliary engines. The enemy challenged with the letter L in Morse from a masthead light, to which we were unable to reply. Fortunately, he challenged twice and only when he received no reply for the second time did he open fire. Their aim was high, either deliberately, or because they were unable to see us clearly enough against the dark shore line.

By the time they had the range, our craft was on main engines and speeding out to sea, having crossed the enemy's bows at what appeared to be point-blank range. We were hit in the stern, which affected the working of the exhaust, but this was hammered open by one of the 357 crew. Shore batteries then opened up with star shell and HE (high explosive). The first casualty was the rubber dinghy sitting on the stern on top of the open foldboat. Then a ventilator cowl. Then Fred Ashton. He was hit in the back by a very small splinter near his spine.

In the meantime, Tony Bloomfield and his craft were busy engaging the enemy and we observed a fast and furious exchange of shot and shell, which was most impressive, green, red and white tracer, star shells and HE all being reflected in a calm sea. When the battle was over, Tony Bloomfield's craft having successfully seen the enemy off, 357 returned to the pinpoint to land the three agents, but not without further excitement.

Chalmers and I embarked in the fold boat with the three agents. Ashton, having been hit, could not accompany us and the rubber boat was completely deflated. With Chalmers rowing, we were soon in sight of the shore, at which time Fowler came through on the walkie-talkie to say that the enemy had returned and that 357 were off and he hoped to see us the following night. No sooner had this message ended when a star shell burst, lighting up the whole area and making our landing that much easier.

It was a very rocky bit of shore, we were not fired on and I am convinced that we were not seen. Having helped the agents up to the railway embankment immediately above the pinpoint, I returned to the boat and Chalmers and I rowed out to sea.

All firing had ceased and all was calm. I remember trying to get through on the radio again but Maxted must have been using his main radio to speak to Bloomfield, as all I got was a continuous hum. On trying again later, Peter Fowler was already calling to say 357 was still off the pinpoint. In fact she had returned. Tom Maxted, who never left a boat party, obviously did not wish to spoil his record.

It was with mixed feelings that moments later I saw a craft to seaward of us. She looked like 357 but could easily have been another E-boat. So again I contacted Fowler over the walkie-talkie, who reassured me, saying that they could see me in the radar and that I was, in fact, going towards them.

Chalmers and I were back on board within minutes. It was not until then that 357 returned to Bastia and home, having successfully landed the agents. Had there been any POWs we would have collected them as well. However, the operation was so late in completion that the POWs would have had to return to their safe houses.

Ashton's splinter was removed the next morning and he was back on duty immediately, suffering only minor discomfort. But the rubber dinghy was never used again.

DESERT VETERANS WITH A TASTE FOR AIRBORNE COMBAT

In June 1944, as the SAS prepared to parachute behind the lines in France in support of the momentous D-Day invasion, soldiers of the LRDG were engaged in similar clandestine airborne missions on the Italian front, many miles behind the German lines. Spud Murphy was one of those who parachuted down into the unknown from a height of less than 500 feet, an operational height deliberately chosen to ensure the least possible chance of detection by the ever-vigilant enemy. Though he landed safely, Spud was later captured after a desperate struggle to evade his pursuers and the following eyewitness account was written by him as he languished in a German prisoner-of-war camp, a fate shared by many of his colleagues.

His description of the risky parachuting mode of entering combat operations is a classic in its own right:

Our mission was to establish a small headquarters from which we would operate at a place named Lama, a small village in Italy at that time 50 or 60 miles behind the German front line. Eighth Army wanted information about certain roads, bridges and rivers and we were to supply that information by means of reconnaissance and the wireless equipment we had brought along with us.

The plan was to be dropped at a spot some 3 miles outside the village and near to a wood in which we hoped to establish a rendezvous. The wireless equipment, food and rucksacks had been packed very carefully. They would be thrown out of the plane first. We would follow at once to ensure that we landed fairly close to them.

It was moonlight, the time was four o'clock in the morning. It was too early for anyone to be about and light enough to look for the equipment and get it safely to our hiding place before dawn. We had enough food for three weeks, by which time we hoped the 8th Army would have caught up with us. Failing that, we felt it would be possible to live off the land for a short time if our rations failed us. As a last resort, we could perhaps obtain food from the Italians, but we wanted as little to do with them as possible. One could never be sure in Italy whether one was speaking to a Fascist or one with pro-Allied sympathies. However, food was our last worry.

We were flying now at about 500 feet. The plane had circled twice over the dropping ground. The pilot was no doubt making sure of his bearings. Suddenly we heard the engines throttle back, a sure indication that the moment for our departure was close at hand. Then could be heard the voice of the dispatcher: 'Action stations! Number one!' The red turns to green. 'Go! two, three, four, five, six, seven, eight.'

It's all over in a flash. I am out of the door. The slipstream hits me with terrific force. I am picked up and tossed about like a cork on the ocean. After what seems like an eternity, but is actually less than two seconds, there is a tug on my shoulders and I am airborne, swaying gently from side to side. In twelve seconds I shall be on the ground and all my attention must be concentrated on the landing. Here the real danger lies.

Strung out in a line on my left I can see the white shapes of four or five parachutes and I make a mental note of their direction. On my right the white buildings of Lama glisten in the moonlight. There is the crack of a rifle shot and red and green Very lights are seen going up in all directions. We've been spotted!

I strain my eyes in an attempt to pierce the gloom. We were told we would be dropped in a cornfield, but the black mass, which I can barely see, suggests I am going to land among trees. A second or two later and my fears are confirmed. Clearly now I can see an orchard below me. At least they will be small trees. No danger at least of dangling from the end of a trapped parachute. The ground is coming up very quickly now and I endeavour to protect myself as best I can against the branches. There is a sharp crack as my feet strike a branch and it breaks away from the tree and the next instant I am lying in a heap on the ground.

Speed is essential if we are to evade our pursuers. The noise of motor cars and tracked vehicles can be heard in all directions. We must have scared them pretty badly. Obviously, they will surround the whole countryside and as soon as daylight comes begin a systematic search.

My parachute rolled up, I hastened in the direction where I expected to find my colleagues, pausing at intervals to listen for the prearranged signal which would indicate that I was close to the patrol commander, Captain Greenwood.

I never heard the signal, nor did I find any of the other members of the patrol. For over an hour I searched among those trees but not a sign did I see of them. Dawn was fast approaching, so I decided to make for the rendezvous, which I judged to be much further north, feeling sure I should find them there.

Much time was wasted hiding in cornfields to avoid being seen by the early risers who were already moving about, and when eventually I arrived at the rendezvous, the sun was peeping over the tops of the hills in the east. But here a surprise awaited me. Instead of a friendly wood which it was intended should hide us, I found a private residence surrounded on all sides by a high wall on top of which ran strands of barbed wire. On further investigation it turned out to be occupied by Germans and from the sentries round about and one or two cars I could see in front of the house, I concluded it must be a headquarters of some kind.

The irony of it! Desperate as my position was I could not fail to appreciate the humour of the situation. What to do next? Had the others been here, discovered the place to be occupied by Germans and moved elsewhere? If so, I felt sure someone would have been left behind to inform me of their whereabouts. Furthermore, in view of the search parties which were out looking for us, it was highly dangerous to go wandering around the countryside looking for them.

Therefore I decided the best thing to do was to get under cover and remain there until nightfall when I could resume my search. My mind made up, I moved off in an easterly direction with the intention of making for the hills but I had barely covered a hundred yards when I heard the crack of a rifle shot.

Had I been seen by the enemy, or was it my own patrol trying to attract my attention? I decided to investigate and set off in the direction of where the sound had come, a hill a mile or so away and to my left. The decision was to prove my undoing. I approached the place very carefully and made use of every inch of dead ground, for it was now broad daylight, but on reaching the top of the hill I could find nobody. I knew then it must have been the enemy I had heard and unless I found a hiding place quickly, I would be discovered.

With this intention I then moved towards a friendly-looking cornfield when, lo and behold, seven Germans armed with automatic rifles popped up from the other side of the hill. Taking advantage of their surprise, I turned and fled followed by bursts from their automatics. Fortunately, they were winded from their climb up the opposite side of the hill and all the shots went wide, but with loud cries of 'Halt!' they were soon pelting after me. Fear of capture lent me wings and I was soon out of sight. Thinking they would expect me to rush on down the hill, I made a sharp turn to my right for a hundred yards then doubled back up the hill, hoping to pass them well off to their right flank. It was successful.

I heard them shouting below me and firing as they went. Now if I could get over the hill I should be safe. But my luck was against me, for I had no sooner reached the top once more when I almost ran into another force which was concealed by the high corn. I was on top of them before I realised they were there. It would have been suicide to attempt to run. My heart sank – I was a prisoner.

Under strong escort, I was taken to the village of Lama where, news of my capture having gone before me, the whole village turned out to gaze silently upon me as I was marched past. Most of them appeared sympathetic and tried to show their sympathy by a wave of the hand when my captors were not looking in their direction. I was amazed to see how obviously afraid they were of the Germans. The Germans, of course, despised the Italians and showed their feelings in no uncertain manner.

I was taken into a house and escorted into a room upstairs where two sentries were left to guard me, one standing by the window, the other by the door with their automatic weapons at the ready. Neither spoke, but intimated by gestures that I must sit down. As neither stool nor chair was offered, I sat on the floor with my back propped up against a wall. I soon found my thoughts wandering back over my many and varied experiences since I had joined the LRDG.

It was a good life – I refused to think of it in the past tense, being very hopeful that eventually I would be able to extricate myself from my present position and ultimately rejoin my unit. There had been plenty of thrills and a great deal of excitement during the carrying out of our many patrols in the desert and later in the Dodecanese Islands.

We had made use of many different kinds of locomotion – trucks, jeeps, destroyers, motor launches, torpedo boats, submarines, fishing boats or caiques as the Greeks call them, aeroplanes and parachutes, and when all else was impractical many a mile had I covered over mountain ranges on the two legs which nature had provided me.

I was as well versed in the art of approaching an objective on skis as I was of stealing ashore on a pitch black night in a rubber dinghy. I had been taught to use my revolver as efficiently as an American gangster of the Prohibition days and was just as much at home in enemy territory as in my own back garden.

During our days in the desert, we had covered thousands of miles over trackless sands to places rarely visited, if ever, by white men. We were familiar with most parts of the desert stretching from the Suez Canal up through Libya,

Cyrenaica, Tripolitania, Tunisia and Algeria. My patrol had been the first to contact the American First Army, two months before the much-publicised meeting of the Eighth and First Army men. We had also been responsible for making the flank attack on Tripoli possible by finding a gap through supposedly impassable mountains for the armour of the New Zealand Division, an occasion on which, whilst acting as guide to the division, I had the honour of taking tea with General Freyberg.

Spud ended up kicking his heels in a prisoner-of-war camp, but one of his fellow prisoners there said he was as indispensable to his fellow POWs as he had always been in his fighting days.

HOW TO DEAL WITH COLLABORATORS

Former prisoner of war Len 'Basher' Inwood tells of a painless, but very effective way of dealing with those who sided with the Nazi invaders, to the shame of their fellow countrymen and women, many of whom repeatedly risked their lives to help the LRDG on the run from a relentless enemy . . .

I would like to bring to notice my own experiences on escaping from Camp 53 at Ancona.

Nina Knight, four others and I had been on the run for some days, at one time going without food for 48 hours, when we came across an Italian shepherd's hut in the mountains. On knocking at the door, we asked the old man there for food, which he wouldn't part with and, in fact, he threatened to report us to the Germans. At this remark, we took over his so-called home and helped ourselves to what was there, which wasn't much.

When we were ready to leave, the old boy asked us to give him a letter to show to the Allied forces, stating how he had helped and fed us!

We gave him a letter, which we got him to sign, which read: 'This man refused to give us any food or water and threatened to hand us over to the Germans. He is very pro-German and anything we had from him we had to take.'

On receiving the letter, which we had also signed, he kissed it and put it next to his heart and thanked us very much.

I often wonder what happened to him if he ever showed that letter to anyone!

A HASTY NAVAL RETREAT!

Mick Keeley was a stalwart member of M2 Patrol from February 1944 to disbandment in August 1945, during which time a peculiar parachute incident occurred which would remain seared in his memory . . .

M2 Patrol were on the island of Ist in Autumn 1944 led by Captain Clough and including Sergeant Swanson, Kip Kiley, Chunky Haynes, Thumper Murray, Signalman Locke and myself. Ken Smith was tragically killed. We were engaged in a shipping watch and were stationed first on Ist, later on Olib and another small island, travelling via MFV *La Palma*. We were all blond and, carrying Schmeisser sub-machine-guns, were taken for Germans. But a German patrol wouldn't have been singing the comic song *The Fuhrer's Face* – the same song Jim Patch recalls singing to German guards when he was a POW in Greece.

We wanted to have a swim and some local girls made swimming costumes for us out of parachute silk. However, when we came out of the water with costumes totally transparent, the girls, who were watching, had a good view and a good laugh!

There were not many other occasions when the LRDG was caught with its trousers down!

CHAPTER 7

Parting Shots and Lasting Fame

Some of the legends and stories of the LRDG do not fit into any particular category, but tell an amazing tale nevertheless. Others have caused headlines decades after the end of the Second World War and are still the subject of controversy, comment and the searchlight gaze of modern-day military scholars.

In many eyes, the unit is assured a rightful place in history alongside the stunning achievements of Lawrence of Arabia, in another desert war more than thirty years before.

The enormous tactical advantage given by the clandestine surveillance of the unit is unquestioned, and today it is a fact that we would not have the world-beating SAS Regiment without the existence of the LRDG, which transported Stirling, Paddy Mayne and their deadly comrades during their early desert raids.

R Patrol receives news at Sirte on the North African coast. (IWM HU16474)

Some of the trucks used by the unit have been found more than forty years later in the desert, where they were abandoned in the heat of action, almost undisturbed – except by the odd passing Bedouin – from that day to this.

As will be seen in this final chapter, one of these authentic LRDG vehicles now has pride of place in London's Imperial War Museum, excellently preserved by the dry, hot desert winds for new generations of admirers to gaze at and wonder how men managed to travel so many thousands of miles in such antiquated lorries, and how they fought and lived to tell the tale.

Other vehicles, however, were halted in their tracks by mines to cause a baffling mystery that took many years to come to light . . .

HOW TO SIT ON A MINE – WITHOUT REALLY TRYING! STAN EASTWOOD'S STORY

A few years after the war, an oil company called Oasis Oil was prospecting in Libya, as were several oil companies at the time, when at a spot between Marada and Zella a party of prospectors came across the remains of a motor vehicle which had been so flattened they wondered what on earth could have hit it. There were unidentifiable bits of the vehicle scattered over a wide area, but one recognizable part was the tailboard, which was found 300 yards from what had apparently been the centre of an explosion. Just discernible on this was the legend 'S4' and nearby were five graves, each marked with a wooden cross. Stan Eastwood fills in the details:

Oasis Oil reported their find and, in due course, the British War Graves Commission turned up with coffins and Union Jacks. Whether the vehicle had been identified as British and, in particular, as LRDG, at this stage, I do not know. Nevertheless, it was the British War Graves authority who arrived to regularize the situation. With due care and reverence they dug at the graves but to their surprise, there were no bodies. They found some spent cartridges and a toothbrush but no bones, and after some discussion and speculation they packed up and came away.

In 1965, the year Rhodesia proclaimed UDI, I was approached by the military attaché who was in the group who came over for negotiations. He wanted to know what had really happened to S4, so I told him and this is all fact.

I can't remember the date, but S1 Patrol left Kufra under Gus Holliman to take up a road watch. We followed the route we had got to know so well and were sailing through the Marada–Zella gap. Suddenly S4 hit a mine and came to an abrupt halt. Cautiously, we gathered round to help. The front wheel of the

A truck patrol negotiates a testing rocky track through hilly desert on the way back to Kufra oasis. (IWM E12384)

truck had been blown off but nobody had been badly hurt. The driver, Ron Lowe, was sitting on the ground in a state of shock. I surveyed the scene and, from the disturbance of the surface of the desert, I could see that he was sitting right on top of another mine! I shouted at him and I swear he leapt 6 feet in the air.

When the rest of the patrol came up we had a conference and were very angry that our nice little way through had been interfered with by the laying of mines. We put firmly at the back of our minds the knowledge that we were at fault for following our old tracks. Some of us wanted to go right away and attack Marada but, after discussion, caution prevailed. Instead, we lifted all the mines we could find, forty-four in total, and piled them up in the remains of S4. We set a time pencil and continued on our way to the road watch. After about 15 miles the air was shaken by the most tremendous blast you ever heard. We knew nothing about atom bombs at that time, of course, but that is what I have likened it to since.

So, what about the graves? I have a theory – what might have happened is that, after the explosion, a patrol was sent out from Italian-occupied Marada to investigate. Having found the devastated truck with nobody about, the patrol put their heads together and concocted a tale of heroism in which the LRDG were attacked, defeated and put to flight, leaving behind five dead to whom the chivalrous Italians accorded a Christian burial with military honours.

Yet another unfathomable mystery of the desert . . .

A CASE OF A BOMB TOO NEAR . . .

Syd Rose takes up the story:

It was towards the end of 1942. I had rejoined the unit at Kufra and after a short spell in hospital, Doc Lawson ran the rule over me and decided I was in need of sick leave. He suggested I might like to spend it in Alex, staying with the Lambiotte family. I had been to dinner with them on one occasion with Bob Anelor and Dick Croucher, so I jumped at the chance to live a civilized life for a while.

A plane was expected in Kufra in a few days' time and it was arranged I would fly to Heliopolis and then on to Alex. The plane duly arrived, a Bombay I believe and I think the crew were in part South African.

During the Italian show in 1940 I had acquired a small, black, Italian valise. This was packed with my kit and off I trundled to the airstrip. On arrival, I reported and was told we would take off after re-fuelling. Leaving my valise by the plane, I wandered off a short distance to where another passenger was

Veterans of Y Patrol relaxing at Kufra oasis. (IWM HU25181)

sitting. I had no idea who he was but his sole topic of conversation was: 'With this [a Thompson sub-machine-gun] and this [a spoon] I can go round the world.' I think he was an SAS chap. I didn't debate the subject because at that moment there was some heavy machine-gun fire from the camp area followed by a couple of planes making an unfriendly approach to our plane.

The strange passenger and I took cover very smartly in some nearby camel scrub and kept well down. After several bangs and rattles I took a quick look at our plane. It was still in one piece – and sick leave was still on.

As the dust cleared, my companion and I decided we could now move. We stood up, to be confronted by a huge, very black Askari of the SDF carrying a very unpleasant-looking bomb, which he casually dumped in the scrub a couple of feet from us. Alex seemed a long way away at this moment. We completed our move: smartly.

Re-fuelling completed, I collected my kit and duly arrived at the Lambiotte's house in Alex. On unpacking, I found every item of clothing had a very jagged hole in it, in quite revealing areas, alarmingly. An enemy foreign body had passed through my valise from end to end! A very embarrassed young man explained the situation to his hosts, who thought it very funny and remarked that now some secrets of the LRDG would be revealed!

THE INCREDIBLE RESCUE OF THE WORLD'S RAREST LRDG TRUCK

One of the original Chevrolet 30-cwt trucks of 1940, 'Waikaha' W8, was found in the Western Desert in astonishingly good condition in 1980, after more than forty years subjected to the ravages of climate and the attentions of passing Bedouin, who 'borrowed' the odd part for spares.

'Waikaha' is the only authenticated, original LRDG truck in existence and currently has a pride of place in London's Imperial War Museum. She has been kept in exactly the state in which she was salvaged and many thousands of people from all over the world have seen and admired her. 'Waikaha' was one of the original nineteen trucks borrowed from the Egyptian Army when the LRDG was first formed as the Long Range Patrol in June 1940. She was originally used by W Patrol until this was disbanded and then taken over by the G (Guards) Patrol when this was raised in December 1940.

When he heard of this amazing discovery, former LRDG CO Major General David Lloyd Owen was desperately keen to bring the vehicle back for display, originally at the Grange Cavern Military Museum, Holywell, Clwyd, and he worked tirelessly to organize and finance a rescue package. An expedition of LRDG veterans and associates was duly dispatched in November 1983 to recover the truck and bring it back to England.

The guiding light at the museum, Tony Pearce, who had been to a number of LRDG reunions, brought in his friend and business associate Steve Griffiths, ex-SAS, who supplied a Bedford 5½-ton diesel truck with a roll-on, roll-off body which was perfect for winching the pricelessly rare truck out of its desert resting place east of the Gilf Kebir.

Gary Owain-Ashbrook acted as treasurer and had been involved in a number of projects with Tony and Steve. David Lloyd Owen's son Piers, another regular at LRDG reunions, was quartermaster and LRDG secretary Jim Patch acted as navigator.

The vehicle was precisely as it had been left all those years ago, fully exposed on top of the sand near the route LRDG patrols regularly used to take from Asyut on the Nile to the Kufra oasis. British Embassy staff persuaded the authorities in Cairo to grant an export licence and after many minor snags, including customs delays, the truck was successfully brought into the UK.

Jim Patch recalls that 'A chap called Abdu Zedan found "Waikaha". She lay about 45 miles west of the road to Dakhla, on the side of a hill, pointing towards the setting sun. There was just a pile of sand under her front wheels.

'She wasn't a wreck, she looked almost ready for service. A closer inspection showed the glass gone from her headlamps, the radiator and carburettor were missing, the top of the gearbox was loose and a snake had taken advantage of the valve springs to divest itself of its skin over successive years! A single round of .303 ammunition stamped 1942 was found near the running board.

'Tony removed the two half shafts so that rolling our prize on to the truck container would not further damage the gearbox, which was full of sand. Steve backed the Bedford into position and lowered the container so that "Waikaha" could be winched inside. The sand was none too stable, especially when disturbed, but with effortless precision the job of getting our precious cargo into the container was done.'

On top of the hill a cairn was built to mark the spot. A piece of Welsh slate, suitably engraved, had been prepared near Holywell and this was cemented to the cairn.

The team returned in triumph on 6 December 1983 with their trophy in good shape, clean, bright and lightly oiled, and ready to go on exhibition at the Cavern Museum. It was later transferred for permanent display to the Imperial War Museum.

A tantalizing mystery remains. Although the truck is definitely an LRDG original, its discovery well away from the fighting areas, in good condition, means that it would not have been used by the LRDG at the time, as the unit never abandoned vehicles in driveable condition. It is almost certain to have been taken over by another unit, perhaps the Sudanese Defence Force, and abandoned for some unknown reason.

Lettering was found carved into the wooden rail behind the driver's cab. This read 'LIBIA CAMPO 117 – FOIS. EGISTO'. The European-type 7 and the wording suggest this is Italian in origin.

The truck was originally part of the New Zealand W Patrol which, under Major Mitford, captured two Italian lorries as they made for Kufra loaded with 2,500 gallons of petrol and official mail which contained items highly interesting to counter-intelligence. The Italian prisoners were transported on the W Patrol trucks and so one of them may have carved the message then with a penknife.

No one knows for sure to this day . . .

FROM DESERT RAIDER TO CLANDESTINE FORGER

Pat Clayton was one of the first men called upon by LRDG founder Ralph Bagnold to join his fledgling band of desert raiders. After spending eighteen years with the Egyptian Government Survey, Pat had an intimate knowledge of the North African desert which few could match. He commanded one of the very first operations carried out by the unit, the Murzuk raid in the Fezzan in January 1941, involving the New Zealanders and the newly formed Guards Patrol, together with assistance from the Free French, based in Chad.

During this raid, which is described in detail earlier, Clayton was wounded and captured, but that was by no means the end of his exceptional contribution to the war effort. While a prisoner of war, he used his skill as a map-maker and draughtsman to produce escape maps, forge identity documents and to aid his fellow prisoners whenever a piece of official-looking paper had to be produced to deceive the enemy. Such was the quality and sheer volume of his work that a section of the Intelligence Corps Museum in Ashford, Kent, has been devoted to him. His is justifiably one of the best-known names in the LRDG hall of fame.

After the war, Pat Clayton returned to the Middle East with the rank of lieutenant colonel, serving until 1953. He then came back to the UK, retired, settled in Hove and died in 1962.

BEWARE THOSE WHO WOULDN'T KNOW SIWA FROM SURBITON

Despite the fact that only a few hundred hardy volunteers were hand-picked to make up the tight-knit ranks of the LRDG, it's a fact that many ex-servicemen – and quite a few who have never been out of civvies in their entire lives – falsely claim to have served in the famous unit.

The reputation of the LRDG has outlived the unit by decades. However, this has unfortunately produced charlatans and envious individuals who wrongly say they were part of the Group, to the embarrassment of genuine members.

It's a problem with which the SAS, with its worldwide reputation for daring behind-the-lines missions, counter-terrorist operations and hostage rescues, is only too well acquainted. In either case, veterans of the two regiments can easily unmask and expose these boasting interlopers with a few well-chosen questions.

When the LRDG Association has been confronted by a claimant wanting to join its ranks, he has been asked to complete an application form and answer questions designed to show with certainty that he is genuine. The system certainly works and even the most determined dreamers are defeated.

As secretary Jim Patch says, 'So many claim to have been in the LRDG that, if all were true, our force would have been enormous!

'One very well spoken chap claimed to have been in the unit since the desert days, but had never heard of Siwa or the 4th Indian Division. Such a pity these trivialities had slipped his mind!'

Another Captain Courageous 'MC, MM', apparently a leading official in an ex-Army outfit in Australia, said he had been in Kabrit in 1942 in No. 7 Patrol of the LRDG under an officer called Player. Unfortunately for our brave captain, there never was a No. 7 LRDG Patrol, nor was there an officer called Player. Also, the LRDG were never based at Kabrit during the entire desert war, though the SAS were.

But then proven facts seldom trouble the highly envious, the highly imaginative, or the terminally boring Walter Mitties of this world. Perhaps the good captain's hard-won decorations were genuine – most likely for cake making!

OLD LRDG MEN NEVER DIE – AND HERE'S WHY . . .

Association member George Wright has penned this wry look at life and mortality entitled 'The Preservation of Man'. Clearly, when he wrote it, he was thinking about the drinking habits of the desert men in particular, to whom a grog of strong service issue rum was nectar!

The evening rum ration became a famous LRDG custom, which was very quickly embraced by all the other irregular outfits operating in the arid desert wastes:

> The horse and mule live thirty years
> And nothing know of wines or beers.
> The goat and sheep at twenty die
> With never a taste of Scotch or Rye.
> The cow drinks water by the ton
> And at eighteen is mostly done.
> The dog at sixteen cashes in
> Without the aid of rum or gin.
> The cat in milk and water soaks
> And then in twelve short years it croaks.
> The modest, sober bone-dry hen
> Lays eggs for nogs then dies at ten.

S Patrol of Rhodesians rests from arduous patrolling at a desert oasis. (IWM HU16679)

> All animals are strictly dry
> They sinless live and swiftly die
> But sinful, ginful, rumsoaked men
> Survive for three score years and ten
> And some of us, the mighty few,
> Stay pickled 'til we're ninety-two!

FIRST OF MANY

The very first LRDG newsletter is a rarity, consisting as it did of a few unbound A4 sheets, issued after the savage war in Europe had ended, but before the Japanese threat was finally extinguished by the terrifying power of the atomic bomb.

The two bombs, dropped by America on Hiroshima and Nagasaki, cost hundreds of thousands of civilian lives but undoubtedly saved the lives of scores of thousands of British, Commonwealth and American soldiers – including almost certainly some of the LRDG's forces – had it been necessary to mount a costly conventional assault on the Japanese mainland.

When the second part of the first bi-annual newsletter arrived in the run-up to Christmas 1945, Japan was already comprehensively defeated and the LRDG was sadly no more, but an unforgettable legend had been forged.

Christmas at Nofilia, 1941. (IWM HU16480)

Copies of the first two newsletters are exceedingly rare, but thanks to former Lance Corporal Arthur Arger of Ormesby, Middlesbrough, it is possible to recall key extracts here. Unlike later issues, the information is related in a condensed staccato style. But the historic nature of these pioneering issues cannot be ignored.

Arthur, of Y Patrol, was on the LRDG patrol which picked up David Stirling, CO of L Detachment, the Special Air Service, when the survivors of that unit were plucked from the North African desert after their first, abortive, parachute raid on enemy airfields in 1941.

The SAS, and Stirling in particular, were always quick to acknowledge the crucial part the LRDG played in the early days of the regiment, taking the raiders to and from their targets with skilful and unerring navigational accuracy.

The units have enjoyed a strong traditional bond, with LRDG Association reunions being held at the Duke of York's headquarters, Chelsea, traditional home of the SAS Regimental Association.

Both associations produce newsletters (the SAS's being *Mars & Minerva*) packed full of pin-sharp memories from veterans of various theatres of war. Here are the opening salvoes from LRDG newsletter issues 1 and 2, 1945:

LRDG Association newsletter no. 1, Italy, July 14, 1945

'It was decided by the War Office in June of this year that the LRDG should be disbanded with effect from August 1, 1945. Honorary secretary Captain S.M. Hamer said: "We may congratulate ourselves on having accomplished the timely formation of the association whilst still together."'

The membership present totalled 381 as follows:

British	243
Rhodesian	88
Kiwis	6
Australians	1
Americans	1
Past British	35
Past Kiwis	6
Past Rhodesians	1

It was expected that by the end of the year, membership would near the 400 mark as more veterans 'joined up'.

For the record, the names of two lady members take a place of honour in the total. Madame Lambiotte and Mrs Doreen Graham, of Cairo, who had long been keenly interested and closely associated with many members of the LRDG, affording them unstinted hospitality, were granted richly deserved Association membership. They were later joined by Mrs Len Adams, of Whangarei, New Zealand, for similar service.

LRDG members were informed that Lieutenant Colonel D.L. Lloyd Owen MC had been awarded the DSO.

Some members, either voluntarily or without chance to volunteer, had taken the first step on the journey out to the Far East and, shortly, the remainder were to disperse over various parts of Occupied Europe and Britain.

The Rhodesians had already formed a branch association in their own country with Staff Sergeant Major Bennett MM as chairman, Staff Sergeant Andrews as hon. secretary and Sergeant Parslee as hon. treasurer. A similar branch association was expected to be operating in New Zealand.

It was not proposed to collect life membership subscriptions until peace with Japan was formally declared and the hon. treasurer, Lieutenant P.A. Mold, was 'ready with open arms to receive innumerable ten shillings!'

It was predicted that there would not be an annual reunion until 1947 at the earliest and until then, members' only link would be newsletters and private correspondence.

Secretary Hamer said, 'We have started well, as most associations invariably do. It is up to us to keep our interest in the Association alive until such time as

Y Patrol at Ain Chetmir during evacuation of Jalo oasis, February 1942. David Lloyd Owen is standing at left back. (IWM HU24961)

we can really get together and from then on there is no telling what further history may be made.' (How prophetic that would turn out to be.)

A nominal roll of membership was included with the newsletter and it was intended that eventually anyone who ever served with the LRDG would be given a chance of joining the Association.

LRDG Association newsletter no. 2, December 1945

Membership increased from 381 to 483 as follows:

British	363
Rhodesian	83
Kiwis	20
South African	6
Others	11

A posthumous George Cross was awarded to Signalman Kenneth Smith and a voluntary fund was set up to help Mrs A.J. Smith, his widowed mother, who was caring for a large family.

Former LRDG CO Lieutenant Colonel David Lloyd Owen DSO, MC was now military assistant to the C-in-C in Italy and had recently been before the Pope.

Signalman K. Williamson, after leaving LRDG, found himself with 6th Airborne Division just in time for their drop over the Rhine which, despite his 16 stones, he managed successfully and eventually was with the division when they joined up with the Russians at Wismar on the Baltic.

Captain J. Hubert was with 1st SAS Regiment, but on its disbandment was looking around for another job, as were so many veterans.

Major C.S. Morris, NZ, of T Patrol and later OC A Squadron, was keen to form the New Zealand branch of the Association as soon as possible.

Trooper A. Sullivan, Lieutenant Colonel Lloyd Owen's driver up until September 1944, had been with 1st SAS Regiment, as had Lance Corporal Cryer. Both famous units, the LRDG and 1st SAS Regiment were disbanded around the same time, 1 August 1945.

The following letters of appreciation were received by the Commanding Officer to all ranks who had served in the LRDG:

From Field Marshal, the Hon. Sir H.R. Alexander GCB, CSI, DSO, MC, ADC

Dear Lloyd Owen, The news of the War Office decision to disband the Long Range Desert Group must have come to you as a great shock – as it did to me.

Long before I first went to the Middle East, I had heard of the exploits of the LRDG in your original hunting grounds in Tripolitania and Cyrenaica and it was with great pride that I first took you under my command in August 1942.

Since then you have continued your fine work with undiminished skill and enthusiasm and it is indeed with great reluctance that I say farewell and good luck to you all.

From Lieutenant General Sir B.C. Freyberg VC

My dear Lloyd Owen, Your letter of 2nd July has just reached me, with the sad news that LRDG is to be disbanded.

Nobody realises better than I do the extent to which their work contributed to the success of the North African campaign and it will always be a source of pride and satisfaction that New Zealanders were able to play a part in your long series of brilliant operations.

Will you please convey to all ranks of LRDG a message of thanks and farewell from their Kiwi friends, both here in Italy and in the Middle East. We wish you all best of good fortune in whatever tasks the future may hold for you.'

THEY WERE 'SORT OF DIFFERENT'

At the end of the war in Europe, the unique role of the LRDG was also rapidly coming to an end and although preparations were made to send some men to the Far East to fight the Japanese, this proposal was rendered unnecessary by the dropping of the atom bombs on Hiroshima and Nagasaki and Japan's unconditional surrender.

The inevitable sadness and regret that pervaded the final days of active service of the desert veterans was not lost on Major Leo Capel, who recorded some years later his feelings on the last days of a proud unit, the like of which the world may never see again. A remark made to him in Benevento, Italy, by the Adjutant of the Infantry Reinforcement Training Depot caught the essence of the men who so boldly, proudly and yet with characteristic casualness wore the Scorpion badge. The remark was 'They're not the usual type: they're sort of different.'

Major Capel completes the unique personal accounts in this book with a telling description which supports the Adjutant's theory perfectly . . .

The camp was full of men waiting for a passage home. Some of the transitees were being particularly troublesome, it was alleged, by simply ignoring all orders and above all by insisting on brewing up on the floor of their barrack room. The men in question, of course, belonged to the LRDG.

I went to see them and was greeted with a minor cheer and a large mug of rum-laced tea. I told them to be kind to the poor fellows who were trying to run the camp and then took my leave of them. They were the last of the unit I ever saw in the LRDG uniform.

It all seems so very much a part of history now but yet, as I write these words, the fog of memory thins and I see some of the scenes as crystal clear as though they had only happened yesterday.

Names escape me, but the faces are there. I have forgotten the places, but the smell of the woods and the dust of the roads is with me.

I'd enjoyed enormously my spell with the LRDG and was stunned, as we all were, by the decision to disband the unit so soon after the end of hostilities. The war had become so much a part of all our lives that it seemed unbelievable that it was now over at last and this coupled with the end of the LRDG was almost too much to take in.

It was all so sudden and it didn't seem true somehow. But true it was . . .

I have vivid recollections of many things in the last six months of the LRDG's war. The skiing and climbing on the Gran Sasso, training for the assault on Hitler's last alpine fortress — which would have been some party if it had come off! David Lloyd Owen saying one day when visiting B Squadron, in all seriousness 'What do you think about the idea of low-level drops into snow without parachutes?'

Everyone paled and Jack Aitken saved the day by offering David another chunk of fruit cake from his latest food parcel . . . and the evening when Ron

Tinker turned over a jeep with about six of us aboard. The doctor swore that the penicillin powder would leave no scars on my hand and he was right . . .

Glissading down the side of the highest peak of the Gran Sasso, bloody fools that we were, taking our lives in our hands and enjoying every single second of it . . . and all the time, that tremendous feeling of being fit and tough enough to take on the whole wide world. Then there was the odd foray into Rome . . .

And, finally, San Nicandro. The wooden floor hard beneath one's sleeping bag and the grenades and Sten gun lying carelessly beside one – the nights spent drinking vermouth and making impossible plans for the future. The feeling of being *sort of different*.

Above all, I remember the final break-up. David and all the officers and most of the men had gone. I, temporarily appointed adjutant for the purpose of disbandment, and a chosen few had closed in on the Signal Squadron base. On the last night of all we sat and talked and all around us the forests were ablaze, for a giant fire had started in the area. Closer and closer crept the flames and I had visions of a Pompeii-like ending to the LRDG. It would have been very appropriate, but it didn't quite happen. However, it was a near thing and we

Memorably different! An evocative study of a typically colourful, bronzed and determined LRDG soldier, Gerrard of Rhodesian T Patrol, with Arab rifle, at Jalo, January 1942. (IWM HU16571)

had to mount a sentry to watch that the flames didn't devour us while we were sleeping.

Next morning we all shook hands and went our various ways. There were still a few vehicles left and the orders were for them to be handed in at the nearest RVD (Return Vehicle Depot). Gilbert Jetley and, I think, Jim Pickles were last seen by me heading towards the north in a heavily laden jeep. They said they'd hand it in at a special RVD they knew of somewhere in the area of Venice.

I and Greenhill, David Lloyd Owen's driver, took off an hour or so later with a small convoy of trucks, which by evening we checked in at an RVD near Benevento. It was sad to see them and their disconsolate drivers, looking so woe-begone when finally we parted company.

It was the end of the road for them and they knew it, but what a long and adventurous road it had been! Then on to Benevento itself and then to some of the other depots, to see how the chaps were faring, and then, finally, to AFHQ (Allied Forces HQ) in their great castle at Caserta. There I handed in a wad of certificates stating that all had been accounted for and that I and my driver were the last of the LRDG; brushing aside a few loaded questions about gold sovereigns and accounts in Bari, I shook hands with the gilded staff and then took my leave. I was really on my own now and it wasn't a very nice feeling.

What that adjutant said in Benevento was true. The men of the LRDG were 'sort of different' – and thank God they were . . .

APPENDIX I

LRDG Commanders and Patrol Designations

LONG RANGE PATROL COMMANDER
(forerunner of the LRDG)

Lt Col Ralph Bagnold   June 1940 to November 1940

LONG RANGE DESERT GROUP COMMANDERS

(in chronological order)

Lt Col Ralph Bagnold   November 1940 to August 1941
Lt Col Guy Prendergast   August 1941 to October 1943
Lt Col Jake Easonsmith   October 1943 to November 1943
Lt Col David Lloyd Owen   November 1943 to July 1945

PATROL DESIGNATIONS

R, T and W Patrols of New Zealanders operated in the very early stages of the desert campaign in mid-1940, when the predecessor of the unit was known as the Long Range Patrol. When the LRDG was formed towards the end of that year, the following patrols evolved throughout the war, principally in the Western Desert and later in the various other theatres of war in which the LRDG was engaged, including the Dodecanese, Italy and Yugoslavia:

> G1 and G2 Patrols = Guards
> Y1 and Y2 = Yeomanry
> R1 and R2 and T1 and T2 Patrols = New Zealand
> S1 and S2 = Rhodesian
> M1 and M2 = Mixed British and Commonwealth
> X Patrol = Italian Campaign

The Heavy Section supplied patrols on long journeys via three-ton trucks and made supply dumps in the desert, also bringing in supplies to oases including Kufra and Siwa.

Honours and Awards

(in alphabetical order)

GEORGE CROSS

Smith, K.   Royal Signals

DSO

Clayton, Maj P.A.	General List	Prendergast, Lt Col G.L.	RTR
Easonsmith, Maj J.R.	RTR	Wilder, Capt N.P.	2 NZEF
Lloyd Owen, Lt Col David	Queen's Regt		

OBE

Bagnold, Lt Col R.A.	RCS	Steele, Maj D.G.	2 NZEF
Shaw, Capt W.B. Kennedy	Intelligence Corps		

MBE

Barrett, Lt D.	2 NZEF	Heywood, Capt G.B.	Middlesex Yeomanry

MC

Browne, Capt L.H.	2 NZEF	Mitford, Maj E.C.	RTR
Bruce, Lt Hon. B.	Coldstream Guards	Morris, Lt C.S.	2 NZEF
Easonsmith, Capt J.R.	RTR	Olivey, Capt J.R.	Rhodesia
Holliman, Capt C.A.	RTR1	Sutherland, Lt J.H.	2 NZEF
Hunter, Capt A.D.N.	R. Scots Fusiliers	Timpson, Capt J.A.L.	Scots Guards
Lawson, Capt R.P.	RAMC	Tinker, Capt R.A.	2 NZEF
Lloyd Owen, Capt D.	Queen's Regt		

DCM

Bassett, Pte D.M.	2 NZEF	Moore, Tpr R.J.	2 NZEF
Browne, Cpl L.H.	2 NZEF		

MM

Brown, Tpr	2 NZEF	Crossley, Cpl J.	Coldstream Guards
Cave, Tpr A.H.	R. Wilts Yeomanry	Dennis, Cpl J.	Coldstream Guards
Craw, Cpl M.	2 NZEF	Low, Pte K.T.	Rhodesia

Dornbush, Tpr C.	2 NZEF	McInnes, Cpl I.H.	2 NZEF
Duncalfe, Gdsman R.	Coldstream Guards	Sadler, Cpl W.M.	Rhodesia
Ellis, Tpr E.	2 NZEF	Sanders, Gnr E.	2 NZEF
Fraser, Cpl M.B.P.	Scots Guards	Sturrock, Pte E.C.	2 NZEF
Garven, Cpl G.C.	2 NZEF	Tighe, Pte A.	RA0C
Gibson, Cpl L.	Scots Guards	Tinker, Cpl R.A.	2 NZEF
Gunn, Pte D.	Seaforths	Tippett, Tpr K.E.	2 NZEF
Hutchins, Sgt D.	N. Somerset Yeomanry	Waetford, Cpl C.	2 NZEF
		Welsh, Gdsmn M.A.	Scots Guards
Jackson, Sgt C.	Rhodesia	Wilcox, Tpr L.A.	2 NZEF
Lewis, L/Cpl T.J.	2 NZEF	Wilson, Sgt	Scots Guards
Dobson, Tpr T.B.	2 NZEF		

BEM

McLeod, S/Sgt A.R.   2 NZEF

MENTIONED IN DISPATCHES

Ames, Sgt S.R.	RASC	Hughes, Cpl W.	RCS
Arnold, Cpl G.	RCS	Hunter, Capt A.D.N.	R. Scots Fusiliers
Arnold, Lt P.L.	General List	Jackson, Sgt C.H.	Rhodesia
Ashdown, Capt T.W.	RA0C	Kendall, Cpl F.	2 NZEF
Atkins, Sgmn R.	RCS	King, Cpl A.T.	REME
Bagnold, Lt Col R.A.	RCS	Leach, Cpl F.A.	Scots Guards
Ball, Sgt C.G.	2 NZEF	Mather, Tpr L.	2 NZEF
Ballantyne, Capt L.B.	2 NZEF	McInnes, Pte D.I.	2 NZEF
Barrett, Lt D.	2 NZEF	McNeill, Pte T.B.	2 NZEF
Beech, Pte R.F.	2 NZEF	McQueen, Lt R.B.	2 NZEF
Bevan, SQMS H.D.	Welsh Rgt	Moore, Tpr R.J.	2 NZEF
Carningham, Sgt J.W.	Warwickshire Yeomanry	Murray, Cpl J.R.	REME
		Penfold, SSM M.	Coldstream Guards
Cave, Cpl A.H.	R. Wilts Yeomanry		
Clarke, Sgt H.R.	RASC	Pritchard, Pte B.	RAMC
Croucher, Lt C.H.	General List	Searle, Sgmn A.D.	RCS
Davidson, Cpl G.L.	2 NZEF	Shaw, Capt W.B. Kennedy	Intelligence Corps
Davies, Sgt A.M.	Intelligence Corps		
Denniff, Lt A.S.	RAC	Shepherd, Sgt J.R.	2 NZEF
Dugan, Cpl W.F.	REME	Spottswood, Pte R.O.	2 NZEF
Gravil, Dvr M.	RASC	Steele, Maj D.G.	2 NZEF
Hammond, Tpr M.E.	2 NZEF	Stocker, Sgt J.P.	RTR
Harcourt, Tpr D.	2 NZEF	Tatton, Sgt F.W.	RA0C
Hickey, Cpl G.	RAMC	Tighe, Pte A.	RA0C
Hough, Sgt W.R.	Middlesex Yeomanry	Timpson, Capt J.A.L.	Scots Guards
		Tinker, Cpl R.A.	2 NZEF

LRDG Association Nominal Roll

During the course of the war, some soldiers served in the LRDG for a period and then left to join other units. Some of these men later joined the Association. However, when the war ended, a few who had served in the unit did not join the Association for various reasons, or subsequently could not be traced, and so there are a very limited number of veterans not accounted for in the Nominal Roll, which is the most complete and unique record of LRDG veterans in existence.

ORIGINAL 1945

UNITED KINGDOM SECTION

(Address at time of joining Association)

Addyman, H. York.
Ambrose, A. c/o Tooting, London.
Ames, S. Redditch, Worcestershire.
Arger, A. Linthorpe, Middlesbrough.
Aspen, R.W. Palmers Green, London.
Astle, J. Aspull, Wigan.
Andrew, F.A. (Lt) Cheadle Hulme, Cheshire.
Ashdown, T.W. (Maj) Hull, Yorkshire.
Bagnold, R.A. (Brig) London.
Baker, L. Seedley, Salford, Lancashire.
Baker, W.J. Barnsley, Yorkshire.
Bamford, E. c/o Northenden, Manchester.
Barbour, K. Toyshill, Nr Sevenoaks, Kent.
Barnes, A.C. Walworth, London.
Bates, A. Northwich, Cheshire.
Bates, H.C. Sefton Park, Liverpool.
Beaumont, G. Worksop, Nottinghamshire.
Bell, E.G. Grimsby.
Benson, C. Macclesfield, Cheshire.
Berry, C.A. Catford, London.
Berryman, J.E. c/o Arundell, Sussex.
Bevan, H. Clydach Vale, Rhondda Valley.

Bishop, J. Brighton, Sussex.
Blackaller, J. Plymouth.
Blaney, G. Dalkeith, Midlothian.
Blease, T. Portsmouth, Hampshire.
Blower, J.E. Widnes, Lancashire.
Bonneyman, W. Glasgow.
Booker, A. London.
Booth, R.B. (Capt) Potters Bar, Middlesex.
Booth, W. Cowley, Oxford.
Boulding, E. Faversham, Kent.
Bowden, G.T. Tipton St John, Sidmouth,
    Devon.
Bowes, F. Wheatley Hill, Co. Durham.
Braithwaite, J. (Capt) Ballater,
    Aberdeenshire.
Bramley, J.B. (Capt) Humberston, Leics.
Brander, D.A.G. (Lt) Stonehaven,
    Kinecardineshire.
Brewer, St Just, Penzance.
Brewin, L. Shelthorpe, Loughborough,
    Leics.
Broadbent, S. Romford, Essex.

Broderick, S. Shipley, Yorkshire.

Brown, J. Ayr.

Browne, L.H. (Maj) London.

Browne, N.G. Watford, Hertfordshire.

Bruce, (Hon.) B. (Capt) Dunblane,
Perthshire.

Buss, C. Heathfield, Sussex.

Byatt, W. Wandsworth, London.

Cade, H.A.P. Harrow, Middlesex.

Cade, R.A.W. Eastcote, Middlesex.

Cain, G. Wandsworth, London.

Callan, P. Glasgow.

Capel, E.L.T. Dawlish, Devon.

Carpenter, R.W. Taunton, Somerset.

Carr, F. Besley Green East, Birmingham.

Carr, R. (Capt) Montpelier Square, London.

Carson, C.I.G. Newry, Co. Down.

Carter, I. London.

Carter, J.D. Aldershot, Hampshire.

Carver, H.E. South Wigston, Leicestershire.

Cashin, D.S. Southport, Lancashire.

Cassavetti, A.J.A. (Capt) Bicester, Oxon.

Caunt, J.D.A. Blackpool.

Cave, A.H. Rode Common, nr Bath,
Somerset.

Chadwick, G. Hugglesgate, Leicestershire.

Chalkley, W. Haultwick, Ware,
Hertfordshire.

Chamberlain, R.E. Upper Norwood,
London.

Chapman, G. London.

Clark, J.E. Kempston, Bedfordshire.

Clarke, H.R. Galston, Ayrshire.

Clayton, P.A. (Maj) The Chant, Oxted,
Surrey.

Clutton, T. Wrexham.

Coker, L.F. St Albans, Hertfordshire.

Colyer, A. Orpington, Kent.

Comerford, C.E. Islington, London.

Cook, P.E. Alum Rock, Birmingham.

Coombes, L.D. Kettering, North
Hamptonshire.

Copp, B.R. Barking, Essex.

Cramond, J. Middlesfield, Aberdeen.

Crichton-Stuart, M.D.D. (Capt) Falkland
Palace, Fife.

Crossley, J. (Sgt) Coldstream Gds, St John's
Camp, High Wycombe,
Buckinghamshire.

Crowest, T. Bickley, Kent.

Crunden, S. Rochester, Kent.

Cryer, R.W. Ashdon, Bristol.

Damsell, F. Harlsden, London.

Davey, G.M.O. (Brig CB CBE DSO) (Hon.
Member) Mere, Wiltshire.

Davidson, F.G. Barrow, Lancashire.

Denniff, A. (Capt) Totley, Sheffield.

Dennis, J. Levenshulme, Manchester.

Devine, F. Glasgow.

Devonshire, H. Wallasey, Cheshire.

Donnelly, J. Hamilton.

Dotlon, E. c/o Old Bond Street, London.

Douglas, K. London.

Downton, W.A. Stonebridge, London.

Duncan, W. Maidenhead, Berkshire.

Eason, N.J.S. Wallington, Surrey.

Edkins, P. Rugby, Warwickshire.

Edwards, D.R. Sandbach, Cheshire.

Enright, F.E. London.

Everitt, V.A.J. London.

Farmer, R.C. London.

Fell, D.W. Disley, nr Stockport, Cheshire.

Fenton, J. Crieff, Perthshire.

Findlay, J.R. Staney, Perthshire.

Fitzpatrick, J. New Southgate, London.

Folland, D. (Capt) Vale of Ask,
Abergavenny.

Ford, G.W. Little Neston, Cheshire.

Foster, A. Olton, Birmingham.

Frost, W.A.T. Moss Side, Manchester.

Frost, W.E. Barnes, London.

Gazcy, H.T. Hansworth, Birmingham.

Gealey, B. Yumble, Llanelly.

Gearing, R. Wilmington, Dartford, Kent.

Gerard, J.W. Bistham, Manchester.

Gibson, A. (Capt) St Frillans, Perthshire.

Gilbert, H. Stoke-on-Trent.

Gillard, J.W.G. Hackney, London.

Gillespie, C.W. (Capt) Cookstown, Co.
Tyrone.

Grant, A. Stafford.

Grant, R.J. Newlands, Glasgow.

Grav, V. Headley, Borden, Hampshire.

Greason, J. Gateshead, Co. Durham.

Greenhill, D.W. Kingsbury, Staffordshire.

Greenwood, A.M. (Capt) London.

Greenwood. Luddenfoot, Halifax.

Gregory, E. Sheffield.

Grover, R. Newich, nr Lewes, Sussex.
Gutteridge, E. Doncaster, S. Yorkshire.
Haigh, J.A. West Derby, Liverpool.
Hall, C. London.
Hall, M. Manor Estate, Sheffield.
Hall, R.A. Heswall, Cheshire.
Hamer, S.M. Fremington, Barnstaple, Devon.
Hansell, G. Southend-on Sea, Essex.
Harding, C. Abington, Berkshire.
Harding, J.E. Gateshead.
Harding-Newman, R. (Lt Col DSO) (Hon. Member) Penrith.
Harper, A. Cutter, nr Aberdeen.
Harrison, F.G. York.
Hartley, T. Stalybridge, Cheshire.
Hartwell, L. Princethorpe, nr Coventry.
Haslam, C. Bispam, Blackpool.
Hay, Court Lane, Birmingham.
Heard, S. Dellapoole, Cornwall.
Hennessay, W. Stowmarket, Suffolk.
Hews, J. Worthing, Sussex.
Heymans, I.F. c/o Christchurch Vicarage, London.
Heys, J. Haslingden, Rossendale, Lancashire.
Heywood, G.B. (Maj) Stonehouse, Gloucestershire.
Hibbert, C.W. Gorton, Manchester.
Hill, W.R. Whitefield, Lancashire.
Hirst, J.D. (Sub Lt DSC) Lindley, Huddersfield.
Holman, F.C. Earl's Barton, Manchester.
Hook, J. Norwich, Norfolk.
Hopkins, L.W. Bourneville, Warwickshire.
Horrocks, F. Pendleton, Salford.
Horton, H. Ruislip, Middlesex.
Hough, W.R. Winchmore Hill, London.
Hughes, J. Westcliffe-on-Sea, Essex.
Hunt, A.E. Leicester.
Hurst, F. Reddish, Stockport, Cheshire.
Hutchins, D.A. (Lt) MM. Llanishen, Cardiff.
Hutchinson, K. Northolt, Middlesex.
Hutchinson, M. Huthwaite, Nottinghamshire.
Igglesden, R. Woolwich, London.
Ingham, E.A. Bethnal Green, London.
Inwood, L. Tyseley, Birmingham.
Izzard, E.H. Clophill, Bedfordshire.

Jackson, C.J. Camberwell, London.
Jackson, H.G. Worsley.
Jarvis, H. Leicester.
Jeffers, A.E. Castle Bellingon, Co. Louth.
Jennings, G.W. Sutton, Surrey.
Jetley, G. Ilfracombe, Devon.
Jex, E.S. Leicester.
Johns, F. Weston-Super-Mare.
Johnson, E. Higher Crumpsall, Manchester.
Jones, C.F. Dry Crook, Gloucestershire.
Jones, D.C. Hayes, Middlesex.
Jordan, A. Hayfield, Cheshire.
Keeley, E.M. Leeds.
Kiley, E. Abbey Wood, London.
Kilpatrick, Culleybachy, Co. Antrim.
King, J.N. Newton Mearns, Glasgow.
Knee, G. Rochdale, Lancashire.
Lawrence, A. Bethnall Green, London.
Lawson, R.P. (Capt) Grimsby, Lincolnshire.
Leach, F. Walthamstow, London.
Leatham, J. Lisburn, Co. Antrim.
Lee, D. Hanworth, Middlesex.
Lennie, R. Glasgow.
Lewenden, P. Alperton, Wembley.
Linnell, F. Walsall.
Littledale, G. (Capt) Fairford, Gloucestershire.
Lloyd Owen, D.L. (Lt Col DSO, MC, Commanding Officer) United Services Club, London.
Locke, G. Hatch End, Middlesex.
Longland, A. Deans Hanger, Northamptonshire.
Loveday, A.E. New Malden, Surrey.
Lowe, A.G. Headington, Oxford.
Lowe, S.R. Gosforth, Newcastle-on-Tyne.
Lunn, H. Hillsborough, Sheffield.
Lyle, D.L. (Gnr, Survey, Training Battery, 24th Field Training Regiment, RA) Larkhill, Wiltshire.
Maine, Bolton, Lancashire.
Marriott, R. Ipswich, Suffolk.
Matheson, West Norwood, London.
Mathews, M. (Lt) c/o Kingsway, London.
Mathews, R.C. Fishponds, Bristol.
Maxfield, J. Cleckheaton.
Maxwell, N. Newcastle.
Maxwell, R.G. (Capt) Lewes, Sussex.

Mayes, G.H. Thornton, Fife.

McArdle, G. Wrexham.

McCafferty, J. Ayr.

McClelland, T.R. NZ Transit Camp, Folkestone, Kent.

McConachie, R.A. Kings Park, Glasgow.

McConnell, T. Glasgow.

McFarlane, Wembley.

McKay, F.W. c/o Hoylake, Moreton, Cheshire.

McKenzie, G.E. Nairn.

McKinnon, J. Fishponds, Bristol.

McLaughlin, D. Dumfries.

McMahon, F.T. Kingston Hill, Surrey.

McMillan, J.A. Drumoyne, Glasgow.

Medine, H. Glengarrock, Ayrshire.

Meff, R.H. Aberdeen.

Mellors, F.E. Mansfield, Nottinghamshire.

Metcalfe, A.G. Pendlebury, Manchester.

Metcalfe, J. New Brancepeth, Co. Durham.

Mitchell, R. Leytonstone, London.

Mold, P.A. c/o Acton, London.

Montagu, C.R. (Hon. Member) Braemore, Hampshire.

Moore, H. Grimsby, Lincolnshire.

Moore, R. Mitcham, Surrey.

Morley, L. Reigate, Surrey.

Morris, A.G. Weymouth, Dorset.

Morrison, W. Clapham, London.

Morton, F. Caterham, Surrey.

Murphy, V.J. Chadwell Heath, Essex.

Murray, J.R. Feirniegair, Hamilton, Lanarkshire.

Murray, R. Coventry Holbrooks, Warwickshire.

Nash, V. Plaistow, West Ham.

Nichols, H.J.J. Dalston, London.

Nicholson, J. Scarborough, N. Yorkshire.

Nolan, J. c/o Staines, Middlesex.

Oddy, E.C. Brentwood, Essex.

Ogilvie, S. Houghton-le-Spring, Co. Durham.

Ollerenshaw, G.A. Ashbourne, Derbyshire.

Osborne, A. Hampstead, London.

Oswald, Sutton, Surrey.

Packer, H.W. Wells, Somerset.

Palmer, A.E. Nuneaton, Warwickshire.

Park, A.W. Aberdeen.

Parsons, H.M. (Capt) Warsash, Southampton.

Parsons, T. Edmonton, London.

Passant, J. Ludlow, Salop.

Patch, J.D. Ilford, Essex.

Patterson, M. Bexley, Kent.

Payne, C. Beccles.

Penfold, J. Hove, Sussex.

Penn, T. Workington, Cumberland.

Perkins, W.W. St John's Wood, London.

Perriment, A. Manor Park, London.

Pickles, J. Eccles, Manchester.

Pimm, R.T. Newport, Monmouthshire.

Pitt, L.A. Highgate, London.

Pratt, J.A. Eyrie, Aberdeenshire.

Prendergast, G.L. (Col DSO) Folkestone, Kent.

Quick, F.R. Wootton Courtney, nr Minehead, Somerset.

Rae, D.O.C. Larbert, Sterlingshire.

Rae, W. North Moulscombe, Brighton.

Reynolds, A. Ilford, Essex.

Richardson, T. Duntocher, Glasgow.

Robb, R.L.R. Bracknell, Berkshire.

Roberts, W. (Gdsmn), Coldstream Gds, The Hayes Camp, Swanwick, Derbyshire.

Rolfe, W.E. Newmarket, Suffolk.

Ross, G. Lowvalleyfield, Fife.

Rowland, P. Gosport, Hampshire.

Rowley, J. Knutton, Stoke.

Salmons, E.H. West Kirby, Cheshire.

Sandle, S. St Winburghs, Bristol.

Satherley, E. Newport, Isle of Wight.

Scriven, T. South Yardley, Birmingham.

Seligman, G. Tottenham, London.

Shaddick, E.W. Barnstaple, N. Devon.

Sharp, c/o Botleys Park War Hospital, Chertsey.

Shaw, H. Carlisle, Cumberland.

Shaw, W.B. Kennedy (Maj) Salisbury, Wiltshire.

Shepherd, G. (Sgt) REME 616 Regt. RA, BLA.

Sheppard, E. Islington, London.

Shute, J. (Capt) Cambridge.

Simms, F.C. (Lt Col MC) R. Warwicks Regt. Khartoum.

Simpson, J.H. Dagenham, Essex.

Sinclair, R.W. Ilford, Essex.

Skipweth, D. (Lt) Bideford, N. Devon.

Slater, H. Dukinfield, Cheshire.

Smart, J.B. Colchester, Essex.

Smart, W. (Sgt) No. 11 Commando, Workshops, Far Cotton, Northampton.

Smeathurst, J. Antwood, Radcliffe.

Smith, C. Thornton, Blackpool.

Smith, C.R.S. Doddington, Kent.

Smith, K. Basingstoke.

Smith, K.G. (Pte) 2nd Bn. Somerset Light Infantry, 'B' Coy. 12 Pln. CMF

Smith, R. Rintre, Rhondda.

Smith, W.G. Abingdon, Berkshire.

Snowden, F. Bradford, Yorkshire.

Spiceley, A.W. Holloway, London.

Springford, V. Warle, Weston-Super-Mare.

Steggles, P. Barnsbury, London.

Stephenson, G.W. Birkenshaw, Bradford.

Stevens, E.G. West Derby, Liverpool.

Stocker, J.B. Southsea, Hampshire.

Stockwell, F. Leeds.

Stormonth-Darling, M.P. (Maj) Kelso, Roxburghshire.

Strachan, A.M. Long Benton, Newcastle.

Stuart, R. Heckmondwike, Yorkshire.

Sturrock, E.C. Ayr.

Sullivan, A. (Tpr) 1st SAS Regt, c/o GPO, Chelmsford.

Swan, C.S. Gillingham, Kent.

Swan, F.G. Longsight, Manchester.

Swanson, J. Castleton, Caithness.

Sweeney, J. Randlestown, Co. Antrim.

Sykes, E. Armley, Leeds.

Tait, N.J. Highbury, London.

Tame, H.J.A. (Capt) Tooting, London.

Tapping, E.J. High Wycombe, Buckinghamshire.

Terry, I.R. Hanover Square, London.

Tew, F. Leicester.

Thompson, A. Harlsden, London.

Thompson, E.L. Buxton, Derbyshire.

Thompson, G. Perth.

Thurgood, L. East Acton, London.

Timpson, J.A.L. (Capt) Scots Gds, School of Infantry, Warminster.

Tinckler, K. Liverpool.

Town, B. Worthing, Sussex.

Tucker, R. Westdown, Ilfracombe.

Tuckey, D. Chingford, Essex.

Tutt-Harris, W. Moordown, Bournemouth.

Twidale, H. Enfield, Middlesex.

Twiss, W.T. (Lt) Sutton Coldfield, Warwickshire.

Walker, N.D. Blundell Sands, Liverpool.

Walkey, J. Old Trafford, Manchester.

Wallace, J. Bradford, Yorkshire.

Warren, R. Barnes, London.

Waterton, A.R.C. Greenford, Middlesex.

Watson, W. Ashington, Northumberland.

Webster, F. Chesterfield, Derbyshire.

Webster, S.C. Stanwell, Middlesex.

Weir, W.R. Bowerham, Lancashire.

Wells, H. Rainham, Kent.

Westlake, W. Petworth, Sussex.

Whitbread, H. Dartford, Kent.

Wigens, R.F. Romford, Kent.

Wilde, D. Ipswich, Suffolk.

Wilkins, L.E. Ifley, Oxford.

Williamson, K.F. Runcorn, Cheshire.

Wilson, J. Guildford, Surrey.

Wilton, S. Liverpool.

Wiltshire, R. Taunton, Somerset.

Wimbourne, J.D. West Southbourne, Bournemouth.

Wooler, P.S. Welling, Kent.

Wren, F.R. Dagenham, Essex.

Wright, G.S. Theydon Bois, Essex.

Yeomans, A. Leicester.

RHODESIAN SECTION

Andrews, S.A.J. Salisbury, S. Rhodesia (S.R.).

Armand, R.E.O. Gwelo, S.R.

Aves, O.H. Salisbury, S.R.

Bailey, A.E.F. Bulawayo, S.R.

Barker, G.J. Odzi, S.R.

Basson, R. Shangani, S.R.

Bawden, R. Shangani, S.R.

Beck, J.R.H. Native Department, Bulawayo, S.R.

Belstead, E.J.C. Salisbury, S.R.
Bennett, A.F. Somabula, S.R.
Bennett, G.J.G. Amber Rose Mine, Umswesme, S.R.
Berry, L.M. Que Que, S.R.
Birch, E. de G. New Fullback Mine, Mtoko, S.R.
Bryant, A.P. Bulawayo, S.R.
Butler, T.G. Umtali, S.R.
Calder-Potts, L. East Qriqualand, Cape Province.
Carlsson, P.V.K. Shahani, S.R.
Cleete, L.C. Greystone, S.R.
Cooke, W.C. Avondale, Salisbury, S.R.
Cooper, A.J. Greendale, Salisbury, S.R.
Coventry, D.T. Fort Victoria, S.R.
Davies, D.W. Railway, Kafue, N.R.
De Maine, D.B. Bulawayo, S.R.
Du Preez, A.M. Macheke, S.R.
Eastwood, S. Salisbury, S.R.
Edwards, A.J. Hotel Chipinga, S.R.
Edwards, R.C. Bulawayo, S.R.
Enslin, G.E.K. Enkeldoorn, S.R.
Evans, J.A. Odzi, S.R.
Frost, B.E. Bulawayo, S.R.
Gifard, E.F.C. Banket, S.R.
Greef, F. Marula, S.R.
Gundry, C. Salisbury, S.R.
Hacking, E.S. Odzi, S.R.
Haddon, T.C. Bulawayo, S.R.
Harding, B.H. Gwelo, S.R.
Hawkins, D.G. Selukwe, S.R.
Hein, H.A.H. Gwelo, S.R.
Hogan, P.J. Bulawayo, S.R.
Jackson, C.J.O. Wanderer Mine, Selukwe, S.R.
Kaplan, E.W. Mtoko, S.R.
Kroeger, J.A. Pietermaritzburg, S.R.
Krog, B. Salisbury, S.R.
Lambert, R.C. Que Que, S.R.

Legrange, J.P. Bulawayo, S.R.
Lewis, T.J. Bulawayo, S.R.
Low, A.T. Bulawayo, S.R.
Low, K. Bulawayo, S.R.
Lowenthal, J.M. Gwelo, S.R.
Light, H.F.N. Salisbury, S.R.
McCullough, R. Rusapi, S.R.
McCullough, R.A. Bulawayo, S.R.
McNeilage, D.W. Umtali, S.R.
Neikerk, E.P. Dett, S.R.
Page, A.S. Salisbury, S.R.
Parsloe, R.S. Bulawayo, S.R.
Poole, P.L. Bulawayo, S.R.
Potgieter, G.F. Umvuma, S.R.
Reynolds, M.J. M.C.c/o Lone Hand Mine, Gwanda, S.R.
Richards, P.S. Salisbury, S.R.
Rizgate, M. Gwelo, S.R.
Robinson, J.E.T. Gwelo, S.R.
Saunders, R.T. Marmendellas, S.R.
Savage, S.S. Balawayo, S.R.
Schadie, E. Salisbury, S.R.
Scott, T.R. Umtali, S.R.
Selmon, W.R. Bulawayo, S.R.
Sherwood, C.D. Salisbury, S.R.
Simpson, D.F. Salisbury, S.R.
Smith, H.J. Salisbury, S.R.
Solomon, E.D. Bulawayo, S.R.
Speares, D.G. Salisbury, S.R.
Stopforth, N. c/o Gwelo, S.R.
Southerns, W.H. Salisbury, S.R.
Utterton, F. Shabanie, S.R.
Valentine, D.J. Lonely Mir, S.R.
Waller, R.C.R. Salisbury, S.R.
Westergaard, E.G. Salisbury, S.R.
Whale, J.C. Salisbury, S.R.
Whitehead, A.V. Salisbury, S.R.
Windell, F.H. Que Que, S.R.
Wood, G.M. Bulawayo, S.R.
Young, W.R. Salisbury, S.R.

SOUTH AFRICAN SECTION

Marshall, N.H. Vincent, East London, S. Africa.
Olivey, J.R. (Capt) Special Service Signals, Durban, S. Africa.
Pitt, G.V. (Lt) Capetown, S.A.

Rundle, R.O. Mahalapye, Bech Prot., S.A.
Stokes, S.A. (Maj) Johannesburg, S.A.
Taylor, P.E. c/o Country Club, Aukland Park, Johannesburg, S.A.

New Zealand Section

(Ranks are given where known. LRP indicates also served in Long Range Patrol (the forerunner of the LRDG):

Adams, D.J.	LRP	Crammond, A.R. (Lt)		Ferguson, I.C.	LRP
Adams, W.R.	LRP	Craw, M.H.		Finnigan, C.F.	
Aislabie, W.P.	LRP	Crawford, A.B.		Fisher, C.L.	
Aitken, D.J. (Capt)		Crisp, J.E. (Lt)		Fleming, D.A.	
Baldwin, I.	LRP	Cross, M.W.		Fogarty, D.M.	
Ball, C.G.	LRP	Crossley, J.		Fogden, M.F.	
Ballantyne, L.B. (Maj)	LRP	Croucher, C.H.B. (Capt) LRP		Forbes, W.D.S.	
Bambery, W.R.		Curtis, M.W.	LRP	Franks, J.A.	
Barber, J.A.		Dalziel, L.D.		Frost, L.H.	
Barker, R.F.T. (Capt)		Dale, A.		Garland, P.L.	LRP
Barrett, D. (Lt)	LRP	Dale, A.R.		Garrett, J.L.	
Bassett, D.M.		Dally, A.E.		Garven, G.C.	LRP
Beale, D.O.		Davies, J.	LRP	Gedye, N.M.	
Beech, F.R.	LRP	Davies, R.C.		Gerrard, W.G.	
Bourgeois, V.C.		Davis, J.L.D.		Gibb, A.D.	LRP
Bowler, J.T.		Davidson, A.G.		Gibbons, J.	
Boys, A.		Davidson, D.		Giles, J.	
Brown, F.R.	LRP	Davison, R.A.		Gill, J.E.	
Brown, F.S.		Davison, G.L.	LRP	Gilmore, J.P.	
Browne, L.H. (Capt)	LRP	Davoren, J.A.E.		Gold, I.	
Burgess, W.H.		Dean, L.G.		Goodall, F.H.	
Burke, P.J.		Derrett, W.A.		Goodwin, V.C.	
Burnand, W.D.	LRP	Dobson, D.G.		Gorringe, E.F.	
Butler, W.G.	LRP	Dobson, E.J.		Gorringe, R.O.	LRP
Cameron, E.A.		Dobson, T.B.		Greason, J.	
Cameron, W.		Dodunski, A.F.	LRP	Greenstreet, B.W.	
Campbell, K.	LRP	Doel, L.G.		Gregory, D.N.	
Campbell, L.T.		Donaldson, L.		Grimsey, C.O.	LRP
Campbell, M.C.		Dornbush, C.A.		Guild, A.I. (Capt)	
Campbell, N.R.		Duncan, J.E.		Haddow, R.G.	
Carter, E.G.	LRP	Edmundson, F.B.	LRP	Hamilton, W.J.	LRP
Chaney, M.F.		Ellingham, S.W.		Hammond, M.E.	LRP
Church, M.H.		Ellis, E.		Hankins, A.E.	LRP
Cleaver, H.H.	LRP	Ellis, L.A.	LRP	Hare, R.E.J.	
Clemens, D.L.		Ellis, N.		Hardyment, C.H.	
Coates, J.	LRP	Ellis, R.		Harcourt, E.	LRP
Collett, C.		Emeny, A.V.		Hawkins, L.J.	LRP
Collins, T.		Emslie, J.	LRP	Hay, R.E.	
Connell, E.M.		Eyles, J.W.	LRP	Hayes, R.D.	
Connelly, A.		Eyre, C.W.	LRP	Heard, V.J.	
Cosgrove, F.W.		Faithful, W.G.		Hewetson, H.P.	
Costello, P.		Fanning, V.S.		Hewson, C.D.	LRP
Cowes, H.W.		Farmer, D.		Hiscoke, A.P.	
Crabbe, R.H.		Ferguson, A.G.		Hobson, N.W.	

Holland, H.T.R.		McBean, R.		Parker, S.D.	
Hood, A.W.	LRP	McCallum, F.R.		Parker, N.J.	
Houston, J.W.		McCorkindale, A.	LRP	Parkes, G.C.	LRP
Hughes, L.T.	LRP	McConachie, C.I.		Partington, H.	
Hunter, M.A.		McCulloch, I.G.		Payne, L.	
Hutchinson, E.Y.M.		McDonald, D.O.		Penhall, A.J.	
Ineson, K.C.J.		McDonald, T.		Pickering, C.	
Jacobs, K.S.		McDowell, G.F.		Pope, J.F.	
Jacobson, G.		McGarry, T.J.	LRP	Porter, R.T.	
Jalfon, H.H.		McGarvey, O.S.		Potter, F.P.	
James, W.		McGregor, P.	LRP	Proctor, W.A.	
Job, A.J.	LRP	McHardy, T.		Rail, W.H.	
Johnstone, L.R.B.		McInnes, D.J.		Ramsay, R.A.	
Jones, J.H.		McInnes, I.H.	LRP	Rawson, R.	LRP
Jopling, F.W.	LRP	McIntyre, J.S.		Reid, E.E.	
Joss, P.M.	LRP	McIver, L.A.		Reid, J.L.	
Judge, I.J.		McKay, F.R.		Reid, P.G.	
Kearns, P.		McKay, H.L.W.		Renwick, A.P.	
Kelly, K.		McKay, W.M.		Respinger, A.E.	LRP
Kendall, F.	LRP	McKeon, D.M.		Rhodes, F.D.	LRP
Kerr, S.		McKenzie, C.B.		Richards, J.	LRP
Kidd, C.		McKeown, F.J.W.		Richardson, M.D.	
Kidd, S.J.	LRP	McLauchlan, K.F. (Lt)		Ritchie, T.E.	
Kitney, E.W.R.	LRP	McLellan, G.I.	LRP	Roberts, N.	
Knowles, G.S.D.		McLelland, T.		Robinson, F.M.	
Knudsen, K.E.		McLeod, A.F.	LRP	Rodgers, R.K.	
Lamb, G.		McLeod, D.C.		Roderick, L.	LRP
Lambert, B.W.		McLeod, R.F.		Rollinson, N.J.	LRP
Landon-Lane, R.J. (Capt)	LRP	McNeil, T.B.	LRP	Ross, D.I.	
Larkin, R.		McQueen, R.B. (Lt)	LRP	Russell, E.T.	LRP
Larsen, L.A.		Middlebrook, L.J.		Sadgrove, A.D.	LRP
Lawson, S.J.		Milburn, T.A.		Sanders, E.	LRP
Lazarus, R. (Capt)		Milne, J.C.		Saunders, A.M.	LRP
Lennox, F.		Mitford, P.V.		Saxton, C.K. (Maj)	
Lennox, G.M.		Mooney, P.		Scott, L.D.	
Lewis, D.A.		Moore, R.J.	LRP	Schaab, J.L.	LRP
Lewis, R.W.N.		Morgan, R.J.		Shaw, A.G.	
Lilley, L.H.		Morris, C.S. (Maj)		Shepherd, B.F.	
Lord, H.		Murphy, F.J.		Shepherd, J.R.	LRP
Loughnan, H.M.		Munro, D.		Simonsen, J.M.	
Lucas, J.C.		Murdoch, A.A.		Simpson, R.A.	
Macassey, J.L.P.		Naden, C.H.		Smith, E.B.	LRP
Macready, D.M.		Nelson, G.H.	LRP	Smith, G.T.	
Mackay, H.D.		Nelson, J.B.	LRP	Smith, R.C.	
Magee, J.B.		Nicholls, L.R.		Spain, V.C.	LRP
Mallett, H.L.		Nutt, A.H.C.		Spedding, A.J.	LRP
Martin, A.C.		O'Keefe, J.R.		Spotswood, R.O.	LRP
Mason, C.B.		O'Malley, N.		Steedman, B.	
Mather, L.F.	LRP	Ormond, A.R.W.	LRP	Steele, D.G. (Maj)	LRP

Stewart, A.M.D.
Stewart, M.W.
Stone, F.R.
Stuart, J.B.
Stutterd, E.C.
Sutherland, G.M.
Sutherland, J.H. (Lt)   LRP
Sutherland, J.M.
Talbot, J.R. (Lt)
Tant, R.D.
Taylor, J.H.E.
Thompson, J.H.
Tilbury, H.
Tinker, R.A. (Capt)   LRP
Tippett, K.E.

Tomlinson, D.J.
Treadwell, C.J.
Treanor, R.A.
Tyler, F.W.
Vincent, A.
Vining, L.J.
Waetford, C.   LRP
Waetford, E.B.
Walsh, M.C.
Walsh, T.E.
Warbrick, D.P.
Watkins, A.R.
Watson, A.
Wells, T.
Wheeler, D.E.

Whimp, S.W.
Whitaker, F.J.
White, R.F.
Wilder, N.P. (Capt)
Willcox, L.A.   LRP
Williams, R.R.
Williamson, J.M.
Wilson, A.
Wright, O.W.
Wrigley, F.M.
Wynne, J.   LRP
Yates, A.
Yaxley, C.A.
Yealands, K.
Zimmerman, J.   LRP

MIDDLE EAST, INDIA, AMERICA, ETC.

Buckwald, N. Haifa, Palestine.
Cluer, R.E.D. c/o Kingston, Jamaica.
Enright, F.E. (Cpl) Royal Signals, Airport Camp, Belize, British Honduras.
Graham, Mrs D. (Hon. Member) c/o Seliman Pasha, Cairo.
Lambiotte, Mrs E. (Hon. Member) Rond Point, Alexandria.

Landman, A. Sydney, Australia.
Lazarus, K.H. Nairobi, Kenya.
Price, D. Rue Hachim Pasha, Cairo.
Scott, R.W. Kolar Goldfields, Mysore State, India.
Tuttle, J. (Lt) c/o The Williams Club, New York City, U.S.A.
Vincent, A. Secunderabad, Deccan, India.

APPENDIX IV

Patrol Commanders

LRP Patrols

R (New Zealand)   Capt D.G. Steele.
T (New Zealand)   Capt P.A. Clayton, Capt L.B. Ballantyne.
W (New Zealand)   Capt E.C. Mitford.

LRDG Patrols

G1 (Guards)   Capt M.D.D. Crichton Stuart,
                     Capt A.M. Hay, Capt J.A.L. Timpson.
G2 (Guards)   Capt J.A.L. Timpson, Lt Hon. R.B. Gurdon,
                     Lt K.H. Sweeting, Lt Hon. B. Bruce.
R1 (New Zealand)   Capt J.R. Easonsmith, Capt A.I. Guild,
                     Capt L.H. Browne, Lt K.F. McLauchlan.
R2 (New Zealand)   Lt C.H. Croucher, Lt J.R. Talbot,
                     Capt K.H. Lazarus.
S1 (Rhodesian)   Capt C.A. Holliman, Capt J.R. Olivey,
                     Capt K.H. Lazarus.
S2 (Rhodesian)   Capt J.R. Olivey, Lt J. Henry.
T1 (New Zealand)   Capt L.B. Ballantyne, Capt N.P. Wilder,
                     Lt J. Crisp.
T2 (New Zealand)   Capt C.S. Morris, Capt N.P. Wilder,
                     Capt R.A. Tinker, Lt A.R. Crammond.
Y1 (Yeomanry and other units) Capt P.J.D. McCraith, Capt F.C. Simms,
                     Capt D. Lloyd Owen.
Y2 (Yeomanry and other units) Capt D. Lloyd Owen, Capt A.D.N. Hunter,
                     Capt E.F. Spicer.

Indian Long Range Squadron

Indian 1   Lt J.E. Cantlay.
Indian 2   Capt T.J.D. Birdwood.
Indian 3   Capt A.B. Rand.
Indian 4   Lt G.W. Nangle.

Long Range Desert Group

ROLL OF HONOUR

P.L. Arnold	H.L. Mallett
L.C. Ashby	G. Matthews
F.R. Beech	L.A. McIver
J. Botha	L. Oelofse
J.T. Bowler	N. O'Malley
W.H. Burton	A.J. Penhall
D. Davison	A. Redfern
E.J. Dobson	G. Rezin
J.R. Easonsmith	C. Richardson
J. Easton	R. Riggs
S. Federman	L. Roderick
S. Fleming	R. Savage
K. Foley	D. Singer
M. Gravil	K. Smith
R.B. Gurdon	A. Tighe
J. Henderson	H. Todman
J. Henry	J. Vanrensberg
C.D. Hewson	P. Wheeldon
A. Hopton	G.F. Yates
B. Jordan	R. Young

Bibliography

Bagnold, Ralph. *Libyan Sands*, Hodder & Stoughton, 1935

Churchill, Winston. *The Second World War*, Vol. IV, 9 vols, Chiswick Press, 1948–53

Cowles, Virginia. *'The Phantom Major'*, *The Story of David Stirling and the SAS Regiment*, Collins, 1958

Crichton-Stuart, Michael. *G. Patrol*, Kimber, 1958

Farran, Roy. *Winged Dagger*, Collins, 1948

James, Malcolm. *'Born of the Desert'*, *SAS in Libya*, Collins, 1945

Kennedy Shaw, W.B. *Long Range Desert Group*, Collins, 1945

Landsborough, Gordon. *Tobruk Commando*, Cassell & Co., 1956

Lloyd Owen, David. *Providence Their Guide*, Harrap, 1980

Lloyd Owen, David. *The Desert My Dwelling Place*, Arms and Armour, 1986

Maclean, Fitzroy. *Eastern Approaches*, Jonathan Cape, 1949

Peniakoff, Vladimir. *Popski's Private Army*, Pan Books, 1950

Strawson, John. *A History of the SAS Regiment*, Grafton Books, 1986

Warner, Philip. *The Special Air Service*, Kimber, 1971

Index

Page numbers given in italic refer to illustrations. KIA = killed in action